# FROM CLASSROOM
# TO BATTLEFIELD

BARRY GOUGH

# FROM CLASSROOM

# TO BATTLEFIELD

VICTORIA HIGH SCHOOL AND
THE FIRST WORLD WAR

HERITAGE

VICTORIA · VANCOUVER · CALGARY

Heritage House Publishing Company Ltd.
heritagehouse.ca

LIBRARY AND ARCHIVES CANADA CATALOGUING IN PUBLICATION

Gough, Barry M., 1938–, author
From classroom to battlefield : Victoria High School and
the First World War / Barry Gough.

Includes bibliographical references and index.
Issued in print and electronic formats.
ISBN 978-1-77203-005-1 (pbk.).—ISBN 978-1-77203-037-2 (cloth).—ISBN 978-1-77203-006-8 (html).
—ISBN 978-1-77203-007-5 (pdf)

1. Victoria High School (Victoria, B.C.)—Students—Biography. 2. World War, 1914–1918—
Biography. 3. Soldiers—Canada—Biography. 4. World War, 1914–1918—Campaigns. 5. World War,
1914-1918—British Columbia—Victoria. I. Title.

D639.E52C3 2014      940.4›12710922      2014-903469-5 C2014-903470-9

Edited by Audrey McClellan
Proofread by Karla Decker
Cover and book design by Jacqui Thomas
Front cover photos (top to bottom): *The Victoria High School building at its opening in May 1914*
(courtesy of Victoria High School Archives); *Officers of the Victoria College Cadet Corps, 1910*
(courtesy of Victoria High School Archives); *The Second Battle of Ypres, 22 April to 25 May 1915*,
by Richard Jack (Beaverbrook Collection of War Art, Canadian War Museum 19710261-0161)
Back cover photo: *Victoria High School Cadet Battalion No. 112, 1914* (courtesy of Victoria High
School Archives)

The interior of this book was produced on 100% post-consumer recycled paper, processed chlorine free,
and printed with vegetable-based inks.

Heritage House acknowledges the financial support for its publishing program from the Government
of Canada through the Canada Book Fund (CBF), Canada Council for the Arts, and the province of
British Columbia through the British Columbia Arts Council and the Book Publishing Tax Credit.

Canadian Patrimoine
Heritage canadien

The Canada Council | Le Conseil des Arts
for the Arts | du Canada

BRITISH COLUMBIA
ARTS COUNCIL

18 17 16 15 14  1 2 3 4 5

Printed in Canada

# CONTENTS

## To the Memory of the Fallen

*And* also to those half a thousand whose names are inscribed on the Roll of Honour, 1914–1918, Victoria High School, Victoria, British Columbia, Canada. They fought for Canada and the British Empire in the First World War to maintain the right and to protect the liberties of civilized societies.

Almost one hundred soldiers, sailors, airmen, teachers, and nurses connected to Victoria High School made the supreme sacrifice in the terrible cataclysm known as the Great War. We hold them high in memory. We owe them no less.

# In Flanders Fields

— MAJOR JOHN MCCRAE —

*In Flanders fields the poppies blow*
*Between the crosses, row on row,*
*That mark our place; and in the sky*
*The larks, still bravely singing, fly*
*Scarce heard amid the guns below.*

*We are the Dead. Short days ago*
*We lived, felt dawn, saw sunset glow,*
*Loved and were loved, and now we lie*
*In Flanders fields.*

*Take up our quarrel with the foe:*
*To you from failing hands we throw*
*The torch; be yours to hold it high.*
*If ye break faith with us who die*
*We shall not sleep, though poppies grow*
*In Flanders fields*

The Canadian Army fought its first terrible battle in the early spring of 1915 in the Ypres salient, Belgium, Western Front. Major (later Lt. Colonel) John McCrae (1872–1918), specialist in clinical medicine and pathology, McGill University, Montreal, wrote this poem on May 3, 1915, while sitting on the back of an ambulance beside the Yser River. A gentle east wind blew the poppies that day. "I wish I could embody on paper some of the varied sensations of that seventeen days . . . seventeen days of Hades! At the end of the first day if anyone had told us we had to spend seventeen days there, we would have folded our hands and said it could not have been done." The poem first appeared in the London magazine *Punch*, December 8, 1915.

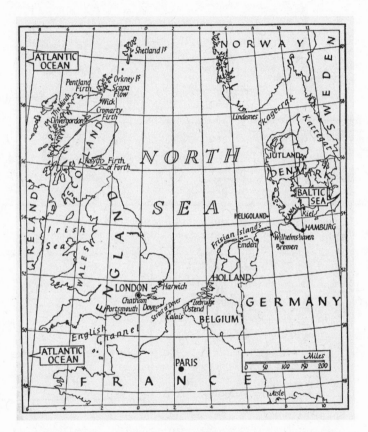

The North Sea, the site of key navy battles fought between the Royal Navy and the German High Seas Fleet. **MAP COURTESY OF CORRELLI BARNETT**

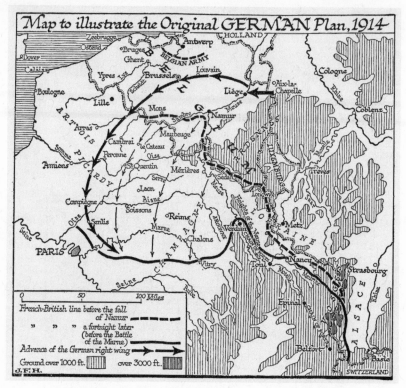

SOURCE: H.G. WELLS, *THE OUTLINE OF HISTORY*, 3RD ED. ILLUSTRATED
BY J.F. HORRABIN. NEW YORK: MACMILLAN COMPANY, 1921.

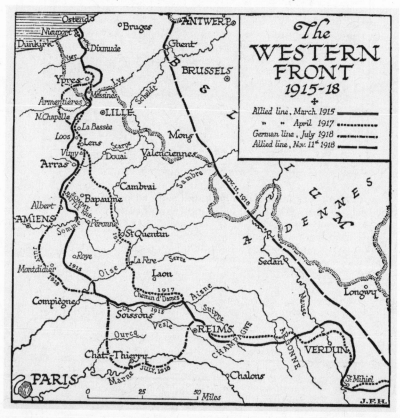

# INTRODUCTION

*T*his is a portrait of a Canadian high school that virtually went to war and was forever changed by the experience. It forms a chapter in the heroism and horror of war. Winston Churchill had it right when he said, "History with its flickering lamp stumbles along the trail of the past, trying to reconstruct its scenes, to revive its echoes, and kindle with pale gleams the passion of former days."[1] Each and every historian faces challenges presented by the dimensions and characteristics of the subject being addressed. For me, the challenge was bringing Victoria into the larger Canadian and British imperial story.

This story is about individuals of the greatest generation in Canadian history, if those who fought the Second World War may somehow be set aside. Most were born in the mid-1890s. They lived in an imperial age. When they were youngsters, men of their fathers' ages may have gone to South Africa to fight the Boers. They came to maturity just as the Great War was starting, or in the next four years. They joined as soon as they could possibly "sign up." They were volunteers and they were patriots. Most of them were born in Victoria or raised there. Many of their families derived from old colonial stock. The forebears of others arrived in the early days of steam navigation or in the early railway age, the 1880s. The rest of Canada was a far distant place—and a subject of federal-provincial difficulties, for British Columbia often demanded special terms. For the men and women of this age, England was their emotional home, by blood, tradition, and institutions. Their parents had celebrated the Golden Jubilee and then the Diamond Jubilee of the great Queen-Empress Victoria. And their parents had known about Canadians fighting for the British Empire in the South African (Boer) War.

As the greatest generation, they helped create the concept of Canada. They put the maple leaf on the maps of the world. That so many of them were killed in battle or otherwise died in service—66,000 out of 600,000 enlistments—is a source of never-ending regret. That most of them were unmarried adds another dimension to the tragedy. The ones whose lives are remembered in this book were well educated. Almost all were high-school graduates and were part of a literate class. Most of them were Christians and identified mainly with Protestant denominations. Some were members of the Masonic Lodge. Few if any were farm boys. They lived in the city or on its immediate outskirts. Most of them came from the professional or business class. Had they lived, it can hardly be doubted that they would have made outstanding contributions to Canada and the world. As it was, their lives were snuffed out far too early—and, in their regrettable passing, they left a pathway of sorrow.

From their sacrifice, the legend of Vimy Ridge has been built up and now enshrined as a symbol of nationhood and of Canada "coming of age." This may need rethinking by other historians braver than me. It is clear, however, that the government of the day made sure that Canadian autonomy in the British Empire would be advanced in consequence of the sacrifice of Canada's soldiers. It is terribly ironic that though most of this greatest generation were born in Canada and were not recent arrivals from the United Kingdom, as has so often been stated in error, they did not enlist solely to fight for Canada: they had something more important on their minds, something that had given them international identity with the strongest political entity then in existence, the British Empire. That the politicians exploited this war for their own benefit lies outside the bounds of this book.

My concern is, as it always has been, to examine the faces in the crowd, those individuals whose contributions and sacrifices deserve far more consideration than the governments and jurisdictions that have received so much attention. So many Canadian history books give the impression that Canada was somehow at war with Mother Britain when in fact Canada was at war against three great empires—the German, the Austro-Hungarian, and the Ottoman. Nor do I subscribe to the argument that Britain could have stayed out of this war and should have stayed out of this war. One has only to consider the mentality and the conformation of the Kaiser, the government, and the military and naval intentions of Germany to understand that Britain and the empire could not stand idly by. Austria-Hungary was determined to crush Serbia, and that invited Russia's intervention, Germany's reaction in turn, and France's response. All of this does not mean that the War was not a mistake. It was a mistake, and the causes were not only complex but also depended on the possibilities of chance, coupled with misfortune. Volumes have been written on these themes. In life, persons find themselves in situations not of their own choosing or design; the same is true of nations and empires. The "what ifs" will always exist, the counterfactuals will abound, the arguments continue without end. Having said this, one cannot turn back the hands of time. And it would really be a tragedy if somehow the sacrifices of the Canadian boys, particularly those of Victoria High School, were to be dismissed as made in vain. Let us put ourselves back in their shoes and boots, for they were the greatest generation.

I have sought to link the changing circumstances of the home city, Victoria, British Columbia, with influences and experiences that came upon it from distant fields of battle. As such, the narrative moves from Victoria to scenes far away, then returns to home. I have chosen a year-by-year approach, one chapter for each year of the First World War, with preliminary and succeeding chapters to put the conflict into the larger perspective of war. Peter Smith in *Come Give a Cheer! One Hundred Years of Victoria High School, 1876–1976* (Victoria High School Centennial Celebrations Committee, 1976) brilliantly told the story of the school's early history, where its achievements as a very Canadian institution are portrayed. It is worth keeping in mind that in its teaching staff and administration the emerging Canadian model was followed from the beginning. In no sense was Victoria High School a spinoff of some Britannic model or some English private school. Nor did it follow any American pattern.

From the outset, I have been aware of the challenge of dealing with the problem of distinguishing Canadians from other citizens of the British Empire, notably the English and Scots who formed such a conspicuous part of Victoria's population in that age. I have concluded that such differentiations are futile and even incorrect: being born in Canada did not necessarily give anyone who fought for the British Empire in that war a special status. Furthermore, it would be wrong to think those of British birth who were connected to Victoria High School and who fought for King and Country were any less or any more significant than those born in Victoria. At the time we are dealing with, Canadian-born persons were the majority of the populace in Victoria (though there was no Canadian citizenship until 1921).[2] On the other hand, the First World War clearly created a Canadian identity, or sharpened one that was already developing. It has been said that the War made Canada a nation. Certainly, the Canadian Expeditionary Force (CEF), as the Canadian official historian Colonel C.P. Stacey declared, was the biggest and most important endeavour Canada ever undertook. I, too, believe this, and I believe that effort has never been surpassed. The Canadian Corps, formed from the CEF, did not act alone: it fought as an integral part of the British Army. In this book I also, as the same official historian did, use the term "the British Armies"—that is, those armies still under British direction in the War, which were from constituent parts of the empire. In this category fall the British Army and those of Canada, Newfoundland, Australia, New Zealand, South Africa, and India. They fought in a common cause.

Our subject is necessarily the Canadian contribution, and Victoria High School's distinctive part. The 1914–1918 war shaped Canada in so many ways. It seemed to end an era of innocence, a long and splendid afternoon. It was a time when "the crust of civilization cracked and crumbled and collapsed"—or as A.E. Housman put it famously, "when earth's foundation fled."[3] The War brought Canada to the support of Great Britain and the British Empire, of which Canada was a part. It brought us to the battlefields of Belgium and France, there to wage an unimaginably terrible war. It also brought us into the war at sea and in the air. It led us to some sideshows of conflict—Salonika and Mesopotamia. It brought us, eventually, to victory over Imperial Germany and the other Central Powers. It gave us a seat in the Imperial War Cabinet and in the councils of the British Empire. It gave us an international status never before imagined. Canada became a signatory to the Treaty of Versailles as a separate dominion of the British Empire (later Commonwealth of Nations). The War gave us pride of achievement in both our collective efforts and in the unique accomplishments of our combatants and non-combatants. In all these ways, Victoria High School, in the most British of all Canadian cities, and one of the youngest, played a remarkable role that heretofore has not been known or appreciated. This book has been written to rectify this state of affairs.

Equally significant is the story of sacrifice and remembrance, and therefore of memorials, remarkable in their variety and extraordinary in their magnificence. I know of no other school in Canada with such treasures of the Great War, Canadian cultural treasures that have been little advertised until now. History is about process and is never static. What was it like in that age for the survivors, those left behind, and those grieving irreparable losses? The collective loss to the school stirred staff and students to action. I describe how the school provided tributes to the Fallen and to those others who served and survived. In its Memorial Trees, Kitchener Memorial Oak, Roll of Honour, Memorial Tablet, Banner of Honour and Sacrifice, and Stained Glass of Victory and Sacrifice, we have a rich variety of material features that are daily reminders of sacrifice and achievement by members of the school in the Great War. In addition, Victoria High School Archives preserves numerous head-and-shoulder photographic portraits of the Fallen. In the days when I was a student at the school (1956 being my graduating year), those individual portraits of lives cut so tragically short by the War hung side by side along the front hallway, forming a long and continuous gallery. How many friends of these lost persons, how many kin, had passed and paid silent tribute to those who had made the ultimate sacrifice? In those days of my studenthood, echoes of empire still could be heard, but gradually all that was swept away, though the sentiments remain in certain circles. Rudyard Kipling had it right in "Recessional," written in the year of Queen Victoria's Diamond Jubilee, 1897:

> *Far-called, our navies melt away;*
> *On dune and headland sinks the fire:*
> *Lo, all our pomp of yesterday*
> *Is one with Nineveh and Tyre!*
> *Judge of the Nations, spare us yet,*
> *Lest we forget—lest we forget!*

It would have been wonderful to tell the story of each of the Fallen and, indeed, of each of the members of the school who answered the call to arms. That has proved impossible due to lack of information and lack of space. Some stories stand out. As will be seen, certain individuals are of central importance; their names are given in the list of Principal Persons.

Many stories could be told of those who survived and went on to other notable achievements. I have selected a few that fall into this category. Some notable names are to be found on the Roll of Honour. Byron "Boss" Johnson, later premier of the province, is one. He was a well-known goalie in lacrosse. Another is Saanich-born Private (later Lt. Colonel) George Bissett, who enlisted when he was at McGill studying medicine, went overseas, was discharged to complete professional training (which he did in 1917), then served with the British Army Medical Corps in France and India.[4] Joseph B. Clearihue, Victoria High School's first Rhodes Scholar, was a lieutenant in the 5th British Columbia Regiment of Garrison Artillery, Royal Canadian Artillery (RCA), and served overseas. He returned to Victoria and became a lawyer, city councillor, member of the Legislative Assembly, judge of note, and also chancellor of the University of Victoria. Captain Stanley Okell, who won the Military Cross, was a Victoria West athlete, born to a pioneering Victoria family, and became a machine gunner in the 67th Western Scottish Battalion. He returned from the War and had a diverse career thereafter. Brothers Robert Ernest Burns and Frederick Dawson Burns, both born and educated in Victoria, served overseas in the CEF and returned to British Columbia, Robert to become superintendent of Lands for the Province of British Columbia and Fred to be golf professional at Royal Colwood Golf Club. Victoria High School has always been connected to the press of this city and province. Archie Wills, marine editor of the *Victoria Times*, wrote about his life in "the Great Adventure of War," and his experiences are included in Kenneth Roeche's *A Fairfield History* in a chapter entitled "Archie's War." I could cite many others who came home.

Many are left out of this story, sadly. Some I have not been able to trace; Douglas Scott, for instance, one of the galaxy of academic stars of the school— prefect, actor, and debater—who went to war in late 1917 and survived.

Nor can this book tell of those who suffered such physical or mental anguish that they took their own lives after the War or otherwise died early deaths. It cannot tell the tales of grieving families and neighbours, or of the grey generation of women whose loved ones were lost in the War and who never married. It is one of the peculiar jobs of the historian that he or she can see, on the one hand, the magnificent achievements of the age, and at the same time the total horror of this terrible catastrophe. Writing this history has brought me bouts of acute sadness. At the same time it has spelled out the essential truth that the persons whose lives are recounted here were caught up in human relationships, particularly a discovered comradeship which, as Frederic Manning put it in *The Middle Parts of Fortune,* "rises on occasion to an intensity of feeling which friendship never touches." Others wrote that the War gave the most human experience that could be revealed.

Readers will note that the terms First World War and Great War are used interchangeably. The latter was in common use until 1939, when Hitler's Germany invaded Poland, prompting an international response, including Canada's declaration of war against Germany. In attempting to recreate the age and the dynamics of the struggle, my own preference has been to call it the Great War, for it was that at the time. I hope I may be excused this historical inaccuracy, for all of us now know that even greater horrors were to follow in the 1939 to 1945 conflict. The Great War turned into a war of cultures, but I have not addressed this theme here except to say that when I was a lad and would talk to survivors of the Great War who wore their pins in their suit lapels, I noted with interest this inscription: "The War for Civilization." What did this mean? Because the causes of the War were so complex (and Europe plunged helter-skelter into it), and the length of it was such that national survival became the order of the day, it is natural that differences between British liberalism, Canadian nationalism, Empire solidarity, United States zeal for saving the world, and French efforts to survive were seen as less dramatic than the difference between those philosophies and German "Kultur." I have also avoided discussion of propaganda wars and the use of the pulpit for recruitment purposes.

I have based this book on various kinds of historical data. Of foremost importance is the student-owned and -operated magazine *The Camosun,* a comprehensive record of school life. This periodical, which appeared first in 1906 as a magazine of Victoria College, was entirely a commercial venture. In the years just preceding the War and those of the War, it owed much of its distinction to successive literary advisors, the teachers Arthur Yates and Ira Dilworth. I have also used the two local Victoria newspapers, the *Daily Colonist* and *Victoria Times.* These reported progress of the War as closely as official censorship and information management allowed. They printed many important sidelights on the conflict and details of family not to be found elsewhere. Various memoirs and biographies, oral interviews made by CBC, and holdings in the University of Victoria enrich the documentation, as do official military records in the United Kingdom and Ottawa. The attestation papers for the CEF are a gold mine, as are the rich-in-detail service records, both of which are in Library and Archives Canada, Ottawa. Many are now available online; more are to follow. I have also used various family letters, photographs, and other records, directly gathered for this book or previously acquired. It is intended that many of these materials will find a home in the Victoria High School Archives or on the website of the Victoria High School Alumni Association and others maintained by Victoria High School.

Royalties from sales of this book, and of any future editions, will go to the Victoria High School Alumni Association for the benefit of its student scholarships or other activities. Contributions to the Victoria High School Archives, custodian of papers and museum items, can be made to Victoria High School Alumni Association, 1260 Grant Street, Victoria, BC, V8T 1C2, Canada.

When I was well into the research for this book, I realized I was undertaking a mission in salvage—a salvage of sociological detail, not only for those mentioned in this book but for all of the community. The work epitomizes what we might well find in any other older community in Canada such as Victoria. I have been delighted to meet so many people who maintain family records and who have expressed to me their thanks that such a book has been published.

When I finished this book, I felt that gnawing regret so many historians feel when they are obliged to leave a topic and send it out to the wider world as a published work. I have been a working historian for most of my life, and many grand and exciting topics have come my way, but in all honesty none has captured my interest as has this story of my old school in the Great War. It is a quintessential Canadian story that deserves to be widely known and widely read. If this book inspires other historians, other students, other schools to salvage the essentials of their own experiences of this war, or the Second World War, I will be eternally grateful. I leave it now, to repeat, with regret, but the fascination of the topic—the heroism and the horror of this war—will remain of imperishable importance in the annals of civilization. This was not just a "great war": it was the greatest catastrophe to Europe, and it embroiled all the world in war. It goes to show that the insularity of Victoria is only a paper fabrication. Of all the episodes of our history, none made Victorians more Canadian than this great adventure of war. It is one of the oddities of our collective experience that although we proclaim ourselves a nation of peacekeepers, we were in fact forged by war—the one described in this book.

While every attempt has been made to keep the memories green and the record accurate, I am aware that errors creep in and also that oversights do occur in any historical enterprise. The publisher and I will be pleased to take note of any corrections that could be included should another edition be published.

In the Acknowledgements, I have listed names of individuals and institutions that have given assistance. I alone am responsible for errors of omission or commission.

Barry Gough

VICTORIA, BC, AUGUST 4, 2014

## PRINCIPAL PERSONS

**John Gibson Anderson,** graduate of the school, student at McGill University, and teacher, enlisted in the Canadian Expeditionary Force at the outset of the War and fought in all its battles, including Vimy Ridge. "Lucky Star," as Major Anderson called himself, was killed at Passchendaele. Early on he won the Military Cross for courageous hand-to-hand combat in the trenches against the enemy. His was the first Military Cross to be won by a Victoria High School soldier.

**Henry Forbes Angus,** Victoria-born and educated at Victoria High School and McGill, won a scholarship to Oxford, then joined a British regiment and served as a staff officer in the Mesopotamia Campaign. In 1919, he taught law in the Canadian Khaki University. Later one of Canada's greatest civil servants and outstanding educators, he was a celebrated "pioneer" of the University of British Columbia.

**Herbert William Boggs**, Victoria-born graduate of Victoria High School, rugby star, and lieutenant leading a platoon of No. 3 Company, 7th Infantry Battalion (British Columbia Regiment), died in February 1915, the first Canadian officer killed in action.

**Harold Lane Campbell**, graduate of Victoria High School, enlisted and served in the medical corps on the Western Front in France. The horrors of war left a deep impression on him. He later became a distinguished educator, a resident of Victoria, superintendent of education, and then deputy minister of education for British Columbia. His brother **Claude Lane Campbell** also became a soldier but did not go with the intended Siberian expedition. A teacher, then vice principal, of Victoria High School, he served as a naval officer in the Second World War. After his return to his old post, he became superintendent of schools for North Island.

**Earl W. "Bunny" Clarke**, graduate of the school and its valedictorian, art teacher, sculptor, and designer of the school's war memorials, he left a great legacy: "By his memorials shall he be known."

**Cecil John Clayton**, graduate of the school and *Daily Colonist* employee, enlisted in the Royal Naval Air Service, earned his "wings," and then flew fighter craft and tactical bombers in the areas of the Dover Patrol and Felixstowe. He was credited with successful action against German U-boats and won the Distinguished Flying Cross. At the Armistice, and now a major in the Royal Air Force, he commanded the air flight that escorted 150 U-boats to their graveyard in Harwich, England. He survived the War and became a Victoria dentist.

**Elsie Collis**, a nursing sister of prominence, served in Salonika and elsewhere in the War and kept a diary of note. She survived the German bombing of her hospital in France, married, raised a family, and lived in the Cowichan Valley.

**Harry Cross**, campus idol, high-ranking scholar, and champion debater, served as a militiaman in the local 5th British Columbia Regiment of Garrison Artillery, RCA, before going to war. He survived a gas attack and later returned to Victoria, where he went to Normal School, earned a teaching certificate, and taught at North Ward School briefly before his health failed him completely. Buried with military honours in Ross Bay Cemetery, Victoria.

**Sir Arthur Currie**, a teacher at Boys' Central School and Victoria High School, promoted the Cadet Battalion; commanded the 5th British Columbia Regiment of Garrison Artillery, RCA; raised a local regiment; became a brigade commander in the First Canadian Division; and rose in July 1917 to command the Canadian Corps in its greatest battles. He was highly decorated and knighted as Canada's greatest soldier; later principal of McGill University until his death in 1933.

**John or "Jack" Dowler**, from a prominent Victoria family, was much admired for his devotion to the school and its Cadet Battalion. He was a graduate of McGill University. At the time of his death at Vimy, he was a major in the Canadian Army. His sacrifice was memorialized in remembrance trees at Lampson Street School and Victoria High School.

**Fletcher Frederick Elliott** and his brother **George William Elliott** saw going to war as a Christian duty, and they were not alone in this. Born in Japan to a Canadian missionary family, they served in the 7th Battalion of the 2nd Brigade, First Canadian Division. George was killed on April 24, 1915, in the Second Battle of Ypres. On May 7 the Victoria press inaccurately reported that both brothers had been killed. Fletcher had only been wounded. He survived his wounds but was killed just over a year later, on June 3, 1916, while leading No. 1 and 3 Companies in a counterattack on the enemy at Mount Sorrel. Both Fletcher Frederick and George William Elliott are memorialized in the Menin Gate, Ypres Memorial Panel.

**Robin Gray**, graduate of the school and a pilot in the Royal Flying Corps (RFC), was shot down and badly injured, saved by a French family, and then was made a German prisoner. He died of wounds. Older brother **James Gray**, also Victoria High School, won his "wings" and was commissioned into the RFC, where he logged hundreds of hours on bombing and reconnaissance missions. He was decorated by the Republic of France. He became a squadron leader, Royal Canadian Air Force, in the Second World War. Another brother, oldest of the three, **Lieutenant Andrew Jack Gray**, fought with the 16th Battalion at Ypres, was wounded at Festubert (losing an arm), and returned to Victoria, where he died age eighty.

**Bruce Hutchison** was prominent in school debating and thespian pursuits, and was an acclaimed editor of *The Camosun* during the war. He and others who were editors, **Roy Daniells** and **Ursula (Edwards) Jupp**, fell under the wing of successive teaching masters and literary directors **Arthur Yates** and **Ira Dilworth**. Hutchison could not enlist as he was too young, only eighteen in 1918. He went on to become Canada's outstanding journalist and author, later recording his school and other experiences in *The Far Side of the Street*.

**Percy James**, graduate of Victoria High School, joined the Royal Navy and at the outbreak of war was an Able Seaman in the doomed British cruiser *Hawke*. He found a watery grave, the first Canadian sailor to die in the War.

**Albert Nelson King**, top student of the school in 1906, worked for the *Daily Colonist* newspaper, was a gold medalist in Classics at McGill, and won the Rhodes Scholarship. While at Oxford he enlisted in King Edward's Horse, became a lieutenant in the Royal Horse Artillery, and was killed in action in May 1916. His sister **Jessie Nelson King**, Royal Jubilee Hospital (1916), was the last Canadian nursing sister to die in the War.

**Paul King**, an air ace, was prominent in school affairs, head of his matriculation class, and highly spirited. His Irish-American mother did not want him to go to war, but he joined the medical corps and then enlisted in the Royal Flying Corps, where his daring tactics helped destroy German aircraft and win the War on the ground in its last months. Decorated for his achievements, he became a medical doctor and later served in the Second World War.

**Herbert William Lacoursiere** was prominent in the school's Cadet Battalion. He enlisted in 1915 as soon as he reached age eighteen. He fought courageously in many campaigns and returned to Victoria a decorated hero, but died tragically in 1923 in a Saanich fire after a gallant attempt to rescue his brother from the inferno. Buried with military honours in West Saanich Cemetery.

**Herbert Cridge Laundy,** graduate of the school, enlisted in September 1914 and went overseas with the first contingent. He distinguished himself by his brave conduct during the Second Battle of Ypres. He won the Military Medal and later the Military Cross. His brother **Everard Lynne Laundy** enlisted as a private, rose to captain, and fought through most of the Somme engagements. He won the Military Cross at Vimy Ridge. Their brother **Cecil Eastman Laundy** also enlisted and survived the war.

**Lieutenant John Angus MacDonald** was a graduate of Queen's University and one of the school's masters or teachers. His teaching subject was French. He won the Military Cross and was killed in action at the Somme.

All four **McCallum brothers,** born and educated in Victoria, became officers in Canadian or British units. **Captain Arthur McCallum** of the Royal Flying Corps was shot down and became "a guest of the Kaiser" for the duration of the war. His wife, **Mary Frances Mackenzie McCallum,** went overseas to England in nursing services. **Major Eric McCallum** won the Distinguished Service Order (DSO) for conspicuous gallantry at Ypres in 1916 while serving with the Royal Canadian Regiment. **Flight Commander Kenneth McCallum** lost a foot when he was shot down while covering a bombing mission. He went on to teach young pilots and was awarded the Military Cross. **Lieutenant Richard McCallum,** RFC, was killed in an airplane accident. They all distinguished themselves in various ways.

**James McNaughton Pottinger**, graduate of Victoria High School, fought side by side with his slightly older brother **Claude Pottinger**. James was killed in action November 1, 1918. News of his death reached Victoria after the Armistice had been signed.

**Robert B. "Bobbie" Powell**, Canada's most famous tennis ace of the age, was also a lawyer and colonial administrator. "Don't worry about me, dear mother, I am only trying to do my duty and that is all that matters." He fought at Vimy Ridge and died in the after-action of that campaign.

**Blayney Scott** earned fame by saving the aircraft in which he was flying as observer by plugging a leak in the fuel tank. Died of wounds from a plane crash. Earned the Military Cross and the Distinguished Service Order.

**Henry George Sivertz** was born in Victoria to an Icelandic family of note, and he and his brothers **Gus** and **Christian** became soldiers. Henry George won the Military Medal and two bars, and he was a sergeant at the time of his death. A campus favourite and student leader at Victoria High School, his passing was much lamented.

**Sara Ellen Spencer** was awarded the Order of the British Empire in 1919 for distinguished services to the Red Cross. This Victoria-born lieutenant in the Canadian Comforts Field Commission was the go-between linking the school to the convalescing Canadian soldiers in the big Canadian hospital at Shorncliffe, Kent. Later a businesswoman and philanthropist, she gave the family house to the Art Gallery of Greater Victoria.

**Arthur Yates** was a teaching master at Victoria High School before the War and during its early years, and a hockey, lacrosse, and rugby player and coach of note. He won a Rhodes Scholarship, then taught at the school until 1917, when he could not longer resist the call to arms. He became a gunner. While at the school he contributed in major ways to its well-being and student life: he was literary director of *The Camosun* and directed the boys' debating society (Beta Delta). He sent home delightful stories from the Western Front, which were published in *The Camosun*. Later a literary agent and a professor at Long Island University, he is credited with being the leading proponent of collegiate rugby in the United States.

*Prologue*

---

## THE LONG AND SPLENDID AFTERNOON

*F*rom time immemorial, the Songhees and Esquimalt First Nations called the locality home. One of their ancestral territories was *Camosun* or *Camousack*, a term generally applied to the area but more specifically to the reversing falls of the internal waterway, the Gorge. Altogether, it was a fine place of settlement and trade. (The name *Camosun* is important to our story, for it was given to Victoria High School's student magazine, founded in 1906.)

Many a European had passed by on reconnaissance, perhaps seeking the entrance to a northwest passage linking the old countries to the land of Kublai Khan. There were so many false starts in this line of discovery. The Spaniard Francisco de Eliza came as close as any to putting down a marker for the king of Spain in 1791, but Madrid's influence was on the wane. The rising tide of British commerce, backed by steam navigation, brought Chief Factor James Douglas on a mission of commercial examination for the Hudson's Bay Company, and in 1843 the firm began construction of a fort, with palisade, on the rocky east side of Camosun, or Victoria, Harbour.

During his inspection of southern Vancouver Island, Douglas found it "a Perfect Eden," one capable of development and habitation. The Island was made a British colony in 1849 to keep out any American squatters, and when the Royal Navy made nearby Esquimalt its Pacific Station headquarters in 1862, that sealed the social fabric of the community. Esquimalt, with its fortifications, dockyard, and artillery garrison, became an imperial watchtower on the North Pacific. This was the origin of what became a mighty cordilleran empire under the name of British Columbia. From these early days the promise of a link with eastern Canada, or British North America, spurred thoughts of a great transcontinental dominion under the Union Jack, a counter to the United States south of the line. But the great mountains of the Continental Divide and the vast sweep of the prairies, to say nothing of the pre-Cambrian shield along the north shore of the Great Lakes, posed difficulties. For that reason, until the Panama Canal was opened in 1914, Victoria and the coast that it served (to its benefit) were joined to the British Isles by 18,000 miles of sea lane. In a country that looked much like Scotland, with its rocks and braes, and given the English and Scots nature of those who directed the affairs of Fort Victoria, it is not surprising that things British were burnished and made much of. Victoria was a creature of empire.

British Columbia, far from the national capital of Ottawa and other eastern cities, was often regarded from afar as "the spoilt child of Confederation." The province grew up in splendid isolation, rich in resources, a hunting and fishing paradise, a place for business capital to flourish, given the governmental regulations of the day. This was Canada's farthest west and the Pacific gateway to Asia. Until the Canadian Pacific Railway reached tidewater at Port Moody on Burrard Inlet, British Columbia had few links with the Canadian west or the rest of Canada. Yet it had been thrown together by circumstances with other portions of British North America and in 1871 became part of Canada. Its independence of perspective reflected its geography, its isolation, its relations with First Nations, and its institutions, religious, social, and educational. British Columbia, and Victoria on Vancouver Island, stood apart from the rest of Canada and uniquely defended from its American neighbours in Washington State and Alaska Territory (the latter Russian before 1867). This uniqueness gave it a political perspective that was not "Wild West" but was more cosmopolitan and worldly than has been imagined. It had not been born yesterday. Rather, it was a seat of imperial power with global interests.

The vegetation was lush, and Garry oaks growing in open glades or on rocky knolls gave the observer impressions of English parkland. Even the gentle, salubrious climate imitated the Old Country. No wonder it attracted so many English and Scots settlers. The process was slow and halting. For a time Victoria became a boom town in consequence of the Fraser River gold rush. The future looked glorious. Already, as an early observer remarked, Victoria's two favourite themes were in place: "a bit of olde England and our rightful place under the sun."[1] Victoria and British Columbia pulsed to the rhythm of steam engines. The primeval stands of trees soon fell for the construction of wharves, warehouses, offices, and administrative and political structures. The swamps were drained and the marshes filled in. Tramways snaked through the city, and streets, sidewalks, and roads quickly extended the town to the east, north, and west. Bridges were raised, and a railway from up-Island and a light-rail line from outlying communities came into town. Marine industries sprang up, and sealing and fishing fleets crowded the harbour. By the end of the century, Victoria was a hub of North Pacific steam navigation, with links to Seattle, Vancouver, and northern points both on Vancouver Island and north to Alaska. Trans-Pacific connections by sea and submarine cable forged new imperial links, while the Royal Navy, still stationed at nearby Esquimalt, was an everyday reminder of ties to the Old Country and to sister nations and colonies across the seas. It had never been an American town, though at one time an annexation petition was raised, without success. The colonists and brideships arrived, and the settlement societies and individually organized schemes for bringing family and friends from the British Isles made Victoria into essentially an English town, and few challenged the validity of that. It was home to the first Chinatown in Canada, too, and the races lived in easy harmony until late in the century, when some difficulties arose because of the agitation of white labour and the mistaken importation of substitute workers. The only real tensions that existed before the guns of August were fired in anger involved race relations, and British Columbia was not immune to the sorts of difficulties faced in all parts of the British Empire where European settlement was occurring.

In the early days, Christian organizations provided the essential service of education. There were private or subscription schools as well. But the concept of the public school, free to all, was gaining wide acceptance, particularly in Ontario. In 1872, British Columbia adopted a free school act, modelled on Ontario's 1846 legislation.[2] Control was vested in the lieutenant-governor–in-council until 1891, when school boards were established where the local population warranted. Under the minister of education, assisted by the superintendent of education, a whole apparatus of centralized control for quality instruction and regular schooling was put in place. Gradually the local municipalities found themselves responsible for the costs of the schools. All public schools were free and were to be run on strictly secular and non-sectarian principles. "The highest morality shall be inculcated, but no religious dogma nor creed shall be taught," said the School Act of 1903. Every school-teacher had to hold a provincial certificate, which came in one of four classes, from a three-year one up to the Academic class, the highest, and valid for life. Textbooks were provided free of charge.

The imperial spirit animated those who controlled public education in the province. One article in the Public Schools Act of 1895 specified that holidays were to be granted on Empire Day (May 24, now the Victoria Day holiday, named for the Queen-Empress Victoria) and the King's birthday. So that the students might better understand the meaning of these official days off school, the following note was appended:

> The object of Empire Day is the development of the Empire idea. Consequently, the lessons, recitations and other exercises of the last teaching day preceding Empire Day (May 24th) should be such as to bear directly upon the history and resources of Canada and the British Empire, and to tend to promote a spirit of true patriotism and loyalty. The school Flag (British or Canadian, which it is earnestly recommended that the Trustees shall provide) should be raised on Empire Day, Dominion Day, the King's Birthday, the anniversaries of great national events, the day of opening or closing school in any term, &c.[3]

When Victoria High School opened in August 1876, it provided the only opportunity for accessible public post-elementary education in British Columbia. It remained the province's lone high school until another was opened eight years later at New Westminster. Nanaimo and Vancouver had high schools soon after that, but Victoria High School, the oldest of its kind west of Winnipeg, and the largest in British Columbia, held the premier position in the province into the twentieth century.

In its first year, sixty students attended classes in the small wooden colonial schoolhouse next to the public primary school, a handsome Italianate two-storey building, with a bell tower, that had been opened to public acclaim just a few months earlier. Both sat on ten acres set aside as a school reserve between

Yates and Fort Streets, bordering Fernwood Street. The number of high-school students quickly soared, and eight years later they moved into a purpose-built premises, a single-storey brick addition to the east end of the primary school. The facility was crowded and noisy, and in 1902 the school moved again, into an elegant facility designed by renowned architect Francis Rattenbury, who had also drawn up plans for the provincial Legislative Buildings, the Empress Hotel, and other fine structures. This school bordered on Fernwood Street, on the same public school reserve.

Under Dr. E.B. Paul, principal from 1892 to 1908, the school went from three divisions, with as many teachers, to a school of thirteen teachers in a newer building that was taxed to the utmost capacity. A teaching colleague remarked that Dr. Paul had given the school a high place in public esteem. Not only was the manner in which he conducted affairs most cordial, but the proportion of students graduating had greatly increased, and every year a higher number of students came from other parts of the province seeking admission.[4]

Victoria grew quickly in the late nineteenth and early twentieth century, and so did the outlying suburbs. Students came to the school from the Gulf Islands or from Gordon Head, Esquimalt, Langford, Cowichan, and far beyond. In those days the feeder schools—Lampson Street, Tolmie, South Park, Bank Street, North Ward, and George Jay—were growing quickly, some full to capacity. The intermediate levels of schooling in Victoria were offered at Boys' Central School and Girls' Central School. The Central Schools were an excellent preparation for the senior level, and we have it on the reliable authority of one student that the course of study was rigorous,[5] although successful completion at that level did not necessarily lead to the high school. To be admitted to Victoria High School, potential students had to sit and successfully write an examination, though a particularly bright student who had done well at the intermediate level could find himself or herself admitted before time. (Female students in Victoria schools always made up a strong proportion of the enrolment, and during the Great War their numbers were higher than those of the male students.) College level was another step above this.

To their shame, many historians think that Victoria College began at Craigdarroch Castle, but this was not so. Victoria High School is the cradle of college and university education in British Columbia. British Columbia's growth presaged the need for a university, and in 1896 the Victoria School Board petitioned to found a college, the first step toward university education.

In the meantime, an affiliation was made between Victoria High School and McGill University in Montreal, arguably Canada's top institution of higher learning. Under the arrangement, Arts I and II were taken at Victoria College, and students then completed their degrees with Arts III at McGill. In 1909–10, the McGill University College of British Columbia, with one branch in Vancouver and the other in Victoria, had 152 students; of this number, 98 were male and 54 were female.

Readers will be surprised at the number of times the McGill connection comes up in this history. McGill was also the link to Oxford, then the premier university in England. The wealth of that empire builder Cecil Rhodes, who had Oxford connections, led to the founding of the Rhodes Scholarships, and thus it was that Victoria High School and Victoria College students who went to McGill often found themselves nominated successfully for Rhodes Scholarships. The process worked in reverse, too, for Oxford supplied a Rhodes Scholar to become a teaching master at Victoria High School in the person of Arthur Yates, whose influence on the students of the school before and during the War is central to this story.

In 1903, education at the university level began with the establishment of Victoria College in the same Victoria High School building erected in 1902. From 1903 to 1915, Victoria College flourished. This is important to our Great War history, for many of those who "went to war" were at one time students at Victoria College (as they were previously at Victoria High School)—John Gibson Anderson, John Dowler, A. Nelson King, and Joseph B. Clearihue to cite but four.

George Jay, long-standing school board member, and Mrs. Margaret Jenkins, also of the school board, were the prime movers of the time, the fixers. They allied themselves with a series of prominent educators, notably Dr. E.B. Paul and S.J. Willis, whose advancement of the interests of Victoria College and Victoria High School knew no bounds. Principals as well as teachers at VHS, Paul and Willis laid the foundations, and they likely would have established British Columbia's first university in Victoria had not the interests of Vancouver and "the mainland" triumphed. In 1907 the province set aside lands for this institution at Point Grey, Vancouver, dashing Victoria's hopes.

Even so, under the arrangement with McGill University, and with the full backing of the Ministry of Education, Victoria High School acquired what might be described as super-high-school status: Victoria College brought some of the finest and best-qualified teachers to Victoria, male and female, most with MA degrees and some with PhDs. Because the college was housed within the high school, this not only put Victoria High School in an exalted position in Western Canada; it also had many benefits for aspiring students at the tertiary level, who were able to complete their preparatory courses for matriculation and university entrance in the provincial capital. Some of the masters or teachers taught in both the college and the high school, putting on or taking off mortarboards and gowns as the occasion warranted.

Until 1909, physical instruction had no place in the school's curriculum. That year, however, the minister of militia of Canada sent a circular letter that conveyed the terms of the Strathcona Trust for the encouragement of physical training and military drill in public schools. Lord Strathcona, a noted benefactor connected to the Hudson's Bay Company, who had outfitted Lord Strathcona's Light Horse for service in the South African or Boer War, saw, as did others such as Robert Baden-Powell, founder of the Boy Scouts, the need for physical preparation and muscular strength in times of peace as in war. The Province of British Columbia took up the possibilities, accepted the conditions of the trust, and made provisions for qualifying teachers for the military instruction of pupils. Thus was born No. 112, Victoria High School Cadet Battalion, headquartered at the school. Its role in this history is extensive.

From early beginnings, the Cadet Battalion gained in numbers, reaching a strength of 182 in November 1913. In the background was a general militarization of Canada, with various units being formed and divided into either the Permanent Active Militia (also known as the Permanent Force) or the Non-Permanent Active Militia. The 5th British Columbia Regiment of Garrison Artillery, RCA (with 373 members in 1912),[6] staff, and force at Esquimalt (125 members), and the 88th Regiment, Victoria Fusiliers (411 members), comprised the local forces, to which was added the 50th Regiment, Gordon Highlanders, raised in 1914.[7] The Headquarters Staff of all British Columbia units was at Work Point, Esquimalt. The sum total of all forces, Permanent and Non-Permanent, in the province was 3,133 troops of all arms. "This force is to be regarded as the framework on which in time of war the manhood of the Province can be drafted, and judged from this standpoint it can doubtless be termed adequate."[8]

In December 1912, the VHS Cadet Battalion and the Lampson Street Cadets held a sham battle at Christmas Hill, then a lonely rocky hillside. The bloodless contest involved about sixty cadets, all of them under the command of Lieutenant Andrew Mulcahy, Royal Canadian Garrison Artillery, assisted by Lieutenant Wilby and Mr. MacDonald, MA, both teachers at the school. Major John Dowler, who features elsewhere in these pages—the heart and soul of the Cadet Battalion—headed up the attacking force that successfully cut the Victoria and Sidney Railway and also captured Christmas Hill. Greater obstacles were to lie ahead for these cadets, many of whom became soldiers in the Great War.[9]

In those days the Daughters of the Empire (now the IODE) presented a Ross rifle and a medal to the prize marksman. Every winter there was an indoor gallery practice at one location or another, including near the Work Point Barracks of the Royal Canadian Garrison Artillery. In fair weather, Clover Point offered a 200-yard range. Good scores on the almost weekly rifle competition were being made with the new Ross rifle. The District Officer Commanding, Colonel Alexander Roy, watched all proceedings with a careful eye. Here was a young Canada in arms.

By 1913, Victoria High School had been housed in its third premises—Rattenbury's handsome red-brick building—for just over ten years. The school stood at the top of a gentle rise of spacious ground that extended from the head of View Street right up to Fernwood Street. Its two previous homes, the two-room frame cottage and the brick extension to the government public school, were nearby, and up the gentle slope from the brick structure were assorted frame buildings, including a gymnasium, band room, woodworking shop, and boy's lavatory.[10] However, all signs indicated that the school population had outgrown the existing buildings. Rather than build even more structures on the Yates Street site, it was decided that a new and large plot of land needed to be found, and quickly.

At this time the cities and towns were being pressed by the provincial government of British Columbia to assume a greater share of the costs of education, and thus the City of Victoria, in considering what sort of new high school was to be built and where, had a specific civic duty that it could not leave to some other branch of government. This shift played strongly to Victoria's civic interests. That an outstanding principal and administrator of wide vision, perhaps the greatest on record, S.J. Willis, guided the whole process in close association with the Department of Education, headed up by the affable, logical, and eminent minister Henry Esson Young, remains an example for all interested in the history of educational administration. Willis was a giant figure in the aggregate, though in person modest and unassuming, and he brought professionalism to his appointment that was a model for many others to follow, both in what became School District 61 (Greater Victoria) and in others farther afield.

In the search for a new site for Victoria High School, one in particular had abiding attraction: the city's gravel and sand pits that stood on a rise at a place called Spring Ridge, one of the early sources for city water. After a complicated land assembly, and some considerable discussion among interested parties, the City, through a 1910 bylaw, donated the three-and-a-half-acre property to the school trustees. Keen to make the site handsome, the City also granted $7,000 for landscaping.[11] Thus a magnificent campus became available for what would be an equally magnificent building. The south boundary faced Grant Street and was also approached by Camosun Street. On the east was Fernwood Street, with Vining Street running into the school grounds as a road access. On the north side lay Gladstone Avenue, and apart from a church (now the Belfry Theatre), the property ran all the way west to a boundary line that lay behind a row of dwellings facing Chambers Street. At the same time, the engineering infrastructure of the Fernwood district was put in, and so the new school site would be served by good roads, sidewalks, and a streetcar, No. 3, "The Vic High Special."

On March 12, 1910, the school board chose C. Elwood Watkins as architect.[12] The project was sent to tender, and Dinsdale & Malcolm's bid was accepted. The costs of this project were unprecedented for schools in British Columbia, and one reads between the lines concerns about cost overruns. In any event, the site development and building went on marvellously well. Watkins designed one of the iconic buildings of the city, and the school matches in age the McPherson Playhouse (formerly Pantages Theatre) and the Royal Theatre, centrepieces of Victoria cultural expression. The three buildings are character-defining elements with enduring legacies and regenerative futures. Watkins showcased the best of the Beaux Arts principles. His classical conservatism is disclosed in the building, notably in the granite main entrance, symmetrical facades, the two-storey main entrance crowned by a balustrade, Ionic pilasters framing second-floor windows, and handsome use of rough-cut granite and terracotta and glazed tile. Technically, the school was state of the art, with a teacher's telephone in each classroom, a centrally regulated wall clock, and thermostat-controlled ventilation. Structurally, too, it was robust: it had reinforced concrete and steel girders, making it seismically stronger than many a building built later.

On Saturday, September 14, 1913, the cornerstone of the new Victoria College and High School—note the name—was laid by the Minister of Education, the Honourable Henry Esson Young, MD, LLD. A large number of students witnessed the ceremony, as did the teaching staff. The school's Cadet Battalion formed the honour guard. "The event marked one of the most important steps in Victoria's progress in the educational line during the last few years," commented *The Camosun*. "Next fall we hope to see the opening of the new structure, which will be an added attraction to the city."[13]

High expectation was in the air. *The Camosun* again: "It is very satisfactory to know that the construction work on the new building is being pushed forward as quickly as possible by the contractors. Everything indicates that the school will be ready for use next fall. When completed it will be one of the most modern of its kind on the continent."

On a much-anticipated day in April 1914, students lined up at the Rattenbury building and, joining hands, walked north to the new building. Before long, teachers and students had found its various nooks and crannies, perhaps peeped into the boiler room where the mighty heating plant stands, or taken lunch in the cafeteria on the ground floor. The maple-floored gymnasium, with its gallery, was the theatre of unimagined athletic prowess. Way up and under the roof lay a short shooting range. Stained glass windows added light to auditorium and stairwells. Marble entry steps provided grandeur and safety, the magnificent railings and external lighting giving an aura of permanence, of solidity. The front entrance stairs brought visitors to the upper hall, the civic space, while at ground level a Girls Entrance and a Boys Entrance provided the designated points of arrival and departure directly into the school. On the east side of the school, another Girls Entrance gave an approach to the first floor; on the west, similarly, was a second Boys Entrance. This design gave easier and private access to respective washrooms, shower-rooms, and gymnasium facilities. All students had their own locker, a first. Because so many of the teachers had at one time or another attended the same institution, we can imagine their delight at taking up their work in the enhanced space, with room to grow. Classes began on April 20.

When Lieutenant-Governor Thomas W. Paterson formally opened the building on May 1, the *Daily Colonist* described it as "the finest educational institution of its kind west of the Great Lakes."[14] The handsome auditorium was thronged to capacity. The pupils sat with their teachers on the main floor, while parents and friends of the scholars filled the large balcony. Ferns, flowering broom, and potted plants decorated the stage, while seated on it was the greatest gathering of the principal individuals who had brought about the achievement. The Board of School Trustees were hosts on the day, for it was their achievement. Mr. George Jay, the driving agent, was in the chair. Mrs. Margaret Jenkins, powerful and popular chair of the finance committee, had steered the project to success at an estimated cost of about $500,000. The Honourable Dr. Henry Esson Young and Mrs. Young were in proud attendance, delighted by the process.[15]

S.J. Willis, the principal, received a finely crafted gold key (the whereabouts of which is unknown) with the school's coat of arms on one side and an inscription on the obverse denoting the presentation. In his response, Willis pointed out that the excellent facility would inspire students to do their best, and he noted the gymnasium, without which a student's education would not be complete, and the new library. The public could use the magnificent auditorium for its benefit, and he hoped that in the future, noted visitors to the city would speak to the students on matters of moment.

Dr. Young, in his remarks, said that the erection of the new high school reflected credit not only on the pupils and teachers but also on the people of Victoria. The people of British Columbia, he noted further, should be proud of the support given by the government to education, and it was a pleasure to the government, and especially to himself as minister of education, that the people provided so much support and sympathy in all matters pertaining to the betterment of educational matters in the province. Not least, great credit was given to Elwood Watkins, the architect.

Prayers of opening and closing were said, "God Save the King" sung, and the whole lovely afternoon concluded with the high school girls giving a physical drill in the gym. In the evening the school was open for public viewing (thousands came, it is said), and again the girls executed a maypole dance and physical exercises. "The gracefulness with which the girls exercised the various movements won for them the praise of the onlookers."[16] This had been S.J. Willis's day, for he had guided the process through all its awkward stages. His vision for a great structure to house a great, publicly supported institution of learning for the public's benefit had materialized. The greatest gift had been given to the City of Victoria.

The new building spoke to civic pride and to expectation of greater things to come in the educational line. Here was the school on the hill, visible for miles around, the focal point for the final years for those advancing from elementary levels and for those of academic brilliance who could go on to college-level work. At its opening there were eighteen divisions and an estimated 450 students. There was also room to grow. For many years the high school had offered a Commercial Class for boys and girls. Technical training classes came after the War. As mentioned earlier, students entered by passing an examination. They would enter junior matriculation, and then, if able, senior matriculation. The Arts I and Arts II years were for those who were in Victoria College. Many of the graduates from senior matriculation went into public-school teaching, which they could do on a provisional permit, and many of the women from the same classes went into nursing, teaching, or secretarial work. All the hopes for the future of the society of British Columbia, and of Victoria in particular, rested on the success of the high school, now given its bright new home. With the best teachers that could be hired—for Willis was a stickler on "quality hirings"—a rich history was opening before Victoria High School in 1914.

In many respects this was the last age of innocence, and certainly of serenity under the security of *Pax Britannica*. Men and women of Victoria were aware of this security, and the reason was clear: nearby Esquimalt served as a calling place for British warships on tours of duty in the Pacific and the Bering Sea. Victorians had opposed the fleet reorganizations, part of the naval reforms that began in 1904, but they had happened anyway, and the Royal Navy had largely disappeared from the coast, except for surveying work. An alliance with Imperial Japan in 1902 had solved some British problems of imperial overstretch. In the face of the British withdrawal, the Canadian government assumed control of Esquimalt naval base, and the 5th BC Regiment of Garrison Artillery, RCA, looked after the fortifications and guns there. This regiment, which recruited cadets from the high school's Cadet Battalion, was to play a unique role in the War, and many of the soldiers mentioned in this book had their initial training in it. The militia system was a strong and integrative force in national development. At Macaulay Point, on the north shore of the entrance to Victoria Harbour, and on Macaulay Plains, the army had a training establishment for officers and men, headquartered at Work Point Barracks. As well, at Willows Beach in Oak Bay, the Esquimalt naval base, and in Sidney were camps for newly formed Canadian Army units. From these beginnings grew mighty centres of training during wartime. All the same, few in 1913 could imagine that possibility.

That was the year Rupert Brooke, a young Cambridge graduate, visited Victoria as part of a North American tour.[17] He had not yet become immortal: war had not yet claimed his life. His poetry had imperial attraction, and it was very much a refuge from the encroaching sounds and fears of impending battle. Linked closely to the ruling Liberal Party in Great Britain, he was the doyen of old Liberal England—and the last victim of the old order. Before he died, of blood poisoning, in 1915, he had written some elegiac verse that became popular at Victoria High School. His poems often were reprinted in the pages of *The Camosun*. From Brooke's "The Soldier":

> *If I should die, think only this of me:*
> *That there's some corner of a foreign field*
> *That is forever England. There shall be*
> *In that rich earth a richer dust concealed;*
> *A dust whom England bore, shaped, made aware,*
> *Gave, once, her flowers to love, her ways to roam,*
> *A body of England's, breathing English air,*
> *Washed by the rivers, blest by suns of home.*

Brooke, a sub-lieutenant in the Royal Naval Brigade during its vain defence of Antwerp, Belgium, was en route to Gallipoli when his life was cut short. He was buried on Scyros. His passing was much lamented. The poetry of the age soon passed to other hands, to those known as the War Poets—Robert Graves, Siegfried Sassoon, Wilfred Owen, and others—who wrote about the horror and pity of war, and the ignorance of higher command. Brooke did not write much about Victoria, though the waters, mountains, and wraith-like clouds that surround it transfixed him: he thought the scene half Japanese.

As of 1913, the old order still existed. It is true that Great Britain was preoccupied with major domestic issues—Irish home rule, demands for female suffrage, temperance, and the licensing of pubs. Canada was caught up in a railway boom, English-French discord, settlement of the west, and diversified immigration. In British Columbia, politicians were concerned with Asian immigration and labour-management issues. But all hoped for the continuance of peace and the age of progress. Indeed, Britain's Liberal government was dominated by pacifists, as was the Canadian government.

The War came upon the British Empire as an unexpected and unwelcome storm.

For some considerable time, however, the Royal Navy had been going through a shakeup the likes of which it had never before seen, and the reason for this was the rise of the Imperial German navy. The key date was 1902, when Germany's naval plans and shipbuilding showed every indication that Germany intended to challenge Britain's power on and over the seas. In London, the Admiralty and the War Office watched with alarm. But no manner of planning and no manner of diplomatic dealing could put a stop to the desire of Imperial Germany and Kaiser Wilhelm II to increase the naval, maritime, and imperial power of that state. The most competent historians have since wondered what Germany hoped to gain, for that land-based nation lacked the resources to dominate on sea as well as on land. The naval program that was developed by Germany did not, and could not, outdistance British capabilities. The ambitious dreadnought program developed by Berlin merely confirmed the whole experience of modern history by intensifying fear in Britain, a fear reciprocated in Germany. The vicious cycle of naval rivalry added little to the security of the two powers, and it hastened Britain into a military alliance with France (and later Russia). The old British isolation in place at the time of Queen Victoria's Diamond Jubilee in 1897 had come to a sudden end.

Naval rivalry did not cause the war, but it insured that when war did break out, Britain would be on the side of Germany's enemies. The German high command understood this. In 1906, the head of the political section of the German Foreign Office, Friedrich von Holstein, wrote, "Germany stands or falls with her army, and for that every sacrifice must be made. The fleet increases the number of our enemies, but will never be strong enough to vanquish them. We cannot hope, now or later, for an equal fight at sea. The land army must—as in '70 [Prussia's defeat of France]—equalize the inequality of the naval forces."[18] With Britain dominating at sea, any measure to stop Germany's domination of the continent had to be undertaken by armies. Here was the origin of the continental commitment, which Britain had worked so hard to avoid. Popular emotion ran deep on both sides. Governments sought to keep up with these emotional outbursts. And so the march to folly continued, awaiting some odd conjunction of causes major or minor that would set loose the dogs of war.

The War Office, which administered the British Army and the dominion and colonial armies overseas, promoted unity of organization, staff procedure, training, and equipment, and it offered the services of the General Staff to help the colonies in any way they desired. On the eve of the War, uniformity of organization, equipment, and doctrine existed among the armies of the British Empire. Canada conformed in every respect except for its use of the problematic, and later discarded, Ross rifle. Similarly, the Admiralty insisted on a unified command of all imperial fleets, and when the time came, the Royal Canadian Navy found itself under Admiralty control.

And yet the expectations of the age lingered as before—of a long peace, with minor wars popping up from time to time on the margins where the Great Powers still exercised imperial impulses. Visions of a much quieter world, free from global strife, continued to burn bright. Hopes for eternal peace were strong. At the Imperial Conference of 1907, the prime minister of Canada, Sir Wilfrid Laurier, spoke eloquently of Canada's desire to remain aloof from the "vortex of militarism" that was Europe. The dreadnought crisis of 1909 brought a change of opinion and the announcement that Canada's destiny was tied up with that of Great Britain. In 1911, Laurier said that if England were placed in such a situation that her existence was in peril, Canada would step forward and go to the rescue and contribute in any way in her power. The control of the seas had to be maintained by the British Empire, and a European balance of power had to be continued. These were interlocking policies, and they meant that the dominions and the colonies were bound to be dragged into the European vortex.[19] The process was ever so stretched out, and it rose to a torrential rush in the last month of peace. The flags of dawn appeared, and they were those of the warring states, even of Armageddon.

Victoria found itself caught up in quarrels far away. We give the last word on how peaceful Victoria had been vaulted onto the world's warlike stage to the student at Victoria High School who won, in early 1915, the coveted gold medal at the fourth annual oratorical contest of the school's Beta Delta Society, the boys' debating club, held in the school auditorium:

> In the last week of July [1914] the men and women of Europe were leading their usual orderly lives, busy and yet easy, lives which could not be disturbed by shocks such as the world knew of old. A fortnight later hell yawned under the feet of those hard-working or pleasure-seeking

men and women, and woe smote them as it smote the peoples we read of in the Middle Ages. Through the rents in our smiling surface of civilization, the ghastly fires of Death, Destruction, and Misery burned red in the gloom.[20]

This eloquent young man, wise beyond his years, tall and striking of appearance, was Strother Foulkes, president of Beta Delta. Contenders for the gold medal included young Bruce Hutchison, the journalist of later fame, Frank Young, and Harry Cross, who features elsewhere in this book. It was a civic event, with the Victoria Canadian Club, the Reverand Jonathan G. Inkster, and His Honour Judge Lampman doing the judging. Foulkes spoke in fine rhetorical language. He used, too, an excellent analogy, that of the great liner *Titanic*, which had gone down in 1912 when it hit an iceberg:

What occurred in Europe is on a grand scale like the disaster to the Titanic. One moment the great liner was speeding across the ocean, equipped with every modern device for comfort, safety and luxury. The men in her stokeholds and steerage were more comfortable than the most luxurious travelers of a century ago. The people in her first-class cabins enjoyed every luxury that a luxurious city life would demand, and all were screened not only from danger but also from the least discomfort or annoyance. Suddenly, in one awful and shattering moment Death smote the floating host so busy with work and play. They were in that moment shot back through immeasurable ages. At one stroke they were hurled from a life of effortless ease back into hideous disaster; to disaster in which heroism burned like a flame of fire, as is the heroism displayed by the soldiers today, who are fighting in Europe, some for their homes, some for their honour, some for their principles, all battling in a terrific struggle.[21]

*chapter 1* # 1914

## VICTORIA GOES TO WAR

O n August 4, the rush of cataclysmic events came down upon the world at midnight Berlin time. Britain's ultimatum to Germany expired then. It was 11:00 PM in London. In the morning of August 5, Victorians awoke to find themselves at war. The *Daily Colonist* printed this proclamation:

> George, by the Grace of God, King of the United Kingdom of Great Britain and Ireland and of the dominions Beyond the Seas, Emperor of India, has in the name of his people declared war against Germany.
>
> We give his whole title [said the *Daily Colonist*] for in this solemn act he has spoken for us all. It may prove to be the most important act performed by a British King since the day our forces were launched against Napoleon and on that never-to-be-forgotten field of Waterloo freed Europe from her would-be master. It is a strange coincidence that on the eve of the centennial of the fateful year 1815 we are again at war to relieve Europe from the intolerable assertion of mastership [this time] by the German Emperor. May the same success that crowned our efforts then attend us now. We are fighting the battle of human freedom.

To all parts of the British Empire, the colonial and dominion offices sent word of the existence of a state of war. The Admiralty sent to Esquimalt (as to all naval establishments and all of His Majesty's ships) this immediate and urgent coded message: COMMENCE HOSTILITIES AGAINST GERMANY. Meanwhile, Sir Edward Grey, the Foreign Secretary, watching from his windows in the Foreign Office as the lights were springing out in the gathering dusk, said to a friend, "The lamps are going out all over Europe; we shall not see them lit again in our lifetime." Indeed, the world would never be the same again.[1]

In the days leading up to the British declaration of war on Germany, London had been abuzz with rumours of an impending clash. The prime minister of the United Kingdom, Herbert Asquith, wrote that he heard a "distant roaring" and that "war or anything that seems likely to lead to war is always popular with the London mob," to which he added: "You remember Sir R[obert] Walpole's remark. 'Now they are ringing their bells; in a few weeks they'll be wringing their hands.'"[2] Outside Buckingham Palace, a throng was cheering and singing "God Save the King."

Victoria got its news from London and New York by various channels. That which reached the city from the imperial capital commanded special attention, for London directed foreign policy for the British Empire. In the circumstances, Canada alone would decide the degree and means of its contribution to any war effort, a fact that had already been demonstrated in the South African, or Anglo-Boer War, which ended in 1902. But given the British nature of the local populace, with so many recent arrivals from "the Old Country," the news copy that arrived from Fleet Street and was used by the local newspapers, the *Daily Colonist* and the *Victoria Times*, counted for a great deal.

*Four days earlier,* on August 1, Colonel-General Hellmuth von Moltke, who commanded the Field Army of the German Empire, learned that Russia had rejected Germany's ultimatum to cease mobilization. Late that afternoon the Kaiser authorized the general mobilization. The French ordered mobilization at the same time. Germany planned to strike first against France with full force, then turn on Russia. Moltke told the chief of the Austrian General Staff that France would be routed in six weeks; then the army could be shifted to the east to smash Russia in turn. Count Schlieffen, Moltke's predecessor, had first sketched this campaign plan in 1905. It involved railway timetables, unit deployments according to schedule, supply arrangements worked out in advance, and a victory that would be won by a wide flank march around the powerful French fortresses between Verdun and Belfort. Such a march obliged Germany to violate the neutrality of Belgium and Luxembourg. This last requirement would bring in the British, who were otherwise not involved by formal alliance in European quarrels. The plan therefore called for a fast strike, one that would yield the fruits of victory before other powers could close the gap or mount stiff resistance.

The German high command miscalculated, and circumstances in the field forced them to abandon the plan. They nevertheless came to the very edge of victory by destroying the French railways and intercepting communications. For a month the Germans maintained the offensive, while the French made successful tactical withdrawals, though at great expense. Moltke confessed on September 7: "Today our armies are fighting all the way from Paris to upper Alsace. I would give my life, as thousands have done, for victory. How much blood has been spilled and how much misery has come upon numberless innocent people whose houses have been burned and razed to the ground. Terror often overcomes me when I think about this, and the feeling I have is as if I must answer for this horror, and yet I could not act otherwise than I have."[3] Moltke himself collapsed in October 1914 and had to be replaced. Heroically, the Allies (Britain and France) halted the German armies at the Battle of the Marne. This gives us perspective on the rapid train of events occurring in Europe during the first weeks of the War. Meantime, in Victoria, a different scenario was working itself out as the city prepared to join in the fight that was taking place thousands of miles away. Weeks and months would pass before any Victorians were able to enter the War.

*When news of* the War reached Victoria on August 5, plans were enacted to call out the militia and place the local regiments on a permanent footing. Suddenly, the city was alive with military forces. The public, long used to the great peace that had given it such splendid isolation from world affairs, now realized that the young fellows were flocking to join up. Recruiting depots advertised for new enlistments. The War might be over by Christmas, so the call to arms spoke of urgency if one wanted to get in on the action. There was a deeper message: the bugles of England were calling to the men overseas. It was time for the Empire to come to the support of the colours. This was the requirement of imperial citizenship. Rudyard Kipling had been talking about it for some time. The moment had come; the time was now.

One of the first to leave for England and then the European theatre was Arthur William Currie, soon to become Canada's most famous soldier and the personification of Canada under arms. Born in 1875 in Napperton, Middlesex County, Ontario, he had been educated at Strathroy Collegiate Institute. He arrived on Vancouver Island fresh from Ontario in 1894 and began teaching in Sidney. Two years later he accepted a position in the public schools of Victoria. For three and a half years he taught at the Central School and partially at Victoria High School. He then developed an insurance practice, and in 1909 real estate was added to the business. Currie continued in this business till the War broke out in 1914.

He had not been a soldier before arriving in Victoria, but in early 1897 he joined the 5th BC Regiment of Garrison Artillery, RCA, as a gunner. He received his commission in this regiment in 1900 and began rising rapidly, passing through all ranks until he became lieutenant-colonel and was given command of the regiment in September 1909. He held this command until November 1913, when he left the regiment and assisted in the formation of the 50th Regiment, Gordon Highlanders. During the time he was in command of the 5th Regiment it attained a very high standard of efficiency, winning all the top prizes in artillery competitions.

A rare glimpse of Currie on the eve of the War is found in a biographical profile published that year. Western Canada afforded a man of Currie's strength and ambition ample scope. With an imperishable faith in the future great-ness of the country, pluck and industry would bring great rewards. Currie was cheerful and optimistic, if unsophisticated. The growth of Victoria's popula-tion and real-estate prospects favoured him. "During this period of change and expansion Colonel Currie has of course seen Victoria grow out of the swaddling clothes of a mere village and don the more ambitious and better-fitting gar-ments of one of the great commercial ports of the North Pacific." He embraced "a sane Imperialism," said the same authority, "which early led him to take up military training for the defence of flag and empire should the occasion ever demand." He was a Liberal, an Anglican, and a prominent Mason. Over six feet in height, with blue eyes and fresh complexion, "he is a fine specimen of clean, western manhood—and those who know him best feel that his best days are yet ahead of him and that British Columbia will hear more of Colonel Arthur William Currie."[4]

At the outbreak of war, Currie volunteered for overseas service. Ottawa answered by offering him command of an infantry brigade. On formation of the First Canadian Division, Currie was given command of the 2nd Infantry Brigade, which at that time comprised the 5th Battalion (recruited mainly from Saskatchewan), the 6th Battalion from Manitoba, the 7th Battalion from British Columbia, and the 8th Battalion from Winnipeg and surrounding districts. Before the brigade crossed to France, the 10th Battalion, composed of men from Manitoba and Alberta, was substituted for the 6th. Currie therefore commanded a brigade made up of units from the greater west. He was promoted to the rank of colonel in January 1915.[5]

We leave his story now, noting as we do that the times favoured the man, but, at the same time, his character was absolutely suited to the circumstances. A made-in-Victoria soldier was about to see the fields of fire. The call from England was urgent toward the end of August, and Currie, on orders, left Victoria on August 27 so as to confer with Canadian authorities in Ottawa and then get to England as soon as possible.

On Wednesday, August 26, volunteers from the 5th BC Regiment of Garrison Artillery, RCA, crowded aboard the CPR steamer *Princess Mary* in Victoria's inner harbour and sailed for Vancouver, there to entrain for Valcartier Camp, Quebec. An estimated sixty officers and men comprised Victoria's initial contribution to the First Contingent. On August 28, the 50th Regiment, Gordon Highlanders, and the 88th Regiment, Victoria Fusiliers, around 500 men, left Victoria in the *Princess Sophia*. A company of men known vaguely as No. 2 Foreign Service Company also left on August 28. Who knew what fates would await them.

Among the first to enlist was thirty-four-year-old Edwin "Ned" Sherwin Tuck, a true soldier of empire. Born in Saint John, New Brunswick, and then come west with his family, he had fought with the 2nd Canadian Mounted Rifles (South Africa) against the Boers. He had been awarded the Queen's South Africa Medal with Transvaal and South Africa 1902 clasps. He was the only Victoria High School "old boy" who was decorated before going into the Great War. Married in 1913 to Alice E. Tuck, he gave his address as "Rocca-Bella," Quadra Street, Victoria. By trade and training he was an expert in communications, specifically telephones, and had worked for BC Telephone Company. He had been in Nelson, BC, for a time and also worked for Northern Pacific Railway in Washington State. Tuck was well known in Victoria military circles because for a time he was in the 5th BC Regiment of Garrison Artillery, RCA. He went overseas as a sergeant in the 16th Battalion (Canadian Scottish) and, truth to tell, was likely saved (at least for a time) because he fell ill at his camp at Salisbury Plain and was sent home. Once recovered, he joined up again, though this time he had to go as a private rather than a sergeant (one of those oddities of being a non-commissioned officer). He fought through the war with the 47th Battalion and died age thirty-seven, on January 18, 1918. He was laid to rest in Sucrerie Cemetery, Ablain–St. Nazaire, France. The devastating news was reported in the Victoria press. He was much lamented by a large circle of friends, for he had spent most of his boyhood in Victoria, a student at Boys' Central and Victoria High. "His widow is now living here with her little child," reported the *Daily Colonist* with sorrow on February 2, 1918. His sister Isla Tuck also lived in the city. His brother, Lieutenant Douglas Tuck, a student of law at the time he enlisted in 1916 (and a militia man of many years), went overseas with the 29th Battalion, fought in France and survived, returned, and was a lawyer in Vancouver. Of Ned Tuck, it could be said that no one had a higher ambition to serve his empire and his country.[6]

Many among the first to go were from the school. Donning the kilt, as *The Camosun* noted, Douglas Campbell, who had joined the 50th Regiment, Gordon Highlanders, was one of the first to volunteer. One patriotic family, the Carters, sent three sons: Elmer, Vere, and Howard. All had been cadets at the school, all belonged to the 5th BC Regiment of Garrison Artillery, RCA, and all left on the first steamer from Victoria. Lieutenant Charlie Brown, of the 88th Regiment, Victoria Fusiliers, and Sergeant "Budge" Paul, an old-time pupil, also in kilts, were among the first to go. Arthur Beaumont Boggs and Herbert William Boggs, whom we meet later, had gone early, though in different ways. Shirley Yuill, once leader of the cadets, went to McGill and then joined a regiment. Lieutenant F. Carleton Hanington, who was to win the Military Cross and was for years a cadet leader at the school, went on to McGill like so many others and was commissioned through the Officers' Training Corps. He made a quick return to Victoria and joined the 5th BC Regiment, and by December 1914 was reported as being on Salisbury Plain in training. Lieutenant Henry L. Robinson, a law student at McGill, had blithely changed his career to that of "arms." They were all "off to war."

"As to the boys who were with us last year," noted *The Camosun*, with sadness, "very little need be said. We feel their loss so much that we need not be reminded of their deeds." The same story listed Captain Richard Wallis, Private Proctor McPherson, Sergeant E. Ferrar Hardwick, Private Cecil Milloy, and Private Dono Heyland. These last six were rugby men who had become soldiers. "All were on our famous team last year; who can take their places? But as they brought the old school glory on the Rugby field, what honour will they not win on the battlefield?"[7] They were some of Arthur Yates's prodigies in this first great age of rugby at the school, which was cut short by the War. The last few years before 1914 had seen a surge in the number of boys' athletic teams—rugby (junior and senior), soccer, two school basketball leagues, and three grass hockey teams. From the number of balls being pursued on the school grounds after classes closed for the day, it seemed that every boy played something.[8] The girls were similar. Two grass tennis courts were also laid out. "Play up, play up, and play the game" was always the credo of sports at the school, an essential part of its student pride and institutional identity. But for the moment, that was generally held in abeyance.

This was the first time and the last in Canada's history that the pressure of war was turned directly on the whole youth of the nation. Those already in employment, and out of school, had freedom to answer the call to the colours. Many of them had been in the Cadet Battalion (with all its training and attention to discipline and marksmanship). Many, too, had gone on to join militia units (see Appendix 3). As for the students in the school, those enrolled in 1914 stayed in; they could not enlist in the Canadian Expeditionary Force (CEF) until they were eighteen, though many fudged their age and got early entry (some of them were found out and sent back home). As one year passed into another, and with no end in sight for war's end, the students, particularly the brighter ones—that is, those in the matriculation class—made plans to enlist as soon as they could. Thus, members of the 1915 class were at the Front by 1917. In that year and particularly the next, the heavy casualties occurred; 1918 was a particularly savage year in the school's history. Right to the end of the War, news kept coming back to Victoria of another "killed in action." In the years after 1915, the upper echelons of the school's males seemed to empty out, much to the sadness of the female students (who had always been in the numerical majority). These fellows had been destined for the professions, and the losses they sustained were sustained by society as a whole. Taken all together, the four years of war brought untold damage to Victoria society, and the War interrupted the enlightened progress that the past several decades had demonstrated. In 1904, the great dawn of Canadian civilization, Sir Wilfrid Laurier, the prime minister, had pronounced that the twentieth century would belong to Canada. All that was spoiled by the dizzying slide into disaster that began with young nationalists in Serbia, who assassinated the archduke and archduchess of Austria-Hungary and set in motion a series of blunders that brought the ruination of Europe. In Victoria, those at the school, as well as those in the city and its suburbs, realized that their best interests could be served by supporting the imperial cause. Given the almost total absence of Canadian nationalism at the time, and the plurality of Canadian political opinion by region, province, or ethnicity, it is clear that the support for the British Empire and even "the Mother Country" was the true extension of the Canadian emotional and material effort. The brightest and the best, who had got to the school by virtue of their success in an admission examination, were the certain vector for support to the colours. All their traditions, all their blood ties, all their sympathies were with empire. In Victoria they gave unqualified support, as indeed was the case in most cities in the Dominion of Canada, as the nation was then called.

The frustrations felt by the female students must have been acute as they saw their boyfriends going off to the combat zone. They also often had a brother or two going overseas as well. The War changed the home front. Before long, trenches were dug at Dallas Road near Clover Point, and dugouts were erected downtown to help with recruitment. Few people in the city could not know that there was a war going on. But as the new school year began in August 1914, no one could have realized that they would be involved in the most stupendous struggle, a battle for civilization, for that was what it was.

At the school, in October, a patriotic fund was established, run by the Victoria High School Patriotic Aid Organization. Records were closely kept and results published about which of the twenty divisions, or classes, contributed the most. With the $135.20 collected, various materials were purchased, and with these the female students made articles for "our soldiers at the front, the unfortunate Belgians and the destitute at home." Balaclava caps, wristlets, socks, and covers for water bags were sent on to "the defenders of our Empire."

Dresses, bonnets, nightdresses, bloomers, rompers, and quilts were acceptable for the Belgian Relief Fund, recently established, and to those in need of help in the home city of Victoria.[9] From the outset, the school's student body followed the War and its social consequences, at home and abroad.

*Now we turn* to the war at sea. On August 2, the First Lord of the Admiralty, Winston Churchill, had ordered the main fleets to their battle station in the North Sea. The Grand Fleet now used Scapa Flow in the Orkneys as its main base. The Navy was to win no Trafalgar. But the blockade that it established became a decisive agency in the struggle. The Navy's many duties were to protect troop transports, guard the English Channel against the German threat, control the North Sea and all approaches to the British Isles, destroy enemy shipping, and prevent enemy invasion of the British Isles or any part of the British Empire. Its further obligations were to sustain the merchant shipping supplying the Home Islands and British forces fighting against the enemy. The main intention was to blockade the approaches to German ports. The Grand Fleet hoped to engage the German High Seas Fleet in major combat. This it did in 1916 at the Battle of Jutland, but without decisive result. By this time the German navy had mounted a U-boat (that is, submarine) campaign against British and Allied commerce, and this becomes important to our story—not only in the sinking of the Cunard liner *Lusitania*, carrying to his death the son of James Dunsmuir, British Columbia's famous business tycoon and politician (James Jr. had been in the 2nd Canadian Mounted Regiment but had resigned so as to join a British regiment), but also as it relates to the first episode of the Great War involving a student of Victoria High School.

The salt water of the oceans was in the blood of Vancouver Islanders and others in British Columbia. Many Victoria boys had joined the famed Royal Navy or the new (1910) Royal Canadian Navy. Percy James, Victoria High School class of 1910, enlisted in the Royal Navy. At the outbreak of hostilities, he found himself an Able Seaman in HMS *Hawke*, one of five vessels in the 10th Cruiser Squadron steadfastly maintaining its northern patrol. The *Hawke*, like other vessels in the squadron, was a protected cruiser of 7,350 tons, with an excellent armament and good speed but ill equipped to deal with a lethal torpedo fired by the enemy.

The young Lieutenant Otto Weddigen skippered *U-9*, one of the German submarines sent out to search the area between the Orkney and Shetland Islands and Norway for British men-of-war. This officer was already an "ace" on account of the fact that on September 22, 1914, he had sunk three light British cruisers—*Aboukir, Hogue,* and *Cressy*—off the coast of Holland. On that occasion, *U-9* had sent torpedoes, one after another, into the unsuspecting British cruisers: the second victim thought the first had struck a mine and stood by to take on survivors, and the third victim followed suit. From the British point of view, this was one of the catastrophes of the naval war. Never again would a warship stop to take on survivors. But it might carelessly stop to take on mail.

At 10:30 AM on October 15, off the east coast of Scotland, near Aberdeen, the *Hawke* took a torpedo amidships. She sank in eight minutes, without even getting off a radio report. A British destroyer and a Norwegian steamer found some survivors in a raft and the ship's dory. Nearly 523 officers and men were lost. VHS's Percy James was not among the survivors. He lies buried on the floor of the North Sea.

The report on proceedings that recorded the event, and the many histories of the episode, tell a tale of British failure to appreciate the range of the U-boats.[10] The loss of the *Hawke* also revealed how warships without adequate "bulges" (to guard against torpedoes) were vulnerable to U-boat torpedo attack. It turns out that the *Hawke* had slowed to pick up her mail from a delivery boat, making her an easy target. "Seldom has a ship sunk so quickly and carried so many men to the bottom of an icy sea," says the German report. "The two other cruisers were vanishing on the horizon. At the moment the torpedo explosion crashed out they turned tail and ran as fast as they could. It may have been inhuman for our adversaries thus to abandon the survivors of the *Hawke*, scores of men struggling in the icy waters, but by this time the British had learned not to repeat the mistake of September 22nd."[11] Weddigen was the first submarine ace but he, too, perished in naval operations when the U-boat he was commanding was sliced in two by HMS *Dreadnought*.

The loss of the *Hawke* so close to Scapa Flow, where the British Grand Fleet was headquartered, forced the commander-in-chief to shift to temporary bases at Loch Ewe, Scotland, then Lough Swilly on the north coast of Ireland. Almost to war's end, U-boats continued to be the greatest peril to the future of the British Empire. Meanwhile, the Grand Fleet's inability to defeat the German navy tied down endless naval resources and lengthened the war on land.

*Percy James holds* a unique place. He is the first Canadian, and the only known sailor connected with Victoria High School, to have died in the war at sea. His name is inscribed on the Chatham Memorial that stands above the River Medway; he is one of 8,500 First World War Royal Navy sailors with no known grave.

Already, as early as the time of James's death, the deadly peril of the U-boat was making itself known and blunting the aggressive spirit of the Royal Navy, which was forced to be cautious in all areas where a U-boat might be lurking. To a degree, as mentioned, this also extended the War on the European continent. No great victory came to the Royal Navy during the war, and in Victoria, as in any other city or town of the British Empire, this caused disappointment. The British Empire was grappling with an undersea force of the enemy that it did not know how to contend with, for the means of anti-submarine warfare were primitive and unscientific. In 1917, we will return again to the naval war involving one of Victoria High School's naval aviators, Cecil Clayton, and in his story we will find how the British had developed new methods of hunting U-boats and keeping the North Sea and English Channel clear of enemy shipping. It is also worth mentioning that many Victoria men would have entered the new Royal Canadian Navy, but it saw little action (though it had much "steaming time"). Most of Victoria High School's male students entered the army and principally joined the CEF. They are thus our main story.

By the time the readers of *The Camosun* were taking note of their old schoolmates, now overseas preparing for deployment in Flanders Fields, the British Expeditionary Force (BEF) had suffered mighty tragedies. The BEF, consisting of five divisions, was in position by August 20, though unaware that the Germans were anywhere near. Some divisions advanced into the mining town of Mons. There, on August 23, the two armies blundered into one another. Overwhelming enemy numbers attacked two British divisions. In the event, British riflemen put up fifteen rounds of rapid fire a minute, which the Germans concluded was machine-gun fire. The British would have stayed and fought it out, but on their right the French army was falling back fast. The British fought again at Le Cateau, then retreated again. The retreat from Mons saved the British Army in the field, but in subsequent battles late that year and early the next, the old Army, perhaps the finest ever put on the continent, was a shadow of its former self.

Meanwhile, the Belgians had abandoned Antwerp to the Germans but saved their army in the process. The so-called race to the sea had prevented the Germans from seizing all Channel ports, though they added Ostend and Zeebrugge to Antwerp—and held them to the end of the war against Allied attack by sea, air, and land. The German army occupied Mons, Belgium. The British Army retreated. The mediaeval university town of Louvain was torched under the German strategic policy of "frightfulness." The occupying forces killed civilians as an act of what they called reprisal. Moral indignation was expressed in many English, Canadian, and American newspapers, giving another reason for joining a military unit to liberate Belgium. (Mons enters our story later, for it was the beginning of the War in the field for the British Army and the end of it, too, when the Canadian Army under Currie forced the German surrender there.) It is important to note that the French army had suffered even worse casualties in 1914, losing over 200,000 men in the field. A section of France from the Marne up to the border with Belgium, then east to the Somme and to Amiens in Picardy, had been fought over at great cost to both sides. These essential details give the context of the situation in which the First Canadian Division found itself in February 1915 when it began to take its position on the Western Front.

*By the year's* end, the short period of mobility had come to a crashing halt. The Western Front had been established from the English Channel all the way to Switzerland and the conflict settled into "siege warfare in the field."[12] Opposing armies took up entrenched positions. The Germans had not attained their major objectives. They had not captured Paris and rolled up the French army. The Ypres salient in northeastern Belgium, where the British held the town of Ypres under the pulverizing bombardment of German guns, became the new battleground of the British Armies, including, within a few months, the First Canadian Division. The horrors of trench warfare now began.

In Berlin there were tempting thoughts about ringing the bells of victory. At the foreign office a confidant to the minister of state wrote: "One is already beginning to make plans for the victory booty . . . We looked at the map today. I always preach the erection of vassal states . . . We Germans have . . . awakened powers in ourselves the magnitude of which we could never have imagined. Above all, we have discovered a spiritual essence through which we can concentrate these powers." The German press held similar views: "The mind is scarcely able to grasp the news being given to the German people about their victories in both east and west. It represents a divine judgement, as it were, branding our antagonists as the criminal originators of this fearful war."[13] The bells of victory could not be rung, though by year's end the German armies had achieved many a triumph. Their encounters with the British Army alone are the stuff of legend and had forced its massive withdrawal. The French army had not come to its promised aid.

The end of 1914 left little of the original and regular British Army, probably the best army Britain had put in the field in all the history of war, with its excellent cavalry and superb infantry of brilliant riflemen. The list of lieutenants and subalterns had been trimmed severely by the heavy fighting that began in August. The ranks had been decimated. The British had sent one army to the Western Front in 1914; the Germans, seven. France had deployed the greatest number on the Allied side. A remnant of the Belgian army survived. By the end of the winter, just as the Canadians were approaching the battle line, the numbers comprising the British Armies had to be kept up. Somehow, too, the spirit of invincibility had to be nurtured, somehow kept alive. There might have been a lot of happiness in skipping off to war, but now the question of how long this conflict would last was on everyone's mind. By the end of 1914, nearly one million had poured into the recruiting stations and enlisted in the British Army, and the British Empire as a whole had a prodigious and hitherto unheard-of two million under arms. This smacks of madness, but all nations and all empires were at the same business.

The First Canadian Division reached England in October 1914 and deployed to France early the next year. Later in 1915, the Canadian Corps was formed. In August 1916, it reached its full strength of four divisions. The First Division was placed under the command of an English officer, Sir Julian Byng, later Viscount Byng of Vimy and Governor General of Canada, who subsequently was promoted to command the Canadian Corps. In June 1917, Lieutenant-General Sir Arthur Currie became Corps Commander. The Government of Canada had actively promoted this change. A new Canadian consciousness was stirring within the Corps itself, and it grew with the War. The victories and sacrifices of the Corps became, in fact, the vehicle in wartime of a new national consciousness and national pride, and the memory of these things continued to be influential in peace. That, however, is the view from

1918 and later. In 1914, Canadians went to war with different aspirations, and they were anxious to get in on the action before the end of the conflict, which, it was said so optimistically, would be over by Christmas.

In its December issue, *The Camosun* featured a story titled "Old Boys at the Front." We have already seen who the "old boys" were—the scholars at Oxford who now found themselves at war, the early enlistments for the 5th BC Regiment of Garrison Artillery, RCA; the 50th Regiment, Gordon Highlanders; the 88th Regiment, Victoria Fusiliers; and a few sailors serving on distant stations in the greatest of navies. The boys had gone as soon as they could, dutifully answering the call to arms. The school magazine expressed these sentiments: "Among the many old High School boys now scattered over the land there are none of whom we are so proud as of those who have left us for the Front. Quite a number of these were only lately in the old High among us and any news from them is welcome; and they in the distant camps would surely appreciate being remembered at Christmas time. An appropriate suggestion is that Christmas letters would be sent to each of these by all their school-fellows."[14]

*chapter 2* **1915**

## WELCOME TO FLANDERS FIELDS:
## SECOND BATTLE OF YPRES

*T*he departure of students to join the cause was watched by those who remained behind. *The Camosun* mentioned Linden E. Fairbairn, who had left the Beta Delta Society, so prominent in student body public affairs, in "his endeavour to serve the Empire during this great crisis, which is calling for the services of every able-bodied man in the Dominion."[1] The call was strong, and the flow of students outward incessant: one at a time, sometimes in groups as friends, usually into the CEF, but also into the Royal Naval Air Service or British regiments. How many joined the Royal Navy or Royal Canadian Navy will never be known. The women, if they had the necessary qualifications, went into the Canadian Army Medical Corps as nursing sisters, and became lieutenants. Sara Ellen Spencer became a lieutenant, one of only seven such, in the Canadian Field Comforts Commission.

The pull of family and friends is strong in our story, for numerous are the instances of brothers enlisting, sometimes at the same time. In other cases, chums at the school joined up together, or members of sports clubs, notably the James Bay Athletic Association, went at the same time. The school's Cadet Battalion was a natural feeder for those wanting to go into the regular forces. The militia units, notably the 5th BC Regiment of Garrison Artillery,

RCA, which provided so many gunners for the Canadian Field Artillery, and the 88th Regiment, Victoria Fusiliers, and the 50th Regiment, Gordon Highlanders, which became part of the 16th Canadian Scottish, are the main ones. In early 1915, Victoria's own 30th Battalion, mobilized at the old Willows Fairgrounds in Oak Bay and numbering some 1,100, went marching off to a tumultuous farewell.

In their pay books was pasted a message reminding His Majesty's troops to be "courteous, considerate and kind . . . and always look upon looting as a disgraceful act." The Canadians were warned that in "this new experience you may find temptations both in wine and women. You must entirely resist both temptations, and while treating all women with perfect courtesy, you should avoid any intimacy." As one reliable authority has observed, "Kitchener's admonition against wine did not survive the train trip to Hazebrouck, in French Flanders. Whether the admonition against "intimacy" survived any longer is unknown. However, given the 1,249 cases of venereal disease treated at Bustard Camp, and the fact that by the end of the war the Canadians had the highest rate of venereal disease (150 per 1,000 men, as compared to 30 per 1,000 for the rest of the BEF) of any army on the Western Front, one might doubt it."[2]

As mentioned in the previous chapter, by the New Year the War had bogged down as both sides sought the protection of the trenches, free from the devastating fire of musketry and machine guns. It was now a desperate struggle for the area between the trenches, "no man's land." In these circumstances, artillery—from the trenches in the form of trench mortars, from the immediate rear of the trenches in the form of field artillery, and from the far rear in the form of heavy howitzers and other large guns—became the new order of the day. Overhead, aircraft worked in reconnaissance and spotting, relaying positions to the gunners. But movement had come to an end. Even breaking the line and forming a salient, or curve, would lengthen the front and make it weaker to defend. In the circumstances, generals hardly considered the potential gains of a breakthrough, and it was only in 1918 that the German general Erich Ludendorff made the mistake in what is known as the Spring Offensive. This explains why generals, most notably the widely criticized Sir Douglas Haig (later Earl Haig) thought in terms of attrition. Throughout this war the British Armies came under the general command of the French and did not act as independent units.

It was into these static circumstances that the Canadian units arrived on the battlefield by February 15, 1915. For a time some of them were attached to British battalions as part of the process of gaining experience, but by March they were positioned by themselves. These were months of appalling losses, for the enemy had compensated for a comparative weakness in infantry with powerfully massed artillery. British guns, throwing lighter shell, could not dislodge the Germans from their field fortifications. The defence had the advantage. Meantime, the temptation to carry on a trench battle with an attempted breakout could not always be contained. And behind enemy lines, the German chemical units made preparations for releasing chlorine gas.

The Ypres salient was always a crowded scene, and it was here, in the Second Battle of Ypres, from April 21 to May 25, that the Canadian Army received its baptism of fire. The Ypres salient formed a "V," the apex pointing east to German lines. The city of Ypres stood midway in the middle of the open gap between the two arms of the V. Canadian and British troops manned the southern flank; French Algerian, and Belgian troops the northern. Orders from headquarters demanded that the line be held at all cost.

Unknown to the Allies, German pioneer companies had organized batteries of cylinders containing 150 tons of chlorine gas. Awaiting an essential westward-blowing wind, the Germans opened the gas nozzles at 5:30 PM on April 22. The Canadians viewed the scene, for they stood to the Algerians' right: greenish-yellow clouds emerged from the ground, spread out, and formed a terrifying bluish-white mist. The Algerians, the first victims, were incapacitated and retreated as best they could. It was impossible to realize what had actually happened, for fumes and smoke obscured everything. Hundreds of men were thrown into a stupor, reported Sir John French, commander of the British Expeditionary Force, and the whole position had to be abandoned, leaving behind fifty guns. The Germans saw the effects of their work: dead men lying on their backs with clenched fists, the field covered in a ghastly yellow cloaking. Until dusk the Germans advanced, then halted, having attained their goal.

Next day, April 23, Canadians plugged the gap against stiff resistance. The Front stabilized once again. At one stage, Colonel Currie found himself roundly criticized by a British superior officer for ordering unauthorized withdrawals. He weathered that storm, though the matter was bound to pop up eventually in the record files of differing British and Canadian official historians.[3]

Chlorine gas was used five times more during the Second Battle of Ypres. By April 26, the Canadians had "Gas Masks, Type I." Until then, and even after, soldiers soaked cloth in water, or urine, and breathed through the cloth to prevent asphyxiation. This was the Canadian welcome to Flanders Fields. News about the forthcoming gas attack had been ignored, perhaps because the Allies believed such use was alien to the precepts of war.[4]

It was at this time, in May 1915, just after the Second Battle of Ypres, that Dr. John McCrae, who was tending to scores of wounded soldiers every day, wrote home to his mother to say that his general impression was of a nightmare. The Canadians had been in the most bitter of fights. The machine-gun fire and rifle fire never ceased even for a minute. And in the background was a constant view of the dead, the wounded, and the maimed. To this was added a terrible anxiety that the line held by his fellows in arms should give way. Had the enemy punched through that line, the road to the Channel ports would have been clear. The damage to the Allied cause, and to Belgium and France, would have been severe. We are now beginning to realize the psychological damage brought on by war in the field. But McCrae had something more immediate on his mind. The day before "In Flanders Fields" was written, McCrae had lost one of his closest friends, Lieutenant Alexis Helmer, who had been given a rudimentary grave and a rough wooden cross. Wild poppies were blooming between his and the other crosses in the area. Today that location is Essex Farm Cemetery, a Commonwealth War Graves Commission (CWGC) burial ground. There is a memorial to McCrae there. Down the lane to a tow path and bridge across the canal stood the earthen dugout dressing station above which McCrae wrote his famous verse. Nearby you can see a group of British concrete dugouts that provided shelter for the soldiers while the war raged without ceasing overhead. The din must have been terrible. McCrae did not survive the war. He died of pneumonia in January 1918 and is buried near Boulogne. The red poppy was adopted as the flower of remembrance for the war dead of Britain, France, the United States, Canada, and other Commonwealth countries. McCrae's birthplace, a limestone cottage in Guelph, Ontario, lies so far away from Essex Farm. There is a memorial cenotaph there, too, in the garden of remembrance.

From May 15 to 25, the First Division took part in the Battle of Festubert, where Canadians took terrible losses yet put up stiff resistance. By June the salient remained stable despite all the artillery, gas, and infantry the Germans had thrown at it, and it remained largely that way until the Passchendaele campaign began there on July 31, 1917.[5] This was the general situation of these days. The Canadians lost more than a third of their infantry in their first battle, and Victoria suffered its first great losses of the War.

Herbert William Boggs, born in Victoria on July 28, 1892, a Victoria High School graduate, was studying law in Victoria when war broke out. As he was the first Canadian officer to be killed in the conflict, his story is particularly noteworthy. His family was of United Empire Loyalist stock from Nova Scotia, and his father, Thomas Frederick William Boggs, the local recruiting officer, had come west as a lieutenant in a provisional battalion during the 1885 Riel Rebellion. Thomas was well connected in business circles, particularly real estate and insurance. Opening up large tracts of land including Gordon Head, supporting local public schools, and advancing the Anglican theological college in Vancouver were features of his life. Herbert and his parents, elder brother, and two sisters, Mary and Dorothy, lived at Maplewood, now 1140 Arthur Currie Lane, Victoria West. The Boggs family showed a keen interest in matters historical, civic, and military, and they held a prominent place in the city and province.[6] The family was attached to Christ Church Cathedral, and Herbert was a member of the James Bay Athletic Association, the longest-lived Canadian sports organization west of Montreal.

At the school, Herbert and his brother, Arthur Beaumont Boggs, one year his senior, had been prominent in the Cadet Battalion, and there is a picture of them and the other officers and non-commissioned officers in 1910 (half of these men would die in the Great War).[7] Arthur decided on a career in the army, became a cadet at the Royal Military College of Canada, and was commissioned in the Indian Army. Captain Arthur Beaumont Boggs survived the war. He was in a cavalry unit of the Indian Army when war began, and he went to France, where he was wounded in action. In 1922, he was awarded the Order of the British Empire.

Meanwhile, Herbert joined the 88th Regiment, Victoria Fusiliers, and at war's outbreak enlisted in the CEF and went to Valcartier. Crossing the Atlantic with the First Canadian Division, he found himself on Salisbury Plain for further rigorous training. By February 1915, he was on the Western Front.

In northeastern Belgium, in the Ypres salient, near La Bassée, Herbert Boggs, now first lieutenant, found himself commanding the left platoon of No. 3 Company, 7th Infantry Battalion (the British Columbia Regiment). As stated, the German "race to the sea" had been halted some months before. Now the heavy siege warfare began, with attacks and counterattacks by opposing forces. The British Armies, which included the First Canadian Division, had been placed to hold against just such a German heavy assault. On February 26, 1915, Boggs was killed in action while commanding his platoon. Colonel Arthur Currie, who knew Herbert and the family as friends, cabled home the sad news, reporting that the young officer had been killed instantly, a blessing. He was twenty-two. Herbert was buried in Ploegsteert Churchyard, Belgium, where he is remembered with honour. News of his death, received the next day, hit the city and the school very hard. As the *Daily Colonist* put it on March 2, for the first time since the war began, the real shadow of it had fallen on Victoria, for Boggs was the first native son to be killed in action. He had, more-over, lived in the city until the time he went to the Front. On the Memorial at Christ Church Cathedral and on the Roll of Honour of the Pacific Club, now hanging in the Union Club of British Columbia, in Victoria, the name of Herbert Boggs can be found prominently listed. It is indicative of his fam-ily's social standing in the community that shortly after his death, his memory was perpetuated in the naming of the Herbert Boggs Chapter of the Imperial Order of the Daughters of the Empire (IODE). *The Camosun* of March 1915 printed details and a fine photographic portrait of the lost warrior.

At the same time Herbert William Boggs enlisted, tall and slender Herbert Cridge Laundy, age nineteen, also joined up. He was in the 5th BC Regiment of Garrison Artillery, RCA. His family was well known in Victoria: his father was in banking, and his mother, Ellen, was from the family of Bishop Edward Cridge, who had been Anglican chaplain and schoolmaster at the Hudson's Bay Company fort in the early days of Victoria. Like many another enlist-ment, Herbert Laundy was "in the ranks." At Second Ypres, Corporal Laundy distinguished himself by his brave conduct. He was awarded the Military Medal, the first Victoria High School alumnus to receive a medal. (Note: the Military Medal was awarded to non-commissioned officers and other ranks; the Military Cross was awarded to officers.) Later he was commissioned lieu-tenant in the 13th Brigade, Canadian Field Artillery, and later, too, he would win the Military Cross. We meet him again at Vimy Ridge.

If one Laundy could join up, so would others. Many families saw all their sons go to war. Herbert Cridge Laundy's older brother, Everard Lynne Laundy, had also been in the 5th BC Regiment of Garrison Artillery. At the outbreak of war, he was in Nanaimo. After disturbances at the coal mines there, the militia had been called out to keep order, at the lieutenant-governor's request.[8] Everard Laundy had hopes of joining up with his brother and going over together in the First Contingent. This was not to be. Accordingly, he went to New Westminster as signalling sergeant in the 47th Battalion, CEF, in 1915. We also meet him again at Vimy Ridge. The third son, Corporal Cecil Eastman Laundy, youngest of the three, also of Victoria High School, fought through the War.

Like his two brothers, whom we meet later, Lieutenant Andrew Jack Gray saw the face of battle in the hard fighting of May 1915. After leaving Victoria High School, he had gone to Columbia University in New York, graduating in 1913 with an honours BSc degree. He had studied metallurgy and the foundry business, hoping to use it in the family's Marine Iron Works. His return to Victoria coincided with the raising of the 50th Regiment, Gordon Highlanders, and he proceeded to the Front with the 16th Battalion. He saw action at Second Ypres and Festubert (Aubers Ridge), May 20, 1915, where, when leading his platoon he was wounded and ultimately lost an arm. That seems to have ended his war, and he returned to Victoria with 800 other wounded Canadians, including Private Ricketts, Private Jock Wilson, Corporal Leighton, and Private John Kirk, all Victorians. He lived on in his native Victoria and died age eighty.

Chariots of fire, soldiers of the Cross, the Elliott brothers were moulded in the missionary cause, and as privates in their early twenties, marched off to war in answer to their captain's call. Their parents, Rev. William and Mrs. Elliott, had been on assignment with the Methodist Church of Canada in Japan when the lads had been born—Fletcher Frederick in Kanazawa in 1891 and George William in Toyama in 1893. The family returned to Canada, specifically to a Christian calling at Cumberland, Vancouver Island. In about 1906, the Elliott brothers arrived in Esquimalt to live with their aunt, Mrs. G.W. (Ella) Robinson, at "Viameda" on Esquimalt Road, so that they might attend the essential Victoria High School, where in time they duly graduated. Both were active members of the YMCA, and both enlisted with the 88th Regiment, Victoria Fusiliers. One of the first soldierly duties for George, a carpenter by trade, was standing guard in support of the civil power at Nanaimo during the miners' disturbances. When war suddenly engulfed the scene, George volunteered for active service in the First Canadian Contingent. Fletcher came fast on his heels. For the moment, and perhaps for all time, his promising career as an accountant with the Royal Bank was put on hold. On August 29, 1914, they sailed on the *Princess Sophia* for Vancouver, and by the time they were at the Front they were in the 7th Battalion (the 1st British Columbia Regiment as it was called when formed) of the 2nd Brigade, First Canadian Division.

At Salisbury Plain the Elliott brothers were placed in the same company, then found themselves side by side in a machine-gun section. Posted to Belgium, they were soon in the thick of things on the Ypres salient. On April 24, when the Canadians were desperately holding the line against the German assault that came in the wake of the gas attack, George William Elliott was killed, one of about 500 of the 7th Battalion who died in the Second Battle of Ypres, to that point the worst episode of the War for Canada. On May 7, the Victoria press inaccurately reported that both had been killed, stating that details of their deaths were scant, but even so, "it is known that they fell with their faces to the foe in an endeavour to stem an oncoming rush of the enemy with the machine gun which they served."[9]

In fact, Fletcher was only wounded in the action. He survived his wounds and was soon back at the Front. He earned a commission on account of conspicuous bravery and resourcefulness on the battlefield. However, the life of a young lieutenant, or subaltern, was invariably short, for as a leader of his section, company, or other unit, he was expected to lead by example, perhaps with pistol in hand when going "over the top," out of the trench and into an unwelcome field of fire. Indeed, Lieutenant Fletcher Frederick Elliott was killed June 3, 1916, while leading No. 1 and 3 Companies in a counterattack on the enemy at Mount Sorrel.

For the remaining family, the shattering effect of his death, a year after that of his brother, can be imagined. Another sorrowful sacrifice to German fire. Such was the nature of the War in this phase. Fletcher and George's sister, who went to Montreal to train as a nurse, went overseas in 1915 with the Red Cross. Looked at from the perspective of Bertram Elliott, youngest of the three brothers and now the only one living (he was residing with his parents at home in Cumberland), his two brothers and his sister had been scattered to the winds of fate by the War. Both Fletcher Frederick and George William Elliott are memorialized in the Menin Gate, Ypres Memorial Panel.

Yet another Victoria High School graduate, arguably the school's most famous soldier, won recognition early in the War. Of a fearsome disposition and of strong heart, John Gibson Anderson had been born in Glasgow, Scotland, in 1885. With his parents he moved to Victoria, attended local schools including Boys' Central School, and then passed on to Victoria High School, where he matriculated. He taught school on Pender Island and in Duncan, and either before or after this he studied electrical engineering at McGill University. His enlistment papers declare him to be an electrician. He had a powerful frame and was a noted athlete as a boxer and wrestler, taking every opportunity for competition in those lines of human endeavour. Twice he was champion wrestler in interuniversity sports. The family home was at Macaulay Point. His father, John Nicholson Anderson, worked in remote areas, including Grande Prairie, Alberta; indeed, in August 1914, John Gibson Anderson was on vacation visiting his father near Grouard, Alberta, when he heard that war had been declared. Without hesitation he enlisted in the 19th Alberta Dragoons, a cavalry regiment. Trooper John Gibson Anderson was off to war. As he had wanted, he was in time to be in the First Canadian Contingent.

For seven or eight months, he was in the thick of things on the Western Front, surviving Second Ypres. He rose through the ranks. In September 1915, Anderson wrote home to his sister, "We are out in rest billets for a few days again, and I am certainly enjoying the rest, for, as you know, we get very little in the front line trenches. We enjoy life, nevertheless, and are holding our share of the line until something stirs, which may be any time. This morning I saw a Bosche aeroplane brought down by a British one after an exciting fight. The machine was one of the latest German type. The four occupants were killed."[10] Anderson saw how his fellow soldiers worked at night, sometimes with a bright moon lighting up the landscape and giving it a macabre appearance. They piled sandbags high and cleared away or drained the trenches. They hammered in pickets for running the communication wires. Sometimes they were driven out of the trenches they had won, then regained them with a bombing party. Overhead passed a continuous exchange of grenades, mortar shells, and canisters. A Stokes mortar did a full day's work until the Germans found the source, putting an end to it or forcing its removal. They gave as hard as they got.

The soldiers also had to contend with a natural world changed by Armageddon. Heavy rain turned the battle-scarred land into a quagmire, destroying natural drainage. Rats came up from the canals and fed on the human remains. At night the men in the trenches had to abide their dreaded arrival. One survivor of the campaign, Victor Raymond "Ray" Parfitt of Victoria High School, for the rest of his life slept with a blanket wrapped tightly round his head to ward off rodents, real or imagined.[11] Trench foot was a widespread malady, and soldiers were forbidden to stand in water. Whale oil was a deterrent. Rubber waders were introduced at last in 1916.

Lice (the vector for "trench fever") were a constant problem, and although people from Victoria sent anti-lice powder, in one case they were asked, by James Pottinger, not to. "It isn't much good and we find the only remedy is creosote of which we can get lots. We sprinkle our blankets and clothes with a strong solution and even sometimes take a sponge bath with a weak solution."[12] Trench fever—possibly rheumatic fever—was a problem, as was "trench mouth," infectious stomatitis, which was very common at that time. Colds, bronchitis, influenza, typhoid, and other diseases took their toll in the cold and constantly wet environment. The dental corps was always busy, dealing not only with casualties from bullets. Soldiers were also kicked by mules and horses. The return to billets was welcome, and rotation in and out of England, "old Blighty," extremely welcome. That London was only 130 miles from the Front meant it was near and yet so far.

In September 1915, Anderson received his commission as lieutenant in the 5th Battalion of the 2nd Infantry Brigade of the First Canadian Division. His battalion was in action near Messines. The situation on this section of the Front was described as "very quiet," perhaps eerily so. What were the Germans opposite up to? What German regiments did the Canadians face? Was there a chance to gain intelligence by capturing prisoners? It seemed a good time to seek out the enemy. Every night, Canadian scouts had been sent out to find targets the artillery could subsequently hit. Why not raid some enemy trenches at the same time?[13] In October, units of the Canadian Army initiated and developed this idea, which became such a popular form of amusement for the whole British Army—and such a serious annoyance to the enemy. It is contended that these raids sadly discomposed the nerves of the Germans and invariably led to some more or less indiscriminate shellfire from them as retaliation.

Anderson was in on the beginning of these dangerous missions. He received orders to make a night reconnaissance of German positions that lay before the 5th Battalion. At 2 AM on the night of October 8, the weather fine and the wind east, Anderson, accompanied by a sapper (military engineer) named Whyte, crept along an old British sap—a covered trench dug to a point near or within an enemy position—and eventually found themselves in one of German making. They now were in the enemy's territory. They inched ahead stealthily. Suddenly they saw two Germans whose rifles lay at their sides. The Germans spotted the Canadians at that precise moment. They lurched for their bombs or grenades, but the Canadians shot and wounded both. The noise of gunfire brought three other German soldiers from around the corner of the trench. Anderson and Whyte opened fire, killing two and wounding the third, who had dropped his rifle and fled the scene "incontinently"—he disappeared through the maze of German barbed wire, watched by the Canadians. Their supply of ammunition exhausted, Anderson and Whyte returned safely to the battalion and prepared for the next escapade.

The next night, the weather dull, Anderson set out again, this time commanding a larger party: three soldiers, bombardiers, carrying hand grenades, and Whyte as scout. The plan called for Anderson and Whyte to make their way along the trench as before, while the others, according to instructions, crawled along the edge of the sap. This time, almost in the same spot as the night before, they found a working party of Germans. Surprise was everything, and the Germans offered no resistance, running back to their lines as soon as they saw the Canadian uniforms. They left behind two rifles, cylindrical grenades with wooden handles, several haversacks filled with rations, and a greatcoat. A clock and a periscope were likewise retrieved. This booty the Canadians took back to their lines. At 3 PM that afternoon the 5th Battalion received congratulations from the senior command at a conference at brigade headquarters. And so the story of the exploits of Anderson, his scout, and his comrades was passed to fellow officers and men.[14]

Lieutenant Anderson received the personal thanks of his brigadier-general. Later he received a letter dated October 10 from Currie, now a major-general, who had been delighted to hear of the encounter of the previous day. He said he had always been interested to know how Anderson would turn out, and he continued: "I am more than pleased to know that you have shown at least that you have 'guts.' It means much to your senior officers, to your men, and to yourself. Now we know that we can trust you. Wishing you every success." The *Daily Colonist* added this: "In explanation of the rather exceptional tone adopted by the general it may be said that Lieutenant Anderson had just been promoted and in the work which he had been given to do was, no doubt, undergoing a test from which he emerged with high honors." Anderson had been one of General Currie's pupils at the Central School when he had taught there. Currie also wrote to a friend in Victoria, Colonel F.B. Gregory, and made specific reference to how pleased he was that Anderson had exhibited gallantry. An extract of Currie's letter to Gregory was read at the Royal Theatre at an event on the Sunday evening. In mid-December came the formal news that the King had conferred on Anderson the Military Cross for "daring and useful reconnaissances." This was front-page news in the *Daily Colonist*.[15] Mrs. J.N. Anderson received this good news along with a report on her son's military exploits into no man's land. Sapper Whyte was also honoured. Their nighttime adventures in search of the enemy out beyond the advanced lines that lay between the adversaries was recounted by Currie in highly complimentary terms.

The year 1915, a hard, disastrous, and bitter one, closed with no peace in sight. The honours of the year lay clearly with the enemy. Russia was in retreat. Serbia had been overwhelmed. We have referred to the Canadian tragedy at the Second Battle of Ypres. Neuve Chapelle, Loos, Gallipoli, and the Dardanelles were names that signified other setbacks. They were not names of good omen. The strain of war was beginning to tell.[16] Alliances, previously weak, were strengthened to counter German's quest for continental dominance.

Opposing armies were locked in mortal combat, separated by only a hundred yards or so. This was a war of the trenches, of gallant and often foolish attempts to gain a quarter of a mile of ground. But a breach in the enemy's line could not possibly lead to victory, only entrapment behind the lines, prison camp, and probably death. All along the Front, the German sniper played his demonic role with the greatest of success. Allied foolishness led to many a death of one of our own, until special sniper training and theoretical application made Canadian snipers the equal and then the better of their enemy opposites. The Ross rifle, slow to use and prone to malfunction, proved a highly successful sniper weapon.

Along the Front, machine-gun crews kept at their lethal work, the bullets spitting out of the chattering barrels. A pair of machine guns set up a few hundred yards from one another could control a whole killing field. At dusk, a party might be sent into no man's land to retrieve the wounded or the dead. On such sorties, an enemy soldier might be found; he might be made prisoner and treated for his wounds, but in the opinion of Robert Graves, the noted writer and poet, who served throughout the War as a British officer, saving the lives of enemy wounded was a matter of much disagreement: "Some divisions, like the Canadians and a division of Lowland territorials, who claimed that they had atrocities to avenge, would not only avoid taking risks to rescue enemy wounded but go out of their way to finish them off."[17] The Canadians considered themselves good trench fighters. When they came up to the Front in relief of some others, they took note of enemy emplacements, bomb shelters, traversing or communications trenches, snipers, and patrols. The gunners were aided by aerial reconnaissance information. But at this stage, maps were often poor or non-existent.

The few minutes before dawn was a precious time for the Canadians, during which they could see the enemy's profiles in the distance. The sun rose behind German lines while Canadian trenches were in darkness. Barbed wire usually lay ahead of any attacking party. Water and mud lay on the ground, and the terrain was pocked with shell holes that claimed many a victim. A soldier stumbling home to his dugout or trench on a night without moonlight could easily slip to his death. Wooden platforms, or duckboards, were constructed for easier walking. Meantime, day in and day out, the supplies came up the trenches, and the burial and clearing parties took away the casualties. The wagons and motor lorries continued to haul up the shells, the ammunition, and the drinking water. No battalion could long stand the human losses experienced, and although new drafts of men came to fill the ranks, the odds of any soldier surviving this beyond one or two wounds received began to lengthen. Young lieutenants who led from the trench, pistol in hand, knew that they might not return. Privates and non-commissioned officers, for that reason, often declined promotions.[18] Stories circulated of the British soldier who finally accepted the offer of a commission, only to be killed the night before that was to happen.

Most Victoria High School lads who enlisted became privates. Few if any of them had gone to a military academy of whatever distinction, and the VHS Cadet Battalion was their preliminary experience in drill and marksmanship. Some had been in the 88th Regiment, Victoria Fusiliers, the 50th Regiment, Gordon Highlanders, or the 5th BC Regiment of Garrison Artillery, RCA, a crack militia regiment and one of the oldest in British Columbia.

The urge to serve King and Country led many to lie about their age and enlist early. John Ellis Fletcher of Victoria High School was one of them. He signed on at age fifteen in Victoria on December 1915. Then he was listed as a deserter, but signed on again April 3, 1916, in Vancouver. He was sent with the Canadian Forestry Corps to England. He was discharged as medically unfit (syphilis) and sailed for Canada May 20, 1919. He lived long and died in North Vancouver in 1963. Not all war stories, we are reminded, are glorious.[19]

*Victoria newspapers continued* to tell of events unfolding in Europe and of Canada's efforts as a British dominion. They would also regularly announce the tragedies of the war. Some of this news, when it involved former students, would be echoed in the pages of *The Camosun*. Lance Corporal P. McPherson had been wounded in the recent terrific battle at Langemarck, northeast of Ypres. Private E.F. Hardwick was believed and trusted so far to be safe. Alva Lowery had left with his old school chum, Fairbairn, and was serving overseas. Fairbairn, it seems, was a campus favourite, highly visible in everything related to schoolwork, spirit, or sports. His fellow students still in Victoria asked the readership "to mingle your heart-felt wishes with ours for 'Good Luck and God Speed.'"[20]

In 1915, a Matriculation Number of *The Camosun* appeared for the first time. Nowadays, we would call it a school annual. It was produced under the inspired guidance of English teacher Arthur Yates. This Englishman, rare on the school staff, where most of his colleagues were Canadian-born, was devoted to student causes on several counts, not least because of his debating experience at Oxford, his literary instincts, and his oratorical capacities. As a Rhodes Scholar at St. John's Oxford, he had taken a degree in jurisprudence (i.e., law). He brought from Oxford a passion for school spirit and may have found Victoria High School a wasteland. He had impressed upon the students about to leave school at the end of their years of study that they were matriculating—that is, graduating. He convinced them they ought to leave some sort of collective personal memorial about themselves and their fellow classmates— and a legacy for the school. There were three "Matric" classes that year, and lovely photos brighten the pages of the May 1915 *Camosun*, one for each class, with the usual commentary and witty remarks about the individuals in question. Each school year after, a single issue of *The Camosun* was devoted to the graduating class and called the Matriculation Number.

A glance at the pages of one of these issues shows that in those years, more girls matriculated than boys, principally because the demand for female education was strong and this was a public, free school, not a private one with fees. The girls had risen to the top of *The Camosun*'s editorial staff, and Hazel McConnell was editor-in-chief. She later became a teacher of great standing in the school. Mr. Yates was her literary advisor.

In keeping with the desire to give females an equal education to males, the Portia Society was founded in 1913, a parallel female organization to Beta Delta, the debating club. "Portia" was the traditional name for women's debating societies in North America, a reference to the eloquent Portia who posed as a male lawyer and amazed all the men of the Venetian court with her brilliant arguments in defence of Antonio, the titular merchant in Shakespeare's *Merchant of Venice*. Miss Jeanette A. Cann, a teacher, was the VHS Portia Society's honorary president. At one meeting of the society she "pointed out that our boys at the front are fighting against the lawless Germans and it stood to reason that we at home should keep the laws." In her opinion, nations could not trust one another if treaties were broken; similarly, individuals cannot trust one another if laws are broken. It was an axiom of the age that the world would be chaos if nobody kept the laws. Miss Cann was another keen supporter of school spirit, and she was discouraged by the fact that so many of the girls had outside interests that detracted from their putting their whole hearts and souls into the school. The seniors should lead and show how things ought to be done, she counselled. Miss Cann never failed in her devotion to the girls of the school or to the school generally. The Portia Society grew during these war years into the powerful force of inspired patriotism. Its members mourned the loss to the War of so many of the male leaders, members of Beta Delta, who were the stars of the male student population.

On May 27, 1915, the Portia Society held its last meeting of the school year, and the young ladies drew slips of paper on which was written a subject for a two-minute speech. Miss Agnes Stevenson drew a slip with the question "Were the Rioters Justified?" The reference was to the riot that occurred in Victoria when news reached the city that the liner *Lusitania* had been sunk by a U-boat. The subject was a difficult one, but offered a chance for her to speak in very good English. "Miss Stevenson," reported *The Camosun*, "held up Aristotle's "Golden Mean" by pointing out that to a certain extent the rioters were justified in giving vent to their feelings and showing the German citizens that they could not have it all their own way. Yet again it was wrong to go so far as to steal, for that helped no one."[21] The *Lusitania* riot resulted in the mayor reading the Riot Act and the militia being called in. For several days, detachments of the 2nd Canadian Mounted Rifles that were waiting to be sent overseas cooperated with the infantry and the civic police in restoring order.

One of Victoria High School's young women, Elsie Dorothy Collis, enlisted at Esquimalt in the Canadian Army Medical Corps (CAMC) in 1915. She was five feet seven inches tall, dark in complexion, with brown eyes and brown hair. Collis, who lived an extraordinary and exciting life in nursing and volunteer work, was born in Harpenden, England, and had arrived in Comox with her parents in 1890 before moving to Victoria, where she attended the school. For Collis, the call to nursing was irresistible. According to a writer who interviewed her, she "had feasted her mind on stories of Florence Nightingale's experiences in the Crimea, she was determined to display the same dauntless courage and conviction if she could fulfill her desire to become a trained nurse."[22] Victoria, in those days, had two training schools for nurses—the Royal Jubilee Hospital (established in 1891) and the Sisters of St. Ann's school at St. Joseph Hospital (1900). Many Victoria nurses had professional connections in Vancouver or Montreal. All their instructors had been schooled in the principles of Florence Nightingale and St. Thomas's Hospital in London, opened in 1860; the modern fabric of medical nursing was erected on that foundation.[23] Collis graduated from Royal Jubilee Hospital in 1911.[24]

On August 21, 1915, wearing their felt hats with CAMC badges, brass-buttoned uniforms of navy-blue serge with scarlet collars, and black buttoned boots, seventy-two nurse-lieutenants paraded along Government Street. A few of them show stern faces of military deportment, but for most of them, pleasant smiles disclose happier sentiments. The women were off to war! The recently held lawn garden parties at the lieutenant-governor's house to the accompaniment of a military band were a fading memory. The Red Cross raised small fortunes by way of help. At "the Plains" at Macaulay Point, they were housed in a tent city, and they did routine and dusty marches, with pleasant swims in the cold salt water at their doorstep, and many a laborious ceremonial parade. Altogether they formed No. 5 Canadian General Hospital under Lieutenant-Colonel E.C. Hart, MD.

Elsie Collis enlisted a month later, on September 15, 1915, and we trace her history beginning in this year. She served, we note in advance, in England, Salonika, and France. She left a diary and an album of extraordinary photos that are featured in Maureen Duffus's *Battlefront Nurses*. From Victoria she would have boarded the *Princess Mary* or *Princess Sophia* for Vancouver, there to entrain for Montreal. After the Atlantic crossing she reached Plymouth (where Nelson's *Victory*, then a training ship, rode at anchor—and the sailors cheered and cheered the nurses as they passed). Then it was on to Shorncliffe, the main Canadian military hospital and staging ground, in Kent, near Sandgate. On visits to otherwise pleasant and majestic London, the pulsing centre of empire, she and her colleagues saw the Zeppelin raids and the search-lights seeking out those lighter-than-air ships that brought down terror once the Kaiser agreed that the imperial capital could be a bombing target. They heard the anti-aircraft batteries doing their noisy work. There was sightseeing in St. Paul's Cathedral and time, too, at William Waldorf Astor's mansion Cliveden, at Taplow, Buckinghamshire, turned over to Canadian medical services for the duration of the war, before returning to the routines of the hospital. Collis writes of tending to "two boys with fractured backs. Some very sad cases. Poor things, you long to do something for them."[25]

Then it was off to Liverpool with No. 5 Canadian General Hospital to board a hospital ship for "somewhere in the middle east," Collis noted in her diary. The hot passage was relieved by a stop in Malta, the British naval station, where British and French warships rode at anchor, while ashore the nurses went to church, bought oranges in the market, and took tea. Malta was essential for the hospital ships—and for the transshipment of the wounded. The passage eastward was wicked in the heavy seas, and all the nurses suffered seasickness. A well-earned and long visit to Egypt, staying in the elegant Semiramis Hotel on the banks of the Nile, and then a trip to the pyramids and a camel ride brought other imperishable memories. Many pleasant days passed in wondrously exotic Cairo before finally, on January 27, 1916, they sailed aboard the hospital ship *Egypt* through rough seas for Salonika on the Aegean Sea.

Salonika was a "sideshow of the war." There was much posturing by the Allies in support of an uncertain Greece, an ineffective power caught up in a familiar quarrel between the king and the archbishop. The Allies, particularly the French, who were in command, sought to establish a strong foothold that was more than anything a political statement designed to keep the Greek government afloat and keep enemy rivals out. It was all connected to the Balkans quagmire and the rescue of Serbia, which the Austro-Hungarian Empire was doing its best to destroy. Bulgarian attacks and German air raids were characteristic. The Canadian nurses were sent where there were no Canadian troops: they were at the disposition of the imperial command. There was much important work to do, attending to wounded from other campaigns and brought there in convoys.

At first sight, Salonika was nice to look at but it grew in time to be a wearying place. Surrounded by barbed wire, it earned the name "the birdcage," and nothing seemed to be a real war here, though routine was broken in various ways. For instance, the famed British submarine *E11* paid a call; it had passed through the distant Dardanelles and had done serious damage to the Ottoman Empire at Constantinople. On another occasion, near where Collis was positioned in Salonika, naval guns knocked down a Zeppelin, the brilliant white flame making a startling display against the vast blue of the sea. Years later Collis recalled the sense of deep pity she felt for the burning crew. A helpless feeling of futility gripped her. There were also pleasant visits to dressing stations in the field. At one time the Italians, who were Allies, arrived to make a military visit; then the Russians did likewise and brought their bands. There was much discomfort and misery—heat and cold, insects, mud, and much else. It was, in all, a dreary war.

General Sir George Milne, commanding the British forces in Salonika, had the highest praise for the Royal Army Medical Corps and the CAMC for their high traditions of efficiency. He wrote to the War Office in London, "The medical services have been called upon to face problems of great difficulty. It can be easily realised that in a climate varying from severe cold to intense damp heat, and in a mountainous country deficient in water, poorly supplied with roads, without local resources, and where dysentery and malaria are rife, the duties and responsibilities of these services must necessarily be heavy." And with specific reference to nurses he said, "By their skill, care and attention, at a time of great stress under trying climatic conditions, the sufferings of the patients have been greatly alleviated."[26]

Although we are getting ahead of ourselves here, it is best to complete Elsie Collis's story to the end of the War. The Salonika campaign wore down, and soon it was time to sail from Salonika to northwest France, via Marseilles and Gibraltar. The nurses wore life jackets at all times, for hospital ships were no longer safe from the U-boat menace. The ship arrived at Etaples, a town lying between Calais and Dieppe, there to set up the hospital. Etaples ("Eat-apples," the British Tommy called it) was one of the largest centres for reinforcements to the imperial forces, with training depots, hospitals, and facilities for 100,000 men. No wonder it became a German target (though German actions were inexcusable). Here, too, the events of the time became embedded in Elsie Collis's mind, as the full misery of war was borne in on her. The cries of the wounded, the smell of death mixed with the odour of strong disinfectant, and the sense of loss and helplessness—all these and more were a regular bill of fare. Today the military cemetery there is the largest British war cemetery in France, and 11,557 men from all over the world, friend and foe, lie buried together.

For the Canadian nursing profession, May 19, 1918, is etched in sacred memory. On that day a rain of terror descended from the air on the medical officers, nurses, and other staff. The savage policy of German "frightfulness" was further demonstrated as four relays of enemy planes bombarded Etaples heavily, mainly its rail lines but with terrible collateral damage to No. 1 Canadian General Hospital and St. John's Ambulance Hospital. The attack was particularly demoralizing to patients, many of whom were suffering shell shock from front line action. Men lying in beds in the wards were trapped beneath falling debris.

Elsie Collis survived and so did her diary. Here's a segment of her entry for May 19, 1918, the day of horror:

> Before I left for supper I heard distant guns but thought nothing of it. Had just got to the kitchen door when bombs began to drop. There were several in the mess quarters and set the rows of huts on fire. Two dropped outside the [nurses'] club, another outside our new quarters. The whole place was wrecked—poor little "Bob" [Gladys Wake of Esquimalt] was buried, she had a fractured femur, a huge wound in the other leg and several smaller ones. A Miss [Katherine] McDonald was killed. She had a tiny wound but it must have severed the femoral artery as she died of hemorrhage almost immediately . . . It was dreadful. We could see the fires through the window, hear the men shouting and calling. Hear bombs dropping, the guns would all stop for a minute until the machines came within range. All one could hear was their continual buzzing—then the guns again, then the bombs . . . We were sure the next one would hit us . . . When there was a lull we hurried back to the wards.

Fifteen German planes carried out that attack while the nursing sisters, at the risk of their own lives, desperately toiled through the night. Of 1,100 patients in the hospital, 66 were killed or died of wounds and 73 others were wounded. "Bob" Wake died on May 22 and was buried the same day. "We all went to the funeral. It was dreadfully trying. 46 of the boys were all buried together in one long grave." The raids did not stop, and as Duffus has explained, the hospitals were chosen targets because the German high command saw them as being in strategic proximity to military rail and port facilities.[27]

Elsie, and others, received Red Cross medals "for bravery in the field." Once back in British Columbia at war's end, Elsie Collis nursed in military hospitals in Vancouver and Victoria and served as matron at Resthaven in Sidney. She was nursing in Vancouver when she met a returned army corporal, Harry Arthur Hunt, suffering terribly from the aftermath of gas and severe shrapnel wounds to the hips, as well as tuberculosis that set in because of months of cold exposure in the trenches. She married Harry Hunt, lived in Cobble Hill, raised a family, and was active in the Women's Institute and various community enterprises. Beloved in her community to the last, she died, this remarkable woman with so many experiences in the business of saving lives, in 1986, age ninety-nine. She was one of nearly 2,000 Canadian nurses, and they and countless others of the nursing profession were the reason so many injured and sick survived the war. Their record of service in the Great War is the stuff of legend and of imperishable pride to those who keep green their memories and continue to write their histories. Duffus writes: "These extraordinary women, who were born during the Victorian age, graduated as professional nurses from some of the earliest hospital training schools in Canada. It would have taken a tremendous leap of imagination to picture these young ladies, so soon after graduation, caring for soldiers sick from malaria, typhoid and dysentery, wounded in battle and horribly burned from gas attacks—all the casualties brought to their hospital wards during the terrible war."[28]

In addition to the name of Elsie Collis we find the names of these other nurses on the Roll of Honour of Victoria High School: [?] Anderson, Hilda Beeston, Jean Mary Denovan, Alice Martha Moss, Joanna Middleton (who trained at St. Joseph's Hospital), M. Redding and [Pearl?] Ross. (A tantalizing detail is that Denovan married Lt. Thomas Norris,[29] also from Victoria High School.) In reading about the lives of Collis and other nurses, one is struck by the dogged continuity of service over the long years—from training, through deployment in fields of fire or of rest, then service in convalescent hospitals and places of rest. Their jobs were never done, and all through the miserable years and the dislocations of their assignments, nurses conducted themselves with good grace and humour, their quiet and reassuring dispositions of immeasurable aid to the suffering and, ever so often, the soon-to-die. Their training had steeled them for the challenges that lay ahead, and in the circumstances they faced there was no substitute for it. Elsie Collis may be the most famous of Victoria High School's nurses, but other stories could be told of the doings of others.


*In November 1915,* for the first time, *The Camosun* printed its Service Roll. This was a partial list of Victoria High School boys, past and present, who were fighting at the Front or had left the province to go to the Front. There were sixty-four in the main list and thirty-six in the category of Enlisted for Service Abroad—that is, likely in training.

The intention of *The Camosun* was to publish the list every month. "If an error appears in the name or rank of any soldier we would be glad to be informed of it and to receive additional names for the list." In some cases, details are given of the individuals: Private James P. Brown was known to be the orderly, or messenger, to Arthur Currie. Lance-Corporal John S. Dee, wounded in action in France, was convalescing in a Birmingham Hospital. Private Charles Hardie was in the Princess Patricia's Canadian Light Infantry. Private Dono Heyland, wounded in action, was now back at the Front. Private John Mudie Milligan was a prisoner of war in Germany. Private Cecil Milloy, who had enlisted with the first draft of the 50th Regiment, Gordon Highlanders, from Victoria, had been wounded and recently returned to Victoria (and, we note here, was thinking about how he might go back to the War). Private Robert O'Meara was serving in the ever-so-essential Sanitary Corps. Sergeant David Valentine Vernon Stevens, 16th Battalion, Canadian Infantry (Manitoba Regiment), had been killed in action on May 20, 1915, at the age of twenty; he was unusually young for a sergeant. Saanich-born Stevens had been a captain in the Cadet Battalion, and later a student at McGill University (likely Victoria College). Corporal Frank Tait had been given an honourable discharge. In the lists of Enlisted for Service Abroad we find Sub-Lieutenant Thomas Brown of HMCS *Rainbow*, Lieutenant Harold Eustace Whyte in the Army Service Corps, and Lieutenant-Colonel W.N. Winsby commanding the 47th Battalion. As the months and years went by, it was harder to place a regiment or unit with a listed name, and so the whole was reduced to one long list in alphabetical order. By the end of the War the names on the school's Service Roll numbered in the hundreds—in fact, nearly half a thousand.

To add literary and patriotic touches, from time to time speeches from Shakespeare would appear. Noteworthy in this regard is *The Camosun* for March 1916, where King Henry V's speech to his troops before Harfleur is given right at the top before the list ("Once more unto the breach, dear friends, once more; Or close the wall up with our English dead!" etc.) And at the bottom of the list, from *King John*: "This England never did, nor never shall, Lie at the proud foot of a conqueror . . . Now these her princes are come home again, Come the three corners of the world in arms, And we shall shock them. Nought shall make us rue, If England to itself do rest but true."

# *chapter 3* **1916**

## THE SOMME: FIELDS OF FIRE

*T*he unnamed valedictorian addressing the Victoria High School graduating class of 1916 summed up nicely the inseparable bonds that joined the school with the War: "Some of us will answer the call of Empire and go forth to battle for the cause of right and honour. But wherever we may be found, the links of the chain of memory will long compel our willing bondage, the unyielding claims of Victoria High School."[1]

The work of the school continued without interruption, and the students passed through their appointed divisions and grades, most of them preparing for other lines of work than going to war. One such was Bruce Hutchison, later Canada's famed journalist.

Born in Prescott, Ontario, in 1901, Hutchison moved with his family to a tiny bungalow on Wilmer Street, Victoria, near the border with Oak Bay. The home, he said, was little affected by the War, though his mother complained that beef prices had soared to unbelievable heights. Hutchison wrote warmly about his arrival, age thirteen, at the brand new Victoria High School in 1914:

> I had entered the grand new Victoria High School and now began,
> strangely enough, to relish education. At night, while Dad read his
> gardening books and Mother sewed, I spent two hours or more on

homework. But over the weekends I found time to raven through the works of Scott, Dickens, Thackeray, Maupassant, and Conrad, among others . . . Persuaded that scholarship was my natural bent, I plunged enthusiastically into the school's debating society [Beta Delta], delivered ponderous well-researched speeches on matters of which I knew nothing, and even debated in Vancouver with a team just as ignorant. Victory in that contest confirmed my singular gifts and exploding self-esteem. Obviously I must become a lawyer.

Hutchison delighted in activities at the school. He played Shylock in Shakespeare's *Merchant of Venice*, paraded as a lieutenant in the Cadet Battalion, wrote stories and penned a few cartoons for *The Camosun*, and rose to become its editor, the first step to making him among the best in that line of work. The *Victoria Times* let him write a column of school news for its Saturday edition, and this gave him an inkling that he might become a journalist. Indeed, the connection with the editor, the great-hearted Benjamin Charles Nicholas, "the immortal Benny," proved important in Hutchison's thinking about what we might call the Canadian fact and Canadian nationalism. Benny Nicholas had agreed to coach the school's boys' debating team, and his connections with Hutchison became close and influential. Just after war's end, Hutchison found himself taking the transcontinental train for Ottawa as a news correspondent, thereby abandoning plans to go to university and become a lawyer. That lay ahead. In 1916, Hutchison was, he said, "already an adolescent intellectual snob and, in retrospect, a rather nasty piece of work altogether." He claimed he paid scant attention to the War, which may be true, and that his "contemporaries and rivals in the fierce politics of our high school" did not do so either, which is an exaggeration.

As to "the depth of a world calamity beyond our comprehension," Hutchison wrote about his fellow classmates now facing the horror of war,

Older boys, some of them our friends, who had graduated ahead of us, were dying in the trenches of Europe. The *Daily Colonist* printed the long casualty lists every morning and Dad read them by the kitchen stove before breakfast. Canada was being drained of its best blood, changed from a colony into a nation. But the anguish and the blood-letting hardly touched our life at school as we prepared for university.

If we thought of it at all, the war seemed far away and bound to end soon in the triumph of Right over Wrong, the birth of an ever-peaceful world, safe for democracy, as President Woodrow Wilson had frequently promised. We sometimes read his speeches in the newspapers and agreed (though Dad was prejudiced against an American who had remained neutral for so long).[2]

The convulsions on the Western Front, this cockpit of the War, were affecting the western world. Canada was not immune. "The New Year's light of 1916 rising upon a frantic and miserable world revealed in its full extent the immense battlefield to which Europe was reduced and on which the noblest nations of Christendom mingled in murderous confusion." This was Winston Churchill, himself an officer on the Front early that same year, writing some time after the War. The struggle would continue to an annihilating conclusion. "There was no escape," he wrote. "All the combatants in both combinations were gripped in a vice from which no single State could extricate itself."[3]

The Battle of the Somme stands like an iron gate across the path of history. It marked the end of the old order and the beginning of a new one. It signified the approach of the end of empires. As Germany was being bled white on the battlefield at the Somme, particularly at Verdun, its reasonable chance of winning the war dwindled away. France had suffered terribly, and these events marked the point at which the burden of the War passed from France to Britain and the British Empire. Imperial Russia was on the verge of revolution. The Austro-Hungarian Empire was in decay. The British Empire was fighting for survival, and, with the aid of its dominions and colonies, it surmounted the biggest challenge it had ever faced. New technologies were coming to the battlefield, and better staff work, too. British artillery, which included Canadian, Australian, and other units, was becoming more powerful and more effective. The tank would soon make its appearance. Aviation was beginning to play a critical part, and the Royal Naval Air Service and Army Air Service started to exert influence in reconnaissance, tactical moves, and victories in the air against strong German air power. The age of the Zeppelin was not yet over but soon would be for military purposes. On the sea, too, 1916 marked a significant development: the great sea fight between the Royal Navy's Grand Fleet and Imperial Germany's High Seas Fleet, May 31 and June 1, known as the Battle of Jutland, failed to result in a British victory, but it left the command of the sea fully in Britannia's hands. And 1916, too, saw the rise of the U-boat peril. By the end of the year Allied shipping losses were so severe that Germany's high command considered implementing "unrestricted submarine warfare." This presaged events to come the following February. In all, then, 1916 was a particularly critical year of the war.

In 1916, too, that iconic figure Field Marshal Lord Kitchener, who had built up the new volunteer British Army and had done so much to aid recruitment in the dominions and colonies, passed from the scene. He went down in HMS *Hampshire* while on a special mission to Russia to put new heart into its war effort. The British Empire mourned a figure of reassuring stature. In Victoria, veterans who had fought under Kitchener in the South African War planned a memorial to the empire's famous soldier. That story is told in the next chapter.

Kitchener's departure from the darkening scene had profound effects on the deployment of the growing and strengthening Canadian divisions in the field, among them: Canada would fight only on the Western Front; Canadian staff training would follow British requirements, to the benefit of Canadian interests;[4] and Canadian politicians would insist on a greater role in the direction of the war effort. The War was becoming an increasingly Canadian one. In January 1916, Ottawa had announced that Canada's authorized forces would be increased to half a million men. No opposition was made to this policy. "By the greatness of the need our future efforts must be measured," said the prime minister, Sir Robert Borden. The appeal brought tremendous response in support, and in early 1916 more than a hundred thousand men enlisted. But 1916 showed that the struggle would exceed all expectations. The Second Division had gone to the Front, then the Third and the Fourth. The need for reinforcements became greater, while toward the end of the year recruitment dropped off. Also that year, the horrific casualties of the expanding conflict prompted Britain to introduce conscription. Manpower was being stretched between domestic and military demands in all the major European nations.

At home in Canada, the industrial base deepened and strengthened in the field of munitions and the preparation of all sorts of war materiel. Some very large profits were made in that sector. Various national agencies were set up by Ottawa to move the economy increasingly into war production. In the economic fields where Canada was already strong, it got stronger. Victoria, as a port, bustled with business. Forest products; canned salmon; ship building and repair; and mineral production in copper, lead, and zinc caused the economy to boom.

Patriotic zeal never wavered, in Victoria or Vancouver, or in other towns and cities of the province. On reaching age eighteen, young men joined up, answering the call and political pressure and propaganda, to help King and Country. This had become Canada's war, and the memories of what had happened in the Second Battle of Ypres, still fresh, were a reminder that there were old scores to settle and big battles ahead.

All expectations of this being a short war had vanished. Maintaining morale in the face of uncertainty as to how the War would end became an essential question. Though some might have argued that the result was never in doubt, in the halls of power and in places of high command much doubt remained, though resolve never faltered. Given the virtual static state of the Western Front, various attempts were made to break the deadlock. The Gallipoli campaign of 1915 ended in disaster, giving no encouragement to the opening of a new front. The campaigns in Palestine and Mesopotamia (Iraq) faced untold difficulties. Only in Africa and East Asia had the Allies exerted such superior power as to close down the German Empire, enriching as they did the interests of the Union of South Africa and the Japanese Empire. The French and British high command knew no other alternative than to wear down the German forces in battle on the continent. General Sir William Robertson, Chief of the Imperial General Staff, when quizzed on this, said that they did not know what else to do. General Haig, the overall commander of the British Armies, held the same view. This is the background to the Battle of the Somme.

All along the Western Front the great guns of both sides continued their lethal work. In the trenches, individual mortar units hurled shells at enemy positions. They could expect something similar in return. Overhead the whirling roar of incoming shells and the explosion of shrapnel shells, the most lethal of all, turned the battlefield into a nightmare above the trenches and far back to the enemy's sources of supply, relief, and retreat. No great battles were to be fought now without sufficient advance bombardment. Tunnelling became a necessity for surprise attack. Overhead, the air crews did the reconnaissance, aerial photography, and target spotting. The new technology of that age had made this an industrial war.

Shirley Duncan Ellis, known as Duncan Ellis, was a star rugby player, the team captain, and one of the finest three-quarters who ever represented

Victoria High School. Born in Victoria in 1892, Duncan, the son of W.H. Ellis, a publisher, and Ada Leslie Ellis (of 50 South Turner Street) graduated in engineering from the University of Toronto, studied at Denver School of Mining, and was employed by the Guggenheims at a mine in far-distant Chile. When war broke out, he shipped for London and joined, apparently on his own artistic abilities, the Artists' Rifles.[5] From there, given his engineering knowledge, he found himself gazetted a second lieutenant in the Royal Engineers, attached to the 173rd Tunnelling Company. His war work was mainly underground, and getting at the enemy below the surface was as necessary a tactic as fighting on the surface. It is said that sometimes the British tunnels opened into those of the enemy, or vice versa. For six months, Ellis was at the Front in Flanders; later his company redeployed to near Béthune, France.

All went well for him until early March 1916. On the 9th he "had a nasty jar," he told a friend, in reference to a shell explosion nearby, "that has added a year to my youthful numbers." On the 14th he wrote his mother: "Just a line to let you know I am still dodging German shells. I have developed a dive from seeking shell holes and deep parts of trenches that would have made me famous at football. I have had a bit of a rocky time lately, slightly gassed, and anxiety told their tale. Then I ate something that disagreed with me, to add to the pleasant round. However, fine spring days are here at last."

Shortly thereafter, according to Sergeant E. Gray, who was with him at the time, Ellis heard that thirty of his men were entombed, and he at once rushed to the scene. The area was dangerous, near the front line trenches. Ellis then worked like a Trojan with his men, under what Sergeant Gray described as the heaviest shellfire he could remember. Three vain attempts were made to free the trapped men. On the fourth they succeeded. Ellis went down into the mine, searched for survivors, and took particulars of the dead (whose bodies could not be recovered for burial until nightfall). "On being brought to the surface, Mr. Ellis collapsed, and had to be assisted to his dugout under shell and machine gunfire. His diligence, manner and example acted as a great incentive to his men," wrote the Sergeant. Ellis's "devotion to duty" was also noted by Captain G.A. Harrison, the company commander.

But exhaustion, and perhaps other illness, as he had hinted at to his mother, took their toll. He became ill, was operated on for appendicitis, but died a few days later, on March 19, age twenty-three. Next day he was buried with full military honours in Béthune Town Cemetery; a cross was being prepared and would shortly be erected by the officers. "It is hard luck," wrote Captain Harrison to Ellis's father, "the poor fellow did not live to know that his splendid act of devotion to duty had been rewarded." The Military Cross was posthumously awarded "for conspicuous gallantry when rescuing, under very heavy fire, some men who had become imprisoned in an old mine. At his first three attempts he was driven back by heavy fire." What compensation this news could have provided at his home can never be known. Duncan Ellis was the first native-born Victorian to win the Military Cross. The War Office sent Lord Kitchener's condolences. Ellis's personal effects—a tobacco pouch, photographs, matriculation certificate, pocket notebook, fountain pen, wristwatch, and others—were sent home by registered post. The Military Cross medal was also sent to the family in Victoria. He had been in military service for 222 days, perhaps close to the average for subalterns.

In the officers' mess of the Royal Engineers, there was an empty chair, as Captain Bryan Fenland, the adjutant, noted with regret. "He was a great favorite amongst both officers and men and we all miss him very much indeed. There is no doubt that his death was caused by overwork and the great strain he underwent during the past fortnight. He was engaged on most difficult and dangerous work in the front line trenches, the success of which was entirely due to his energy and good work . . . These men all owe their lives to his energy and bravery."[6]

Later that spring, in the vicinity of Ploegsteert, Albert Nelson King (generally known as Nelson King) was serving as a lieutenant in the Royal Field Artillery. He had been named for the famous Admiral Lord Nelson. He may be ranked among the school's academic cream and was perhaps the most promising of Canada's sons whose life was soon to be cut short. His name is on the school's student lists, which line the front stairwell, as top student for 1906. He was born in Moodyville, British Columbia. His grandfather had been in the Royal Navy as a paymaster in HMS *Daring*, which had called at Esquimalt. His father, an accountant, died in 1892, and the family—Mrs. King, Albert Nelson King, his brother Cecil Nelson King, and sisters Jessie and Sybil—moved to Victoria. The girls had also attended Victoria High School, and Jessie enters our story a little farther on. As the eldest son, Nelson King had to do much, and he had to earn money. Like many another Victoria High School lad, he was engaged by the *Daily Colonist* circulation department, in route deliveries and then in administration. The connection of Victoria High School with that paper, as well as with the *Victoria Times*, is significant: these were networks beyond the school, but they depended on a reliable supply of conscientious boys to do their work on and off the premises—and to deliver the news.

Upon matriculation, Nelson King took Arts I and II at Victoria College, and then went on to McGill to complete his bachelor's degree. There he had come to the attention of those who saw in him a particularly brilliant fellow. He won the gold medal for Classics. He took the BC exam to qualify as a teacher in the Academic category and was on the staff at Boys' Central when news came that he had been selected Rhodes Scholar for British Columbia in 1912.[7] At that time, Victoria High School was so prominent in British Columbia educational standing that any likely nomination from persons connected with McGill would merit strongest consideration.

While at Oxford, Nelson King joined King Edward's Horse, the King's Overseas Dominions Regiment, whose purpose was to allow visitors to the United Kingdom to be attached for drill and training or to qualify for promotion as commissioned or non-commissioned officers. The regiment dated from the war in South Africa and was popular with "colonials" at Oxford, Cambridge, and London universities. When the War broke out, Trooper King was encamped with his regiment on the Earl of Clarendon's estate, The Grove, near Watford. The sword drills and charges with lances, the order of the day for cavalry, were subjects of amusement. It seemed as if they were preparing for a much earlier war, such as Waterloo or Crimea, when all officers were horsemen.

The Royal Field Artillery had a special requirement for horses and horsemen, for mobility in the field was its expertise. Before long, Nelson King found himself at the Duke of York's Barracks in Chelsea, and in January 1915, he was off to Aldershot. There, Second Lieutenant Nelson King joined C Battery, 53rd (Howitzer) Brigade, one of four four-gun batteries that made up the brigade. That unit was placed under command of the 9th (Scottish) Division. All his aspirations as a classicist had been set aside. He deployed to France and arrived at Le Havre on May 10, 1915.

Exactly a year later, Albert Nelson King was stationed in the area of Ploegsteert Wood, Belgium, which consists of a series of low ridges of tactical importance. These open, rolling features were dotted with thick deciduous woods. Higher-ups determined that the Front must be held at all costs. The German forces were out to the east. Trench warfare was a feature of the fighting. The heavy shells passed and repassed high overhead, doing their lethal work. By this time, C Battery, like the others, had been detached from the brigade. It was likely off to the west, behind a ridge, at the southern edge of the Ypres Salient and probably about two miles back from the Front. Oddly, Hitler was in this same neighbourhood about the same time. A runner, he was wounded. Not far off, too, Churchill, no longer at the Admiralty, was a battalion commander of the Royal Scots Fusiliers.

We do not know how Nelson King died. Perhaps he was situated dangerously exposed to snipers as forward observation officer. We will never know for sure. In any event, on May 10, 1916, Lieutenant Albert Nelson King was killed in action. He was buried with 227 others in a small cemetery, now known as Rifle House Cemetery, which stands deep in the woods near Hainaut, Belgium, only accessible by muddy road and on foot. I located his grave after some considerable difficulty. Like the grave of every other known warrior killed in action, it has a reference: in his case "I.DD. 3. Rifle House Cemetery." Rifle House is one of the CWGC cemeteries that dot the landscape of Belgium and Flanders (and elsewhere). Nowadays, it is a place of absolute peace. Like others of its kind, it is walled and gated, the grass is carefully tended, and English roses are almost always a feature. The area around is well forested now, but in mid-1916 the landscape would have been desolate—hardly a tree standing, only broken trunks and burned and shattered limbs, the ground a thousand craters, and no birds singing. It would have been a wasteland, and even now we can imagine the burial parties making their dreary procession, the chaplain reading the last rites, the detail party firing a last salute over the lowering coffin.

Here a necessary diversion is in order. A year and a half later, in November 1917, Nelson's sister Jessie Nelson King, four years his senior and a Canadian nursing sister, arrived in France. She had been educated at South Park and then Girls' Central School before attending Victoria High School for a time. She began training as a nurse in Montreal when Nelson had been at McGill. On return to Victoria, she entered the Royal Jubilee Hospital and qualified. In 1916, she served at Work Point, Esquimalt, for four months, then joined the service of her country as nursing sister. The enemy tried to kill her several times. The transport carrying her to England was attacked by a U-boat, but all passengers made shore safely. In November 1917, she joined No. 1 Canadian Hospital and was at Etaples during the air raid of 1918 in which Nursing Sister Gladys Wake, of Victoria, and many others were killed.[8]

Before leaving France, a party of nurses planned a visit to the battlefields, and Jessie was one who made what must have been a hard and exhausting journey. On return to the hospital at the beginning of March 1919, she was stricken with meningitis, suffered a long and lingering illness, and died April 4, 1919, age twenty-six, at No. 14 Stationary Hospital, Wimereux, France.

In 1920, Jessie Nelson King was one of the nursing sisters paid special honour (Christina Campbell and Gladys Wake were among others honoured then or later). Beside the tribute there to Jessie we find these words of Percy Bysshe Shelley, evoking enduring memories of events and sensations, inserted, tellingly, by her next of kin and Lieutenant Robert Stephen, her fiancée:

> *Music, when soft voices die*
> *Vibrates in the memory.*[9]

Jessie had respects of her own to pay in her last months on the battle-scarred area that had been the Western Front, where desolation was everywhere though the guns were silent at last. During that battlefields journey, Jessie Nelson King went in search of the grave of her brother Nelson and found it. One can only imagine her personal pain and deep regret. Her last letter home, dated February 22, 1919, told of her visit to her brother's grave. What particularly touches the observer is that within two years of Nelson's being killed in action, she, too, died. She was, according to the official medical services history, the last Canadian nursing sister to die in the War.[10] So here we have a double or compounded tragedy, one of imperishable regret.

When I paid my respects at Nelson King's grave, I set at the base of his gravestone a wreath of remembrance on behalf of Victoria High School's Alumni Association. The life of one of the most promising of persons had been stamped out by war. He was one of thousands who died that year. But I had not forgotten that in Rifle House Cemetery, his grieving sister Jessie had been there before me.

*At the time* of Nelson King's passing, the French and British armies were preparing for a big offensive. It is now known as the Somme.

On July 1, the Somme saw the first great action by a British army of continental size. The British Armies consisted of 57 divisions, most of them from the United Kingdom but many from the dominions. This compares with

95 French and 117 German divisions on the Western Front. The British Armies in France had grown steadily in response to Kitchener's call. Although an incomparable spirit existed in this force, the officers had little knowledge of trench warfare, and the enemy's success was largely attributed to reasons other than the stout use of the machine gun and scientifically planned defences.[11] The idea of manning trenches, then going "over the top" and advancing in a regular line, bayonets glinting in the sun, was the tactical thinking of the old order. Haig, the commander-in-chief, imagined that if he delivered a prolonged "barrage," followed by an infantry assault, it would clear up the wreckage, and then the cavalry could be part of a breakthrough that would operate in open country like a battering ram.

All this was to change on July 1. That day, thirteen British divisions went "over the top" in regular waves. German machine guns knocked them over in rows: 19,000 killed, 57,000 casualties sustained. At Beaumont-Hamel on the same day, 733 of 801 men of the 1st Newfoundland Regiment perished. The British Armies suffered the greatest loss in a single day of any army in the Great War. It was a killing field unlike any other. Haig decided to persist with his battering ram. He delayed for a few days and then began the vain attempt to cut the German lines and make a breakthrough. The British, French, and Australians all paid heavy prices that summer. The Germans put up a stout defence, and their guns and machine guns did excellent work. Their reliance on machinery increased. Letters found on captured Germans reported terrible conditions at home. The longing for peace was strong, but most still thought winning was possible, leading to complete victory. Others were not so sure, thinking that no one would win the war.

For the British Armies the enormous losses continued, and the men who had escaped death were dog-tired. It was impossible to keep men very long in the firing line under such conditions. Troops were relieved frequently. The "Anzacs" of the Australian and New Zealand Army Corps were in the line for six weeks. They captured more ground than any other corps to that time, and they took 900 prisoners. The Somme battle continued to go on as hard as ever.

The Canadian Corps was not there at the beginning, but on September 3, the Canadians began replacing the Australians in the line. They came under heavy enemy mortar and artillery fire. All along the line the British Armies were taking great casualties. Back and forth went the attacks, and the Germans suffered terribly, too. On September 10, the historian of the 10th Canadian

Infantry Battalion wrote, "Nothing out of the ordinary occurred." Four men were wounded, and six were killed.[12] Tanks were used for the first time five days later. The Canadian Corps attacked at Courcelette on the 15th, and the Princess Patricia's Canadian Light Infantry (PPCLI), with many from Victoria, were part of it. Of the PPCLI, it was said that they were "scared of nought but rats." In the shell-shattered landscape, they suffered terribly under withering German machine-gun fire but pushed ahead and took many prisoners.

Private Charles Mawer Hardie of the PPCLI died in this attempt. Son of Gordon and Ethel Hardie of Esquimalt, he had joined the first McGill draft in Montreal. On account of his fearlessness and natural ability, he was chosen as a bomb thrower, and his sunny disposition made him a favourite of fellow soldiers. He was wounded in the right elbow at Ypres, recovered in England, and was back at the Front in time for the Somme. He often talked about the possibility of getting back to the dear homeland that he had left so long ago. The vision faded quickly: he went to the Somme and was one of those who participated in the taking of Thiepval, the fortified ridge that had long held up the Australians but fell to the persistent hammering of the Canadians. Soon thereafter, Hardie was struck on the head by shrapnel. The wound was not thought serious, but three days later an operation was performed, unsuccessfully. He was twenty-one at the time of his death on October 13, 1916.[13]

The British Armies advanced up the gentle slope on September 15, but by day's end showers of rain made it difficult to negotiate the slippery, muddy, and shell-shattered ground. That day stretcher-bearers brought down the wounded. They laboured to the point of exhaustion, even though they were aided by the troops and by German prisoners.[14] Haig ordered a postponement of four days.

German high command, realizing the enemy's determination, decided to build a great line of defence, the Hindenburg Line, placed behind the front lines so they could hold their position on the Western Front. Overhead, the Royal Flying Corps took the offensive, carrying the war beyond the enemy's lines. They bombed German troops in their trenches. In terms of environmental degradation, nothing to that point compared to what transpired on the Somme. On October 11, Lady Helen Vincent (later Viscountess D'Abernon) was on the Front, near Albert, France, where no previous women visitors had been allowed, and witnessed a section of the battlefield come under intense German bombardment. "We stood for a long while riveted by the strange Satanic scene," she wrote, "but, at last, it was a relief to turn away. The ground which we were treading, the shellholes we avoided, are broken patches of a battlefield of only a short month ago." She continued: "The scene had a Lucifer, Prince of Darkness kind of splendour, but uppermost in my mind was a sense of the wickedness and waste of life, the lack of any definite objective commensurate with all this destruction, desolation and human suffering." A visit to a casualty clearing station did not cheer her up: "In the officers' tent the faces were, almost without exception, the faces of mere boys. Special tents are set apart for the abdominal wounds, for chest wounds, for eyes, for gas-gangrene, etc., and of course separate tents for the Boches. Among these, one lonely figure, still on a forgotten stretcher, was lying with his face turned to the wall. Like others he did not speak nor even look round as we passed through, and remains, in memory, a lonely pathetic figure."[15]


We now return to Victoria High School casualties of 1916, most connected with the Somme. However, before the Somme attack, on May 30, 1916, Private Marc Edward Berton (who, we note with curiosity, had been born in France) died age seventeen. He was in the 10th Battalion, Canadian Infantry (Alberta Regiment), and had enlisted before the required age of eighteen. He may have been an American citizen. At the time of his death his parents, Gaston and Jeanne Jacquet Berton, were living in San Francisco. He is buried in Railway Dugouts Burial Ground, Zillebeke, Ypres, Belgium.

In the first Canadian push on the Somme, on September 3, Private Arthur Douglas Belyea of D Company, 4th Canadian Pioneers, died age thirty-two. He was the son of Barbara and the late Arthur L. Belyea, King's Counsel, of Vancouver. He is remembered with honour in Reninghelst New Military Cemetery, Poperinge, Belgium, one of 800 Great War casualties commemorated at this site.

Henry Cuthbert Holmes, lieutenant in the 2nd Battalion, Irish Guards, born in India and educated at Victoria College (Arts II) and then Balliol College, Oxford, was wounded at the Somme on September 15, 1916. He returned home to Victoria on convalescence, married Philippa Despard Pemberton, rejoined his regiment, and at war's end became for two years a secretary to the Peace Commission in Versailles. Along the way he qualified as an English barrister, returned to Victoria, and became a real-estate mogul.[16] He is shown on the school's Roll of Honour as having won the Military Cross.

Another to fall at the Somme was Private Ernest Robertson Elford, native of Victoria and educated at Victoria High School. His family had had connections with the city since gold rush days, when they arrived from California. Many business opportunities opened in lumbering, and his father was part owner, and the manager, of Shawnigan Lake Lumber Company. After graduating, Elford became a surveyor and was in that line of work on northern Vancouver Island when war broke out. He joined the 88th Regiment, Victoria Fusiliers, enlisted in the CEF, and arrived in England. His pay book shows that he was docked occasionally for being away without leave. He was in France with the 10th Battalion by late October 1915 and was much in the thick of things, suffering shrapnel wounds and influenza. He sent a postcard from Paris to his brother Hugh, at home at 1426 Stadacona Street. Elford was almost a year on the front lines. On September 26, when storming enemy trenches near Courcelette, he got hit badly by shrapnel and died almost instantly, age twenty-four.[17] He has no known grave.

Gunner John Henry Austin, 10th Brigade, Canadian Field Artillery, was killed in action October 11, 1916. His body was never identified. Like many others, he is remembered with honour on the Canadian National Vimy Memorial. He is also memorialized by the James Bay Athletic Association and his school.

John Angus MacDonald, the school's valued and popular French master, who was away on leave, died in battle during the last desperate days of the Battle of the Somme. A year earlier, he had left Canada with his battalion, the 47th (Western Ontario Regiment). Born in Montreal in 1885, he had been educated at Queen's University (BA and MA) and then ventured west to Victoria to teach. He had always shown a keen interest in the school's Cadet Battalion, in which he was, in turn, cadet instructor, then lieutenant. He was active in wrestling and basketball at the school. He played rugby for the James Bay Athletic Association. In his spare time, he was a militia soldier, joining the 5th British Columbia Regiment of Garrison Artillery in which so many of the school served, and had risen to the rank of sergeant major, then commissioned lieutenant. Then had come the long passage to the Western Front.

On the night of September 16/17, 1916, in the Ypres trenches near La Clytte (also near Dickebusch village), MacDonald won the Military Cross, the citation reading, "For conspicuous gallantry when leading a raid, he advanced down the enemy's trench in spite of opposition, accounting for five of the enemy in the trench and others in the dugouts. He brought back useful information." From the battalion war diary we learn that the objects of this raid (one of two carried on simultaneously) were to capture prisoners, thereby gaining information and helping operations then being planned farther south, that is, at the Somme. At 12:20 AM, MacDonald, leading twenty-five other ranks, bombed or bayonetted eight Germans, occupied the trench, then at 12:35 withdrew and returned from where they had started. It had been a tidy operation, requiring careful planning and execution. The raiding parties had been assisted by intense artillery bombardment just before the raid, then a "box barrage" for fifteen minutes around the enemy trenches, then, and finally, a repetition of the bombardment such as had commenced the whole operation. The raiders had scurried across no man's land and returned unscathed. Good fortune had attended them, for not all were so lucky in such perilous proceedings.

MacDonald, redeployed to the south with his unit, then fought through all Canadian actions in the Battle of the Somme, almost to the time that ghastly campaign trickled out. On November 11, he was killed while leading a gallant and, as it turned out, successful attack on a German trench.

Mere days before his death, he wrote home to the students of Matriculation A, whom he had bade farewell not much more than a year before: "A tenth part of the story of horrors and desolation caused by this war will never be written, nor the suffering and misery that of necessity follow in its wake." Thinking to the future, he had suggested a topic for the girls' debating society to consider: "I have a new theme for discussion in the 'Portia': 'International Arbitration to Settle all International Disputes, and of course international police to give effect to the decrees of the courts so established.' How do you like it?" Such was the grand and altruistic desire, never realized. But while he lived, the noble Lieutenant MacDonald saw a need for alternate measures to avoid war. "I should like to 'drop in' for a lesson in French," he wrote wistfully in closing, "but must wait for the realization of this darling wish in the sweet by and by."

Lieutenant John Angus MacDonald, MC, died age thirty-one. Unmarried, he left no immediate family. He is buried in Albert Communal Cemetery Extension, Somme. MAY HIS SOUL REST IN PEACE reads his gravestone. It is not an exaggeration to say that his end epitomizes the horror and the heroism of war that was the Somme, and indeed the whole War. His loss was deeply felt by those who knew him in the city and in the school, staff and students alike. Newton F. Pullen, a student, penned a poem that was published in *The Camosun* of December 1916. A few lines printed here serve to show the deep bonds between the school and its late schoolmaster:

> *A real Canadian, and an earnest teacher he;*
> *Of hard and generous work, of mighty soul the slave.*
> *Small portion of this cold, grim world had known his worth,*
> *For young he was, and modest; yet in those who knew,*
> *Respect and admiration found a ready birth.*
> *Betwixt his pupils and himself there quickly grew*
> *An understanding and a friendship which they prize.*

Students had named him "Mac," with deep affection. After his death was announced, "Mac" took on a new connotation, for affection gave way to sadness: "its naming is with speaking silence fraught." MacDonald was a patriot, and Canada was dear to him. He had answered his country's call to honour; he could not but obey it, wrote Newton Pullen, and "he lives on in the living mind." "Another hero has been added to the Honour Roll of Canada," says *The Camosun*'s memorial, to which is added, "To live in hearts we live behind, Is not to die." He is remembered, too, in the Queen's University Roll of Honour.[18]

Late that same year came shocking news of the death on December 20, 1916, of Private Percy Gladstone Barr, whose widowed mother, Mrs. Rose Ann Barr, lived at Colwood with her two daughters. Matriculating from Victoria High School in October 1915, Percy Barr had enlisted while still underage, at seventeen. Trained as a sniper, he was himself shot while carrying out those dangerous duties close to the German lines. A bright student and immensely popular at school, he was also a noted basketball player and a devoted churchman, attending First Presbyterian (now First Metropolitan) Church, Victoria, and was a member of its Bible class. He left Victoria with the 103rd Battalion (Vancouver Island Timber Wolves) but later transferred to the 29th (Tobin's Tigers). Six members of First Presbyterian's basketball teams were at the Front. Of Percy Barr, the *Daily Colonist* wrote: "It is said that no finer boy ever left Canada and no braver or keener soldier ever served in her army."[19] It was also said that he was determined to go to war "and his motive in going was as high as his determination was firm." His brother Private Willis Barr, an architect, had gone overseas with the Canadian Army Service Corps and was a despatch rider. He was twice wounded, though miraculously survived the War.[20]

Kitchener's army found its graveyard on the Somme, but that was not all: the idealism of the old order perished. Disenchantment and cynicism replaced zest and idealism. Rupert Brooke's poetry, like that of Julian Grenfell, who had written in lyrical innocence, was now replaced by the works of a new school of poets who saw horror and suffering at every turn, though the comradeship of the trenches tempered the verse. As F. Scott Fitzgerald wrote in *Tender Is the Night*, such a battle could never be fought again, for men would not have the stomach for it. The old world and the old order had been blown up. On the Somme, one empire advanced slowly, gaining a few inches a day, while another walked backward, leaving a field of death and millions of anxious or grieving hearts at home.

The slaughter on the Somme continued for weeks, then died out in the mud of November to no strategic gain. By November, and the end of this sad campaign, the British had 420,000 casualties (including the injured); the French 194,000; and the Germans against the British 280,000 and against both the British and French armies 465,000. In just 138 days, more than 310,000 soldiers from the British, Canadian, French, and German armies had died.[21]

Officers of the Victoria College Cadet Corps, 1910. *Back row, L to R:* Colour Sgt. E. Steele, Sgt. S. Yuill, Lt. A. Mulcahy, RCA (instructor), Sgt. C. Brown. *Front Row, L to R:* Maj. V. Stevens, Lt. J. Dowler, Capt. Leroy L. Hartman, Lt. H. Boggs, Sgt. C. Hanington. VICTORIA HIGH SCHOOL ARCHIVES

Members of the Victoria High School Boys' Debating Club en route to a competition at King Edward High School in Vancouver. VICTORIA HIGH SCHOOL ARCHIVES

Rowing practice in the Inner Harbour, James Bay Athletic Association, 1912. *Left to right:* O. Sommers, Matthew H. Scott, P. Ogden, Blayney Scott. SCOTT FAMILY

Recruiting barrack on Fort Street, 1916. SCOTT FAMILY

Victoria military parade with Legislative Buildings in the distance, May 14, 1915. SCOTT FAMILY

The 30th Battalion departs for Vancouver to join the Canadian Expeditionary Force, February 14, 1915. SCOTT FAMILY

Professional nurses of the Canadian Army Medical Corps depart Victoria for the Front.
SCOTT FAMILY

King George V and Queen Mary with nurses at Taplow, England. Clara Detweiler is second to the right from Queen Mary. REID FAMILY

*Clockwise from top left:* Gunner S. Gordon Reid, Lieut. John "Jack" Reid, and Private David Reginald Reid, three of four brothers with connections to Victoria High School who enlisted. REID FAMILY

The home front: Victoria High School Victory Garden. VICTORIA HIGH SCHOOL ARCHIVES

Capt. Augustus E.S. Thurburn, died May 28, 1917, age 27. VICTORIA HIGH SCHOOL ARCHIVES

Rugby star Pte. Cyril Sedger,
died December 4, 1915, age 25.
VICTORIA HIGH SCHOOL ARCHIVES

Pte. Fred G. Heal, died January 24,
1915, age 27.
VICTORIA HIGH SCHOOL ARCHIVES

Private Heal's grave at Bulford
Church Cemetery, Wiltshire, England.
VICTORIA HIGH SCHOOL ARCHIVES

St. Martin's Cathedral at Ypres, Belgium, partially destroyed by German gunfire.
BARRY GOUGH COLLECTION

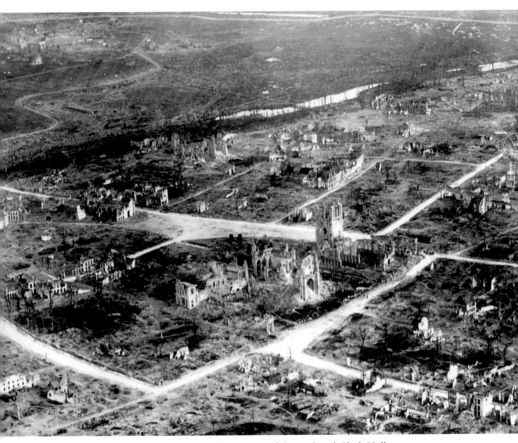

The ruins of Ypres showing the absolute destruction of the medieval Cloth Hall.

Menin Gate memorial to the British Empire missing, Ypres. There are 140 cemeteries containing war graves in the environs. BARRY GOUGH COLLECTION

Sapper W.G. Head, died August 22, 1917. VICTORIA HIGH SCHOOL ARCHIVES

Lieut. Frank M. Dunn, died September 23, 1917, age 27. VICTORIA HIGH SCHOOL ARCHIVES

A familiar sight in 1918: Canadian soldiers escorting German prisoners. CAMPBELL FAMILY

The new British weapon, the tank, Western Front. CAMPBELL FAMILY

Sgt. Harold Lane Campbell *(top right)* with the Canadian Army Medical Corps non-commissioned officers. Transport to and from the Front was by boxcars, known affectionately as "four and X" (four horses or ten men). CAMPBELL FAMILY

Soldiers of the casualty station tend to wounded in Canadian trenches, Western Front.
CAMPBELL FAMILY

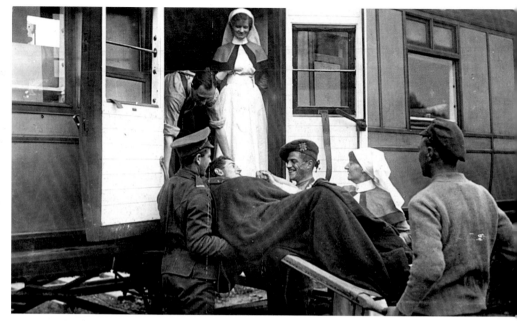

Medical evacuation to England. CAMPBELL FAMILY

Death and dying on the Western Front. SCOTT FAMILY

## VIMY RIDGE AND PASSCHENDAELE

T he year opened with a new recruit to the CEF. Harry Cross of Victoria, VHS Class of 1916, recently turned eighteen, had signed up. Of striking appearance, he had grey eyes, blondish-red hair, and a lovely countenance. At five feet seven inches tall, he stood near the national average. Church of England by religious persuasion, he lived with his parents and sister, Lily, at 1511 Pembroke Street. Military affairs were no new thing to Harry. On September 14, 1916, he had paraded with the 5th BC Regiment of Garrison Artillery, RCA. He was a gunner, became familiar with military routines and law, and drilled with the unit regularly. At the school, he had been at or near the top of his class, and had placed highly on the provincial final examinations. His popularity in the school knew no bounds. Like his contemporary Strother Foulkes, the eloquent speaker whom we have already met, he was proclaimed a campus idol by *The Camosun*.[1] Harry was publicly spirited and gave so much energy and commitment to the school—and all with a happy, witty disposition. He had come under the influence of teacher Arthur Yates, and had developed considerable skills as a speaker and debater. Many prizes had come his way. He was president of the boys' debating society, Beta Delta, and had gone to Vancouver to compete for the school against archrival King Edward High School. He wrote in an agreeable and generous style, and in many ways contributed markedly to the public discussions at the school about the national purpose in the War. He is one of the young men who would have gone to the War earlier if he could have, but age eighteen was the minimum requirement. By the time he had matriculated, he was of age to join up.

If any fellow had the backing of the school in future endeavours, it was Harry Cross. He, Strother Foulkes, and others signed up at about the same time. The flower of Canadian youth, who had been following the War from a distance, was now soon to see it close at hand. Gunner Harry Cross left for overseas in February. The War would forever change him and all those who knew him.

He was immediately assigned to the Divisional Ammunition Column, Canadian Field Artillery, where he would be useful in the big campaigns that were to come that year. Harry Cross fought through the long summer and well into the autumn of 1917. He was gassed by shell at Passchendaele in the last month of that appalling campaign, November 1917. He was hospitalized in England at the Lord Derby War Hospital in Lancashire, his future uncertain. We pick up his story later.[2]

Early 1917 brought devastating news to Victoria that Second Lieutenant Conrad Blackadder Wilson had been killed in action. He was the elder son of Charles J. Wilson, a mining engineer, and Isabella Blackadder Wilson of Laurel Lane. Conrad was born in Altenschlirf, Germany, had been educated in St. Mary's School, Melrose, then George Watson's College, Edinburgh, before coming to Victoria with his family. He was a student at Victoria High School at the time he enlisted in the CEF. He was six feet four inches tall and a Presbyterian. Before enlisting, which he did November 9, 1914, age eighteen, he had paraded with the Victoria-raised 50th Regiment, Gordon Highlanders. He served in France, in the ranks of the 30th Battalion, 16th Canadian Scottish, for a year, and then was sent for officers' training, earning a commission in the 9th (Glasgow Highlanders) Battalion, Highland Light Infantry.

Thus far, Wilson had fulfilled his ambitions and was well trained for what was to come, save for the fact that fate took an awful turn. While serving in a grenade section of his battalion near the small town of Bouchavesnes-Bergen, Peronne Road, Picardy, France, he and other officers, plus six Royal Engineers and fifty-nine other ranks of Glasgow Highlanders, stormed an enemy trench after a four-minute bombardment of artillery, trench mortar, and machine-gun fire. Entering the trench, the party split into three, hurling bombs and thus destroying enemy dugouts, or entering those bombed from above. It was high-risk work, and Wilson knocked out a machine-gun unit and captured the weapon. Still the Germans resisted the assault, and a precious twenty-five minutes passed before Wilson and his party began their withdrawal to their own trench. Wilson was killed in his own line after coming back. He died on February 7, 1917. Two officers in this action were awarded the Military Cross. Second Lieutenant Wilson was not recognized, a matter noted with regret in the *Daily Colonist*. He is buried in Peronne Communal Cemetery Extension. *In Memoriam*, published in *The Camosun*, added this: "A death like sleep, A Gentle wafting to immortal life"—Milton.[3] So closed the story of the Scottish soldier, born in Germany, educated partially in Victoria, enlisted in Canadian forces, and killed serving in a Scottish unit when in France. He is memorialized in Edinburgh Castle. He had done so very much in his twenty-odd years. He had seen war at the sharp end. His brother, Gunner Robin Stuart Wilson, also of Victoria High School and three years his brother's junior, spent most of his war years in the Military Police, mainly putting down riots in Canadian troop camps; he was unlucky enough to be caught in several gas attacks. After the Armistice he was stationed in Germany with the Canadian occupying force until 1920. He returned to Canada, attended the University of California, Berkeley, studying mining engineering, and had a long career managing mines in the American west and southwest. In 1940, he went to manage a gold mine at or near Bulawayo in Rhodesia (Zimbabwe), where his lungs finally failed in 1972.

*We return to* 1917. Earlier that year a new plan for defeating the enemy was developed by France and Britain. For the first time, Canada was to take a significant role as an armed power on the stage of history. Easter Monday, April 9, 1917, marks a day of Canadian destiny. That was when the four Canadian Divisions, fighting together for the first time and forming the Canadian Corps, along with the British Fifth Division and a considerable number of artillery units, seized Vimy Ridge. The Corps was commanded by General Sir Julian Byng, and General Arthur Currie commanded the First Division.

Vimy Ridge, fourteen kilometres in length, commands the Douai Plain, which stretches north toward hugely important, highly industrial Lille, with its rail communications. The locale was highly defended, a significant part of the enemy's defence system. A previous French attempt had failed to dislodge the German defenders. Now a new scheme was devised. The Canadian approach to Vimy Ridge was by way of tunnels cut to within metres of the Ridge. Royal Engineers had begun the work in 1916, and on the eve of battle the underground complex amounted to twenty-two miles of subways, some with electricity and others also with a narrow-gauge railway. The tunnel system proved almost bombproof.[4]

A creeping barrage of lethal shellfire preceded the infantry. Mines had been activated, creating havoc for the enemy. Then came the assault. The Canadians came out of the tunnels at the appointed hour, joining others for the battle. They went over the top at dawn in a broad frontal attack. The attackers soon knew they had broken the German lines. Prisoners in goodly numbers began to come to the Canadian lines. In the next day or so, the objective was made secure, the enemy swept from the field and height of land.

Like the Battle of the Somme, the battle for Vimy Ridge could not be fought without heavy casualties. "We must be reconciled to that in advance," a reporter for *The Times*, the noted British newspaper, wrote on April 10, 1917. He added, "But the enemy will suffer more than we, and we shall break him here as we broke him on the Somme." This was the logic of a war of attrition.

Many Victorians took part in this stupendous event, and many were connected in some way to Victoria High School. Major-General Currie commanded the veteran First Division, which consisted of the first three Canadian brigades—the 2nd Brigade included the 7th Battalion (British Columbia), and the 3rd Brigade included the 16th Battalion (Canadian Scottish). Lieutenant-Colonel Cy Peck, who later won the Victoria Cross, was in the Canadian Scottish. Brigadier-General Victor Odlum, who had been prominent in real estate and newspapers in Victoria and elsewhere in the province, ordered the 7th Battalion to take critically important Hill 145.

Corporal Gus Sivertz, Victoria High School, an optometrist in civilian life, was serving in the 2nd Canadian Mounted Rifles. This unit formed part of the 8th Brigade of the Third Canadian Division. Almost directly ahead, about 2,500 metres away, lay the top of the Ridge. First the Germans had to be driven back. To do this, some heavy terrain had to be crossed and some woods circumvented. Gus Sivertz's story is one of survival in the midst of unremitting horror. This is what he wrote about the great day:

I looked ahead and saw the German front line crashing into pieces; bits of men, timbers, lumps of chalk were flying through the air, and, blending with the shattering wall of fire. We didn't dare lift our heads, knowing that the barrage was to come flat over us and then lift in three minutes. That queer empty stomach feeling had gone. I don't think anyone was scared instead one's whole body seemed to be in a mad macabre dance.

I guess it was perhaps the most perfect barrage of the war, as it was so perfectly synchronized. Then suddenly it jumped 100 yards and we were away. Instead of a German trench there was only a wide, muddy depression, stinking of explosives. Then Lieutenant Christie was hit and just pitched forward, dead. When I straightened up, I tried to hurry to catch up with my group. I tripped on some snarled barbed wire and fell, just as a big Hun shell screamed into the muck alongside me. I was knocked over, and in rising, got a terrific slam on the top of my head. It rammed my tin hat down to my ears.

I ran in a stumbling sort of way to get up with my buddies. It's terrible to be alone one feels that all the enemy guns are pointed at one and one is naked. So I rejoined my group. There wasn't much to shoot at—Heinies were coming back with their hands up, and his counter-barrage wasn't so hot. The man next to me smiled and leaned over to me to say something. I think he meant to say "It's going fine," or something like that. He put his mouth almost to my ear, there was such a helluva noise going on. He never finished the sentence, never made a sound, just pitched on his face.[5]

The three boys of the Laundy family were in the thick of things at Vimy. Lieutenant Everard Lynne Laundy, who we met in 1915, had fought through most Somme engagements with the 10th Infantry Brigade and was with them when they took the Hindenburg Line, the important German fixed defence. He had been promoted lieutenant, and after a period of rest and relief had returned to the line the night before the Vimy Ridge attack. In the event, his company obtained its objective but was to a great extent isolated and under heavy shellfire for several days. He got back to camp, having been posted missing with about six men—all that remained of the company, which was nominally one hundred in number.

Lieutenant Laundy won the Military Cross. The citation reads: "As the only surviving officer of the party detailed for the capture of an enemy position, he personally displayed great gallantry in repulsing several counter-attacks and although severely shaken by shellfire, he carried on until relieved, setting a fine example of courage and duty under most difficulties." He received his medal from George V at Buckingham Palace. He returned home to Victoria at war's end.[6] He had been four years in and out of the line of battle.

Private Albert Babcock, who qualified as a druggist after his years at Victoria High School, was killed in action in the taking of Vimy Ridge. He was born in Winnipeg and died April 10, 1917, age twenty-one. He had been a soldier for a year and a half, enlisting in the 103rd Battalion in Victoria, then transferring to the 29th Battalion, Canadian Infantry (British Columbia Regiment). He has no known grave and is remembered with honour on the Vimy Memorial. He left a grieving mother, Mrs. Annie Babcock, of 1717 Denman Street, Victoria.

"Don't worry about me, dear mother, I am trying to do my duty and that is all that matters." So wrote Robert Branks "Bobbie" Powell, Canada's most famous tennis player of the age, to his mother, at home in Victoria. He had fought through the battle of Vimy Ridge, and now he found himself with the 16th Battalion, Canadian Infantry (Manitoba Regiment), in the attempt to secure the southeastern flank of the Ridge, a vulnerable location. To rectify this, British and Canadian forces launched an attack toward Arleux-en-Gohelle on April 28. Arleux was captured by the Canadians, but the British met with stiffer resistance from the Germans. The village was held by evening, though subsequently Vimy Ridge was made secure, at least for the time being. The casualties were high, and Lieutenant Powell was killed in action. He was deeply mourned. He had led Canada's tennis team at the 1908 Summer Olympics, captained Canada's Davis Cup team in 1913, was a finalist at Wimbledon, and won numerous titles and much fame. Moreover, he was called to the English bar and was registered as a barrister-at-law with the Law Society of Alberta, had served in the British Colonial Service in Fiji and the Western Pacific High Commission, and was private secretary to the lieutenant-governor of British Columbia. He came from one of the most prominent Canadian and Victoria families, the son of Dr. Israel Wood Powell (a friend of Prime Minister Sir John A. Macdonald, who appointed him BC's first Indian Commissioner) and Mrs. Jane Branks Powell. He had been born in Victoria, educated at Victoria

High School, and learned to play tennis on his family's court. He had joined the 50th Regiment, Gordon Highlanders, and was commissioned September 1, 1914. He was a popular and able soldier—and internationally famous, his death noted in the world press. He is buried in Ecoivres Military Cemetery, Mont-St. Eloi, France.[7]

The hard-fought victory at Vimy Ridge was swift, but came at an incalculable cost. Canadians had suffered appalling losses, and the number of wounded and dead in this battle is prodigious—10,602, of which 3,598 were killed, according to one Canadian source.[8] At least one who was following the action, Siegfried Sassoon, an officer in a British regiment, thought the Canadian communiqués had been fudged so as to represent lower casualties.[9] The Germans lost 20,000, equivalent to a division. This triumph soon became the stuff of legend.

In the weeks following, further terrible casualties would be taken. Casualties for the whole Battle of Arras, which contains the battle for Vimy Ridge, up to May 3 are officially given as 84,000; those for the enemy are estimated at 75,000. We now know that 32 German divisions had been engaged, or twice the number engaged on the Somme, for the same period. That the success at Vimy Ridge by the Canadian and British forces had shocked the Germans is clear from the forebodings of Crown Prince Rupprecht of Bavaria: "Is it any use to pursue the war further under such conditions? Only if peace with Russia is speedily concluded. If not . . . we must admit ourselves to be conquered. For if we delay longer, the peace-terms of our enemies will only grow harder."[10]

To that point in the War, the capture of Vimy Ridge had been the greatest British victory. Not only had the Canadians gained the Ridge, with its commanding position, but they had also captured 54 guns, 104 trench mortars, 124 machine guns, and more than 4,000 prisoners. The Canadian Corps had demonstrated that proper planning could lessen the rate of casualties. The psychological effects of the victory were clear, and it gave a boost to the whole Empire effort. The Allied world gave acclaim. The capture of the Ridge, said the French press, was an Easter gift from Canada. Canada would win other victories, but none caught the imagination more than Vimy. One historian of the campaign wrote, "No matter what the constitutional historians may say, it was on Easter Monday, April 9, 1917, and not on any other date, that Canada became a nation."[11]

*By early 1917*, the Service Roll of the school, published in the May issue of *The Camosun*, had swollen to over three hundred names. The compilers, whose names are not known, noted that the list as printed was necessarily only a partial one of those VHS masters (teachers) and students who were either serving at the Front or preparing to take their places there.[12] Keeping track of who had gone away to war and what percentage of the student body was away or had stayed at home is impossible, for school records fail us there. Every year more and more males enlisted when they could—that is, at age eighteen, or earlier if joining the Royal Navy or Royal Canadian Navy. Many of the sailor lads were never heard from again, finding watery graves at some distant burial ground where even their individual names may not be recorded. They are, in a sense, lost to history. On the other hand, there are many names we know about whose stories can be told.

Beside twenty-six names on the school's Service Roll of May 1917 can be seen a cross indicating "Killed in Action": so designated were Lieutenant J.A. MacDonald, M.C., one of the VHS masters; Gunner John Henry Austin; Private Percy Barr; Private Mark Edward Berton; Lieutenant Herbert William Boggs; Private J.J. Brown; Lieutenant Adair Carss; Sergeant Fred Copas; Lieutenant J.D. Dowler; Private Ernest Elford; Lieutenant S. Duncan Ellis, MC; Lieutenant F. Elliott; Private George Elliott; Private Charles Mawer Hardie; Private F.G. "Fred" Heal;[13] Sergeant Edward Jackson; Lieutenant Albert Nelson King; Sergeant J.A. Pascoe; Private Horace "Tod" Paul; Private Harold Roe; Sergeant Cyril Sedger;[14] Sergeant D.V. Stevens; Private William Stewart; Private F. Thompson; and Lieutenant Conrad Blackadder Wilson. By war's end, that number would more than triple.

Each of these deaths has its own story. Readers of *The Camosun* learned of their late friends recently departed. One of them, Sergeant Fred Copas, campus favourite, had left the school to join the 103rd Battalion, with which he went overseas. At school he had been prominent on the rugby pitch under Mr. Yates's tutelage. His winning personality had made him an unconscious leader at school; once in the Army, this same personality had soon raised him to sergeant in his battalion. In fact, he was made drill instructor and was offered a similar post in England. But being parade sergeant was too distant a following for the determined Fred Copas, who itched for action, and he gave up his position and even his stripes to go to France, where he made his sacrifice.[15] Private Copas was in the 102nd Battalion, Canadian Infantry

(Central Ontario Regiment). He died on the opening day of Canada's Vimy triumph, April 9, age twenty-one. His headstone in Canadian Cemetery No. 2, Neuville-St.-Vaast, France, reads THEIR GLORY SHALL NOT BE BLOTTED OUT.

Private Harold Roe was another on the list of the fallen heroes of the school. A popular and clever student, with very bright career prospects, he had graduated with the class of 1915. But as *The Camosun* noted, he would have had "a bright career had he not taken upon himself the greatest of all careers—that of self-sacrifice." He had done well at the Front and had been recommended for a commission. Before this commission arrived, he fell in battle at Vimy on April 10, 1917, age twenty.[16] He is commemorated on the Vimy Memorial.

The litany continued. One by one the sorrowful news of deaths of members of the forces attached to the school reached town. At the school, each death was noted, a cause for grief and sorrow. But as is often the case in the annals of history, some get greater attention, and their passing is all that much more regretted. Such is the case with John—or more commonly, Jack—Dowler.

Lieutenant Dowler died of wounds on April 11, a casualty of the taking of Vimy Ridge. He was twenty-five, the only son of Wellington J. and Elizabeth Sketchley Dowler. Born in Victoria or possibly Saanich, he had passed through the primary, intermediary, and senior departments of the public schools. Few could have been so actively connected with every aspect of public or high-school life. Active in athletics, his particular pride was the Cadet Battalion, with which he was associated for seven years, beginning when he was at Boy's Central School. For three of those years he served as a major and commanding officer of the corps. Under his energetic management and enthusiasm, it had attained high efficiency and excellent morale. "It is an inspiring sight to see Major John striding about the school grounds with drawn sword, looking like a truculent pirate followed by a slovenly mob of martial scarecrows," quipped *The Camosun* in January 1913. He was also captain of the college hockey team. At one time he was assistant principal at Lampson Street School, Esquimalt. In 1914, he joined the Royal School of Instruction at Work Point Barracks (where they wore the old red tunics as if dressed for colonial campaigns) and qualified as lieutenant. In the autumn of 1915, Dowler headed for Montreal to complete his bachelor's degree at McGill, and joined the university contingent training corps for officers, rising from private to lieutenant in three months. On his return to Victoria in May 1916, he was appointed lieutenant of "C" Company of the 11th Canadian Mounted Rifles, and in June he left with that battalion for service overseas.[17]

Dowler distinguished himself in the handling of weapons and became battalion instructor in bombing. In the preparations for the assault on Vimy Ridge, his competence was of particular value. At the time he was in the 47th Battalion, Canadian Infantry (Western Ontario Regiment), and took part in the attack on Vimy Ridge. He fell leading his company in the onslaught. He died of wounds and lies buried in Barlin Communal Cemetery Extension, Pas de Calais, France. Since the beginning of the war, the French and British had been burying their war dead here, and from time to time the Allies had had to dodge German shelling. By the time Dowler was laid to rest there, with the last rites, one thousand war casualties had been commemorated in that site. Among the treasures of the Victoria High School Archives is a photo of Dowler, presented to the school by his cousin May Croft (Mrs. Allison Campbell). The bronzed frame, of the finest of its time, displays the Canadian maple leaf badge at the top, while across the bottom it is marked FOR KING AND COUNTRY. Dowler's death was commemorated by the planting of one of the school's Memorial Trees, and news of his death on the fields of France was a most poignant reminder of how long this war was continuing and how it was bleeding away the blood of Canada's sons.

*On another battlefield,* the dashing Captain August Edward Sedgwick Thurburn, 3rd Battalion, King's Royal Rifles (previously in the 9th Battalion, Essex Regiment), died on May 28, 1917, age twenty-seven. The son of "Thory" and Mary Thurburn of Mount Tolmie, Victoria, Sedgwick Thurburn was born in England and came to Victoria early, where he was educated at Victoria High School. The martial spirit coursed through his veins. His grandfather, Colonel Thurburn, was a veteran of the Crimean War and Indian Mutiny, while his father, T. Vincent Thurburn, an Indian-born banker, fought through the African Basuto campaign and the South African War. A handsome fellow sporting a moustache, with a lovely countenance far from severe, we see Sedgwick not long before his death in a photo that shows him in his prized "British Warm" overcoat. He was the son of empire and was prepared to die for it. While serving with the Essex Regiment, he had been mentioned in despatches by Field Marshal Sir Douglas Haig in recognition of gallant and distinguished conduct, and his good work in the way of sapping and mining. He had gone to the Front in France first, and there, during the fighting at

Festubert in 1915, he was severely wounded, his injuries necessitating hospitalization for nine months. After recovery, in early 1916, he was sent out with a draft of 250 men of the King's Royal Rifles for Salonika. He lies in an unusual Commonwealth War Cemetery, Mikra British Cemetery, near the seaport of Kalamaria, Greece. He is buried with over 1,800 British soldiers. A card from Buckingham Palace, signed by George RI (Rex and Imperatrix, that is, King and Emperor) was sent to his parents: "I join with my grateful people in sending you this memorial of a brave life given for others in the Great War." The *Daily Colonist*, in reporting his death, states that Thurburn was one of eight cousins in service in the War, one of whom was killed leading a charge at Vimy Ridge a few weeks previous, while another was wounded the same day.[18]

On June 2, 1917, news reached Dr. E.B. and Mrs. Ada Paul—so intimately connected with the history of the school, for he had been principal from 1892 to 1908—that their eldest son, Private Horace John Paul, known as "Tod," had been killed in action, age twenty-five. He was in the E Pioneering Battalion. A colour sergeant and lieutenant in the Cadet Battalion at the school, he was a member of the James Bay Athletic Association's football team and had been a clerk in the Provincial Secretary's office before enlisting in the 50th Regiment, Gordon Highlanders, upon the declaration of war.[19] His younger brother, Private Alexander S. Paul, 16th Battalion, had been wounded at Ypres in May 1915 and survived the War.

The young men of Canada and the Empire continued to enlist as volunteers. McGill had always been an excellent recruiting ground, and the Officers' Training Corps there a longstanding and powerful one. Most of the students began in the ranks. One of them was Robert Stanley Stuart Yates, a member of a pioneer Victoria family—Yates Street had been named for one of his forebears, who had also been a member of the old colonial Vancouver Island Legislature. Robert, a law student at McGill in 1917, enlisted in the university's 10th Siege Artillery Battalion. Private Robert Yates went overseas and was the victim of a German gas attack. He survived the War, returned to Victoria after the Armistice, became a lawyer in the family firm, and later achieved the high position of clerk of the British Columbia legislature.[20]

*We usually think* of the coming of peace as the time to put up memorials to the dead of war, but Victoria High School and the citizens of the city could not wait till then to remember those who had already fallen in Flanders Fields. The pain of loss called for some sort of response. Besides, when the War would end was anyone's guess, and the death toll continued to mount. Each issue of *The Camosun* brought the grim particulars to hand, and the local papers published devastating stories every day, at the same time magically putting the best face on the sacrifices of the War. News of the stunning recent victory at Vimy Ridge was also filled with the sad news of Dowler's death.

We do not know when the planning to plant and dedicate the Victoria High School Memorial Trees began, but it was likely early in 1917. The Second Battle of Ypres was on the minds of those who followed the War, and to commemorate the second anniversary of this Canadian sacrifice, the closest Friday to the date of the battle (April 22, 1915) was selected. Therefore, on April 20, fourteen maple trees donated by the Women's Canadian Club were planted on the grounds of Victoria High School, bordering either side of the Fernwood or Vining Street entrance. One of the trees was for Jack Dowler, and on May 2 of that same year a tree-planting ceremony at Lampson Street School also commemorated him.[21]

The Women's Canadian Club also organized the ceremony. Active in the planting and the dedication were the school principal, the school board, and the school Cadet Battalion. Music was supplied by the 5th BC Regiment of Garrison Artillery, RCA. A combined schools choir under Mr. Pollard sang "O Canada." A piece called "Canada's Song of Freedom," with words composed by Dowler's father, Wellington Dowler, was not performed because heavy, wet weather kept many choristers away.

It was entirely appropriate that the Cadet Battalion took a major role in the memorial ceremonies, under its senior officer William McMichael (later principal of Central Junior High School). Prominent in planting the Memorial Trees were Mrs. Margaret Jenkins, the school trustee; the Honourable Harlan Carey Brewster, premier of British Columbia; John Cochrane, president of the Canadian Club; and Miss Grace Burris, president of the University Women's Club. The school staff was in attendance, as was the student body. Lieutenant-Governor Barnard was there, with the high school cadets forming the guard of honour. Nearly 2,500 braved the elements for the memorial ceremony.

The Reverend Captain John Campbell, the military chaplain, delivered the invocation. A local newspaper reported his words as "thanking God for the beautiful country in which they were privileged to live, a country in which all enjoyed civic and religious liberty. The Empire had held unswervingly to the principle of contending against tyranny, despotism and oppression. Might the day soon come when war might cease and matters of international dispute be settled in other manner than by the sword." The drapery of mourning, he said, was spread in many Victoria homes. The dear ones mourned had given life for the freedom of mankind, and he hoped they would "uplift the future generations by the memory of their sacrifice." Then he turned his attention to the trees as living symbols of remembrance. "These trees now being planted would grow up a living memorial to the gallant young men who had passed through the High School and gone on to death in championing so great a cause." They were, he said, an example of sacrifice not to be forgotten but to be remembered forever. That they were maple trees, with their own Canadian symbolism, was not lost on anyone.

In reporting these events, the *Victoria Times* further remarked on the symbolism of the trees: "An avenue of tall young maple trees . . . will bear leaf in a few weeks. While they arrest the notice of the passer-by they will suggest to his inward eye the picture of the boy-students who once gathered with their fellow students in this Alma Mater, but who now lie, heroes of Empire, beneath the sod of France [and Belgium]."

That same day, April 20, the Kitchener Memorial Oak was dedicated on the school grounds on Grant Street, midway between Fernwood and Camosun Streets. It was planted to commemorate the life of Field Marshal Earl Kitchener of Khartoum. Although we have already noted his importance, we return to it now. Horatio Herbert Kitchener was born in Ireland. He was commissioned into the Royal Engineers in 1871, fought in Egyptian and Sudan campaigns, and became famous in 1898 when he led a Nile expedition that overwhelmed Mahdi forces at Omdurman. He later served in South Africa and India as commander-in-chief of British forces there. He was an indefatigable organizer who understood the necessity of consolidating resources before striking a decisive blow in the field. He was the foremost British soldier of the age.

In 1914, Kitchener had become Secretary of State for War. A shy and reticent fellow, he nonetheless inspired confidence in those who knew him. He added to his prestige by his prophecy of the scope and duration of the war. One of the few men to foresee a long war, one in which Britain's victory was far from certain, he organized the largest volunteer army—the New Army, some called it—that Britain had ever seen, and expanded production of armaments and other wartime requirements. Already a famous military figure, Kitchener allowed his commanding presence and luxuriant moustache to be used in a famous recruiting poster: with its message "Your Country Needs You," the poster remains an enduring image and had a powerful impact throughout the Empire, including in Victoria and Canada. On June 5, 1916, the cruiser *Hampshire*, carrying Kitchener to Archangel for military conferences with Russia, an ally, struck a mine off the Orkneys and sank, drowning him and most of the ship's company. His epitaph in London reads: "Coffined in a man of war, he passed to the great beyond."

Of the dedication of the Kitchener tree, the *Victoria Times* of April 21, 1917, reported, under the heading "Trees in Honor of Heroes of Empire: Citizens and School Children Attend Impressive Memorial Ceremony at High School": "A little company of Old Campaigners, bearing two standards, gathered round while the Kitchener Memorial Oak was planted, the band playing 'Rule Britannia.' 'I have the honor to plant this oak in memory of Lord Kitchener, under whom I served in the Egyptian campaign of 1882 and in the Soudan in 1885,' said S.J. Pomeroy, 50th Royal West Kent Regiment, of the British Campaigners' Association." It was in this battle, against the Mahdi, that the British redcoats were seen in battle for the last time. As for this English oak, *Quercus robur*, it had been grown and given by Walter Bernie Anderson of Oak Bay. In the nearly hundred years since its planting, the Kitchener Memorial Oak has grown to be a venerable giant. Recognized as a Heritage Tree by the Victoria Horticultural Society, a bronze plaque, courtesy of Victoria High School Alumni Association, marks its importance for generations to come.

In early 2011, to the shock and sadness of thousands, the thirteen surviving maple trees bordering the Vining Street entrance were felled and disposed of in an act that has many still shaking their heads at the roles of arborists, landscapers, and site planners. The original trees, their planting and dedication, served as a model for commemorations of war sacrifices and pledges of peace in other communities across Canada.[22]


*Canada, like the* United Kingdom, long recruited her army by voluntary methods. But now Kitchener's magic had gone. By 1917, recruits were no longer coming forward in the required numbers. The base from which they could be drawn was thinning. The government instituted conscription, and it was unpopular in many rural areas and throughout the French-speaking regions. Laurier opposed conscription on grounds of race and retreated from an invitation to join a union government. Prime Minister Sir Robert Borden formed a Union Government of Conservatives and conscriptionist Liberals, then appealed to the country for support in a December election. The conscriptionists received an overwhelming victory in Canada as a whole, but failed badly in Quebec, where they won only three seats. In the circumstances, conscription placed a serious strain on the unity of Canada, though its effects were hardly felt in British Columbia.

By August 1917, the world was very different than it had been at the time of Vimy, only three months earlier. Russia was facing revolt. Germany was stronger, a victor on the Eastern Front and shifting its divisions to the Western Front. The Allied advance on Passchendaele began July 31 and would lead Canadian forces into a quagmire of difficulties and seemingly massive casualties. These losses occurred at the time of the conscription crisis in Canada, so the government did not want them broadcast. The Canadians, by their actions, were winning the respect of close observers of the war. David Lloyd George, the British prime minister, commenting on the Canadians as storm troopers, said that any time the Canadians came into the line, the Germans could expect the worst.[23]

Victoria's press continued to promote the cause of enlistment and the worthiness of serving for King and Country. Families "at war" merited special newspaper coverage, not least because, almost invariably, at least one son in a family did not survive the catastrophe.

On June 3 of that year of destiny, photographs of four Reid brothers of 123 Simcoe Street appeared side by side in the *Daily Colonist* under the heading "Four of Family are Fighting Battles of Empire." The four, all natives of Victoria and all connected to Victoria High School, were Private David Reginald "Reggie" Reid, just turned nineteen, who had already died in the Battle of Mount Sorrel on June 3, 1916; Lieutenant John "Jack" Deighton Reid, who would be killed in action, age 28, on May 28, 1918; Gunner S. Gordon Reid, Canadian Field Artillery, who left for the front on June 3, 1917 (his departure prompted the article in the *Daily Colonist*); and Clifford Duncan Reid, Canadian Army Medical Corps. All were connected to the famed pioneer clergyman Dr. John Reid, Sr.

Cliff attended Victoria High School at the Yates Street location in 1913 and continued at the new school on Grant Street from 1914 to 1916, when he enlisted with the CAMC. He had a bad leg from an earlier bout of polio and managed to fool the examining medical officer by doing a quick turn and showing his good leg twice. The witty, eloquent Cliff was an orderly in the operating room and met the sweet and charming Clara Detweiler of Kitchener, Ontario, at No. 1 Canadian Hospital at Etaples, where she was a registered nurse, a graduate of Toronto General. (Her brother, Dr. Herbert Detweiler, was the gold medalist of the Class of 1914 at the University of Toronto Medical School and went on to become a prominent Canadian immunologist.) Clara was on night duty on May 19, 1918, when her dormitory was bombed in the attack by fifteen German aircraft that mortally wounded three nurses (Esquimalt-born Gladys Wake among them) and forty-seven soldiers. German aircraft dropped leaflets warning of air attacks to follow, which prompted the evacuation of all patients who were well enough to be moved. Cliff was among those who volunteered to stay behind with those patients too ill to be relocated. Bombs were dropped on May 30 and May 31, 1918, at Etaples and the surrounding area, destroying a hospital train and resulting in twenty-seven patients and attendants being killed and seventy-nine wounded.

On the return of peace, Cliff was a member of the 1919/1920 Soldiers' Civil Re-establishment Class at Victoria High School (see Chapter 7). Cliff and Clara married in Vancouver on October 9, 1920, and had a daughter and two sons. Cliff joined the Canadian Immigration Service and headed up the Victoria office until he left to serve with the Canadian army as a major in the Second World War, examining military recruits on Vancouver Island and throughout British Columbia. At the close of hostilities the Department of Immigration assigned him to its office in London, England, to head up the movement of British immigrants to Canada, and he was later posted to The Hague as first Canadian consul to the Netherlands, where he was in charge of postwar immigration from the Netherlands to Canada.

There's a more recent Victoria High School connection here, for their son, Reginald "Reg" Herbert Reid, the fourth-generation Reid to reside in Victoria, graduated from the school as class valedictorian of 1943, married Iris Chapman McIvor (VHS Class of 1941) on November 8, 1946, taught at the school from 1957 to 1963, and became its highly popular and respected vice principal from 1967 to 1977. The family retains close ties to the school to this day, as Reg's two younger children graduated from VHS: Janet Reid in 1975 and Linda Reid in 1977.

In addition, Clifford and Clara's youngest son, John "Jack" Reid, attended Vic High before enlisting in the Navy in the Second World War, where he was posted to HMCS *Sioux*. Jack's youngest child, John Reid, was a 1975 graduate of VHS.[24]

*Each issue of* the Victoria daily newspapers was sure to announce the sorrowful passing of yet another local man. The Victoria High School tally continued to rise.

Private Lyall Layzelle Bland, 47th Battalion, Canadian Infantry (British Columbia Regiment), died age seventeen on August 21, 1917, another who had enlisted underage. The son of Joseph and Elizabeth Bland of Alberni, BC, has no known grave and is remembered on the Vimy Memorial. Another from the school, Second Lieutenant Frank Mewburn Dunn, of the 10th Battalion, Durham Light Infantry, died shortly thereafter, on September 23. Dunn was a senior newspaperman in the editorial department of both the *Daily Colonist* and the *Victoria Times* before enlisting in early 1915 in No. 5 Canadian General Hospital, assembled at Esquimalt. With that unit he served in Salonika, then trained and qualified for a commission. He was assigned to the famous English regiment, but, like many a subaltern, his life on the front line was short. He was killed soon after he arrived on the Western Front.[25] He died while entering an enemy trench and is buried in Cabin Hill Cemetery, Wytschaete ("Whitesheet" to the Tommies), Belgium. The ridge there changed hands repeatedly and was not finally held by the British until September 28, 1918. Dunn's name is to be found on the memorial to journalists in the British Columbia Legislative Buildings.

*Out through the* Menin Gate at Ypres and up the rising ground to Passchendaele lay a small town, really, but one now only of immortal memory. It was pulverized in the War. The battles fought for it were the battles of elevation. Higher position gave not only a field of view. It also gave an advantage to snipers, gunners, and traversing machine guns. A hill of even ten metres in height could give precious strategic advantage, and so it was on the long passage to the Passchendaele Ridge; the Germans held the advantage. Only when you stand at the top and look back to the Menin Gate can you grasp the significance of the protracted and desperate fight Canadians were obliged to wage against German machine-gun fire from two opposite positions—one east, the other west—that covered the naked land in the field of fire. This was the Canadian problem and the Canadian challenge. And the purely British Army, in far superior numbers to the Canadians, faced it as well. Even so, the Canadians get ultimate credit for taking the ridge—but at horrific cost. "Here was suffered," wrote an Australian historian, "perhaps the greatest agony of man's history, when shells and bombs had cut and gouged the earth into marshy wastes. It must have been the most desolate and dangerous of all battlefields. Here it was that the Germans belted their line with brick houses or 'pill-boxes.' They were built of concrete and steel. Right to the muzzles of the guns they were to be stormed in the mire."[26] Ultimately, 47,000 Empire soldiers were engaged in the campaign on this "field of death."

With good reason, Canadians always associate Passchendaele with mud. From the Passchendaele Ridge down to the drainage creeks and canals below is one long gentle slope. With the soggy weather off the English Channel and even gently falling rain, a battlefield such as this would quickly turn to quagmire. "Good God, did we really send men to fight in that?" asked an appalled British chief of staff in October 1917. From the viewpoint of the soldier it was much the same. "I got down on my knees in the mud and prayed to God to bring me through."[27]

For three and a half months the British Armies fought under most adverse conditions of weather. The commander-in-chief, Field Marshal Douglas Haig, wrote that the circumstances "entailed almost superhuman exertions on the part of the troops of all arms and services." Looking on the bright side of things, he noted that the Allied armies used up no less than 78 enemy divisions—between July and November, the Germans lost 24,065 prisoners, 74 guns, 941 machine guns, and 138 mortars. Their death toll was massive. "Most important of all," Haig wrote, "our new and hastily trained armies have shown once again that they are capable of meeting and beating the enemy's best troops, even under conditions which favoured his defence to a degree which it required the greatest endurance, determination and heroism to overcome."[28] The cost to the Canadian army was horrendous. Haig will always be in the spotlight for his role in this terrible fight.

The Canadian Corps commander was Lieutenant-General Currie, who succeeded General Sir Julian Byng, the hero of Vimy. Currie had fought through all the battles since 1915—Ypres, Somme, Vimy, Hill 70, and now Passchendaele. He had worried about potential Canadian losses in this last campaign and was very close in the actual estimate. Greater challenges and greater successes awaited him. But the struggle could not be won without losses on the ground.

The Canadian phase of the campaign to take Passchendaele Ridge commenced on October 26, 1917. In the preparations for it, which were of enormous scale, many died. Corporal John Norman Spencer, born in Victoria and educated at Victoria High School, was an electrical contractor before going overseas. He served in 715th Mechanical Transport Company, hauling ammunition for the Royal Army Service Corps. The thousands in this vast and sprawling organization were the unsung heroes of the Army. Using horses and motor vehicles, railways and waterways, the Army Service Corps performed prodigious feats of logistics, delivering food, equipment, and ammunition, an essential part of winning the war. Corporal Spencer was twenty-five when he was killed in action in France on July 13, 1917. He is buried in Gwalia Cemetery, Poperinge, Belgium. Closer to home, on the north face of his parents' headstone at Ross Bay Cemetery, this message gives notice of his loss: SLEEP ON DEAR SON, IN A SOLDIER'S GRAVE, YOUR LIFE FOR YOUR COUNTRY, YOU NOBLY GAVE. He had three brothers, one of whom served on the Western Front in the Canadian Engineers.[29]

Gunner Roy Stewart Clements, born and raised in Victoria, graduate of the school, was killed at Passchendaele October 31, 1917, age twenty-four. He was a Baptist and an excise officer before going to war. Son of John and Emilia Clements, 1427 Harrison Street, Victoria, he had been attached to the 4th Ammunition Column, Canadian Field Artillery. He is buried in Potijze Chateau Grounds Cemetery, Belgium. His gravestone has telling lines: TILL THE DAY BREAK AND THE SHADOWS FLEE AWAY.

Major John Gibson Anderson, a graduate of the school, died at Passchendaele toward the end of the campaign. We have seen him before. He was fearless and in 1915 had won the Military Cross "for conspicuous gallantry" in two raids on German trenches, in which he retrieved important information about the enemy. He called himself "Lucky Star" because he had somehow survived when so many of his comrades had died. Anderson had been commissioned as a lieutenant and then promoted captain, then major.

During the fighting in the Ypres salient in June 1916, he and a subaltern were the only officers of "C" Company, 5th Battalion, to survive.

The lucky star that for two years had followed Anderson was about to fail him. First he was wounded in the head at Vimy on April 9, 1917, and convalesced in a French military hospital. Then, back in the line for the last push at Passchendaele, he was killed in action November 10, age thirty-two. He was in the 5th Battalion, Canadian Infantry (Saskatchewan Regiment Western Cavalry), at the time of his death. His mother, Mrs. Mary Anderson, lived at 318 Thomas Street, Macaulay Point, Esquimalt.

Currie wrote to Mrs. Anderson in words that speak for themselves about this outstanding soldier:

> The officer commanding the Battalion informs me that he has written giving particulars regarding the death of your son, Major John G. Anderson, of the 5th Canadian Battalion. It only remains for me to offer you my sincerest sympathy. I knew John for over twenty years, and it was my privilege to be his teacher in the public schools of Victoria, B.C., in the year 1896. Shortly after that time I lost track of him. I remember the day in May 1915, during the battle of Festubert, that I was brought a message by a mounted orderly, in whom I recognized my old pupil. Later in the year it was my privilege to recommend him for a commission, and I have watched, with a great deal of pride, his military career. He early gave evidence of possessing in a superlative degree those qualities which go to make up a successful soldier. He was gallant to a fault, devoted to duty, loyal to his superiors, and a real leader of men. His loss is most keenly felt, not only by all ranks of the 5th Battalion, but by his Brigade and Division as well. We shall find it very hard to replace him, and you must have been intensely proud of his record in the army, and I pray that the great God of battles may grant you some measure of consolation.[30]

The officer commanding the 5th Battalion to whom Currie refers was Lieutenant Colonel Paul O. Tudor. He had seen Anderson in and out of action since the days he won the Military Cross and been mentioned in despatches. Tudor wrote to Mrs. Anderson:

> I am writing to tell you that your son was killed on November 10 while gallantly leading his men up to form a defensive flank during the

attack at Passchendaele Ridge. I cannot tell you how deeply I feel for you in your sad loss, for your son was one of my best officers and most popular with both officers and men. He was a very gallant officer, too, and always ready to do anything he was asked. He is a great loss to the Battalion and will never be forgotten. He is buried on the battlefield (and I will forward the exact location to you) and Canon Scott, the senior Chaplain of the 1st Canadian Division read the burial service.

With all my sympathy,

Paul O. Tudor, Lt.-Col.[31]

Like thousands of others who perished at Passchendaele, Anderson has no known grave. But we find his name, and those of many others, cut in stone on the Menin Gate, the Ypres Memorial (Panel 18-26-28). Major John Gibson Anderson, M.C., deserves to be recognized as among the greatest Canadian fighting soldiers. He liked the sharp end of war; his personality favoured it, and his muscular and athletic capabilities made him a great leader in the field. Had he lived, he would have gone on to even more senior rank and outstanding responsibilities. In the end, as happened to so many soldiers who saw action, his lucky star faded out. Thousands of others faced life's end that way.

On October 26, the Canadian Corps led the attack toward Passchendaele. By November 6, it had taken the village, and on the 10th more of the ridge. All that Haig had wanted for his winter line, the Canadians had gained: the Germans had been prevented from attacking the French, and they could no longer look down on the Ypres Salient. The taking of Passchendaele Ridge, which in effect closed the war on land for the year 1917, was only a prelude to another campaign and another location. The fighting moved now to Cambrai. And once again the field of battle shifted to the chalk fields of the Somme, and to Amiens.

Tyne Cot Cemetery, perched atop Passchendaele Ridge, is a memorial ground to unimaginable and monumental sacrifice. There are 20,000 graves. As was explained to me, the number of gravestones there equate to a full division standing on parade. It is the largest CWGC cemetery in the world. King George V wrote of his 1922 visit to Tyne Cot Cemetery, "I have many times asked myself whether there can be more potent advocates of peace upon earth through the years to come, than this massed multitude of silent witnesses to the desolation of war." Those who died and had no known grave were commemorated elsewhere, chiefly on the Menin Gate.

I have a personal connection with the events of these hundred days. My wife's grandfather, the Reverend John Morris, was there with Canadian Pioneer companies that were "setting the guns," as he used to say, slogging it out in the rain and the muck. He had enlisted in the ranks and then become a Canadian chaplain, and hence an officer, looking after all those burial parties. "Known only to God" read many of the names of the Fallen. These were the ones made unrecognizable by shrapnel, the ones with maimed bodies, exhaustion leading to death.

Where was hope to be found? Where victory? Should surrender be considered? Could an honourable withdrawal be effected and face saved? No. This was a war to the finish. Here the kin of the Empire spilled their blood: a New Zealander here, a Scottish Highlander there, a Sherwood Forester here, an Irish Fusilier there. Comrades in arms, they were also comrades in death.

One can appreciate that this experience contributed to a fervent call for "no more war." This was born in the mud of Passchendaele. Here, too, lies the origin of appeasement in the 1930s. And also the call for a new kind of war— one from the air, with a strategic bombing campaign that would take the war to the enemy's industries, cities, and strategic points, and thus save horrific casualties on the ground.

*Air power had* been having a growing impact in the War, and it played a large role at Passchendaele. The Royal Flying Corps (RFC) waged a battle in the air against its German opposite, with marked success. The designs, engines, speeds, armament, and manoeuvrability of airplanes were changing rapidly. Pilots in the RFC saw themselves as the "knights of the air," the gladiators, energetic and chivalrous, a special breed of warrior set apart by the prospects of war in the central blue, four miles above earth.

Victoria enjoyed a long-standing history of aviation, with the city's first flights being made on Lansdowne Field in the 1910s. The excitement of war in the air spurred much interest. Small wonder that great Canadian airmen became pilots in the RFC. One-third of all pilots of that service in the Great War were from Canada. Men from Victoria High School, often enlisting first as privates in the CEF, made a successful transfer to the Royal Naval Air Service (RNAS) or the RFC, and then made notable contributions to the air war, some dying tragic deaths, others undertaking heroic assignments, still others completing their missions without incident. There was a good deal of low-level flying, when the enemy machine-gunners could see the faces of the attacking RFC pilots. Mechanical failures were common. Altogether the work was hazardous, the elements often difficult, and the equipment less than completely reliable. It was high-risk work, and it attracted some of the most daring types.

We go back to the previous year, 1916, to note the first of Victoria High School's young men to die in one of the air units. On July 20, 1916, Flight Sub-Lieutenant Douglas Whittier, RNAS, born and educated in Victoria, son of Anson and Amelia Whittier of 1972 St. Ann Street, died age twenty-four. A member of 3 Wing awaiting orders to Luxeuil, France, he attempted a low-level loop in Bristol Scout C1245 near Manston, England, but his machine lost speed, twisted into a sideslip, and made a spiral nosedive to earth. The court of inquiry delivered a verdict of misadventure, for all the controls were found in good order. The verdict of the inquest reads: "This Officer was a good Pilot and his death is deeply felt amongst the Officers & Men of the Wing." Arrangements were made to provide a gun carriage on loan from the Army, a band and a firing party for the funeral. He is remembered with honour in Minster (Thanet) Cemetery, Kent.[32]

Another of these knights of the air was Flight-Lieutenant George Robert "Robin" Gray, RNAS. He was the youngest of three Gray boys, all Victoria-born and graduates of the school, and the best known on account of the circumstances of his death. (The story of his eldest brother, Lieutenant Andrew Jack Gray, has been told in connection with events of early 1915.) Their father, Andrew Gray, born and raised in Scotland, was a mechanical engineer and owner of Marine Iron Works, Victoria.[33] Their mother, Mary, was born in Scotland. Besides the three boys, there was a daughter, Annie, and the family lived at 1135 Catherine Street, now a heritage property, where they had a Chinese servant and other help. Robin Gray had joined the Army Service Corps in November 1915 in Canada and was with it for a few months. He was driver for Colonel James Duff-Stuart, General Officer Commanding Military District No. 11, headquartered at Work Point. Robin wanted more action, and like the famed Billy Bishop, he wanted to see the battlefield from the air. Recruited by the RNAS, he soon found himself a cadet in the RFC, in a class that was trained in England in the summer of 1917. He was commissioned as a temporary second lieutenant on May 14, and on September 27 was promoted to temporary lieutenant. He had barely twenty hours' flying time before he was posted to his squadron. He served in the 84th Squadron attached to the British Expeditionary Force, a highly successful squadron that destroyed 139 enemy planes and many observation balloons.

Gray came onto and indeed above the scene of battle just as the Canadian Corps was making its push at Passchendaele and suffering its terrible tragedies. He was flying the SE5 Scout, a single-seater fighter biplane that was strong, manoeuvrable, and easier for a novice to fly than the Sopwith Camel. Billy Bishop and Albert Ball flew the SE5 with success. The introduction of this plane in mid-1917 played an important role in giving Britain superiority in the air—and keeping it for the rest of the War. Gray's first and second flights passed without apparent incident. In his third flight over the lines, however, and during a dogfight with one of the enemy's Albatros planes on October 30, he was shot down and badly wounded in the chest and arm. A French family saw him land his plane. Apparently fearing that he would be killed by the enemy on the ground, they obtained his wallet, which contained identification papers, and hid it from the Germans on the rafters of their barn. The next day Robin Gray was reported wounded. Nothing was heard from him for some time and he was presumed dead. In fact, he was a prisoner of war, but he died of his wounds on October 31, age eighteen. He was posthumously awarded the British War Medal and the Victory Medal.

Robin Gray was buried among eighty-seven others at Tourcoing (Pont-Neuville) Communal Cemetery, France, which is registered with the CWGC and is not far from the Belgium border and Ypres. His death brought much pain and anguish, not least because it was reported twice. The February 1918 *Camosun* printed a lovely head-and-shoulders photograph of Gray. Proudly displayed on his tunic are his "wings." The inscription reads: "In Memoriam: Flight-Lieutenant Robin Gray, Died in German Prison Camp Christmas, 1917." He was the son of Andrew and Mary Gray, whose headstone in Ross Bay Cemetery, Victoria, invokes divine guidance: IN LOVING MEMORY: THY WILL BE DONE. Robin Gray is also commemorated here with the notation KILLED IN ACTION IN FRANCE. The *Daily Colonist* paid this editorial tribute on February 2, 1918: "With him it was a joyous thing to go forth on the Great Adventure, for, though so young, he prized his country's honour far above his life. His name has now been added to that gallant band of heroes whom death has immortalized and whose memory will be forever sanctified among men of the British race." Making a pilgrimage in memory of their dear Robin after the War, his mother and grandmother found the scene of where he came to earth, and met the French farm family who had perhaps saved him from instant death.[34]

Robin Gray's brother James Leonard Gray, also of Victoria High School, has a story of a different sort. He had joined the 88th Regiment, Victoria Fusiliers. In February 1917 we find him learning to fly the Curtiss JN4 aircraft in Toronto. By August he was in England for instruction in various types of machines, both airplanes and seaplanes, and he was commissioned and rose to Captain, RFC, on September 17, 1917. He was posted to 27 Squadron in France in mid-December, and before war's end had logged 252 hours on 72 bombing and reconnaissance missions. He did not suffer his brother's fate and came away from the conflict unscathed. Captain James Gray, "Jimmy" to friends and family, was awarded the Croix de Guerre avec palmes in addition to the British War Medal and the Victory Medal. As a member of the Victoria Flying Club, he flew the first airmail to Nanaimo on August 15, 1919. In 1940 he enlisted in the Royal Canadian Air Force and retired as squadron leader in 1944. He died in 1985.[35]


*Canadians were transported* back and forth across the English Channel by the hundreds and thousands. The plain adjacent to Shorncliffe, Kent, near the Channel, had been selected for the organization, assembly, and training of the Second and Third Canadian Divisions. As the wounded and broken bodies returned, a Canadian military hospital was needed there too. The Canadian Army Medical Hospital at Shorncliffe was one of several in the United Kingdom, and it has a connection with Victoria High School.

The Victoria High School Patriotic Aid Organization kept "field comforts" work as its focus. It collected pennies, nickels, and dimes for the purchase of two fifty-dollar Victory Bonds as soon as they became available for purchase in November 1917. Day by day the news drifted in of members of the school who were aiding the war effort in one way or another.

"The V.H.S. has just realized that there is in England a former High School girl who is doing important work," reported the February 1918 edition of *The Camosun*. "She is Miss Sarah [correctly spelled Sara] Spencer, or, to be more correct, Lieut. Spencer, who is second in command of the [Canadian] Field Comforts Commission Depot in [Shorncliffe, Kent] England. We are sending Red Cross articles and numbers of *The Camosun* to Miss Spencer, and in doing so we may be sure that they will be distributed so as to be of the greatest use possible."

Spencer is listed as a nurse on the school's Roll of Honour, though no evidence exists that she had that qualification. She was one of seven Canadian commissioned women who were overseas for four years with the well-known Torontonian Captain Mollie Plummer, the officer commanding the Canadian Field Comforts Commission.[36] That organization had been established to make sure that gifts sent to the soldiers overseas reached their intended recipient. It was an offshoot of the Women's Patriotic League.

Sara Ellen Spencer is a heroine who is, sadly, almost lost to history. Born in Victoria in 1885, one of thirteen children of David and Emma Spencer, a noted Methodist family, she grew up in an atmosphere of civic commerce and the social gospel. Her father had founded Spencer's Department Store. Many of her kind undertook the essential paramedical and social welfare work so beneficial to those who had come back from the Front in wounded, and sometimes critical, states of mind or body. She was courageous in her convictions and zealous in her actions.

While working at Shorncliffe (quartered in the Royal Engineers Barracks), Spencer lived in Sandgate, Kent, right on the English Channel. There, she would have heard the guns thudding ceaselessly across the water. In late summer 1918 she wrote Ira Dilworth, a teacher and later principal at the school, who chaired the school's Field Comforts Committee:

Had I been home your kind letter and generous enclosure of thirty-seven dollars would have been acknowledged sooner, but I have just returned from leave. The Victoria High School Field Comforts Committee is indeed doing splendid work. I was so interested in your account of it. I shall turn in its money order to the office tomorrow, when you will receive a formal acknowledgement. In the meantime will you extend to the Committee my very hearty personal thanks for its interest and support? We shall be glad indeed to forward the scrapbooks. We find it difficult to fill all the requests from the front for reading matter of any kind. Thanking you and the other members of the Faculty for your kind wishes, and the Field Comforts Committee for their cooperation in what is, after all, more the work of Canadians in Canada than the few who are "carrying on" for them here.[37]

Sara Ellen Spencer outlived most of those involved in the First World War. Death claimed this quiet, unassuming, and powerful woman in 1983 at her residence, 3610 Cadboro Bay Road, Oak Bay, at the grand old age of ninety-seven. Her obituary noted her as businesswoman and philanthropist, which indeed she was. A benefactor of Victoria and a patron of the arts, among her many generous actions was the gift of the family home, Llan Derwen on Moss Street, to the Art Gallery of Greater Victoria. "She crystalized the dreams of all those people working so hard in the thirties and forties to create an art gallery," said Patricia Bovey, at the time the director of the gallery. Sara Spencer also gave tireless support to the Victoria Symphony, the United Way, and the Red Cross.[38] She received the Order of the British Empire in 1919 for her wartime service for the Red Cross.

*On a wider* field of war, Henry Forbes Angus, born in Victoria in 1891, found himself on a hot and sandy desert fighting the Ottomans in 1917. He was with his British Army unit in Mesopotamia (now Iraq), at Nasiriyeh, near Basra. Those fighting on the Western Front might think this a "sideshow." But in 1917, imperial efforts there against the sagging Ottoman Empire were of vast importance, designed to link interests in the Mediterranean with India and to keep the Germans out of any further, long-term advance to the east at Russian expense.[39] As well, the Admiralty had an interest in the oil. In July, London ordered General Allenby, the new commander in Egypt, to "strike the Turks as hard as possible."[40]

Angus's, it seems, was an exotic war, though not as dashing as the one T.E. Lawrence is said to have had. Out on the hot desert sands and the rivers that run through them, Angus was acting quartermaster—that is, the master resolver of issues, complaints, and quarrels—in the 1st Battalion, 4th Dorsetshire Regiment. How he got there is of some interest. A brilliant student at Victoria High School and then Victoria College in Arts I and II, he went to McGill to complete his BA. There, under the good offices of Sir William Peterson, principal of McGill, he was accepted into prestigious Balliol College, Oxford, to read law. The Vinerian Scholarship, won by some of the greatest lawyers in England, came his way and he was called to the Inner Temple Bar in 1914. Like many another Canadian in Oxford, he joined the Officers' Training Corps. As second lieutenant in the Wiltshire

Regiment, he was sent to India as part of the replacement for regular forces who were going to the Western Front.

Lieutenant Angus was first stationed at Delhi Fort in 1914, a peaceful enough assignment. When a platoon of the Wiltshires went from Poona as reinforcements for the 4th Dorsetshires fighting in Mesopotamia, Angus found himself on the front line. The Mesopotamian war had gone badly for the British: in 1915, General Townsend and his Indian Army had been obliged to surrender to Ottoman forces. While Angus was there, however, a turnaround occurred in British fortunes, and the Turks were defeated, leaving the British in charge of Mesopotamia.

We are tempted to say that Angus had a quiet war. Even so, he rose to staff captain of the 34th Indian Infantry Brigade at Tikrit in 1918. He was twice mentioned in despatches as serving with conspicuous distinction. After the peace, to wind up his story, he took a troopship for England, demobilized there, and spent 1919 as lecturer in law at the Canadian Khaki University, set up in Britain, that provided higher education to 50,000 service personnel. He then returned to Canada and arrived in Victoria looking for new prospects. Upon the recommendation of Professor Walter Sage, a historian at the University of British Columbia, Angus was appointed to teach economics. Although he also joined the law firm of E.P. Davis, having qualified for the British Columbia bar, he chose to stay at the university. His remarkable career as an economist, gifted historian, critic of anti-Asiatic sentiments, and civil servant lies beyond the scope of these pages. Suffice to say that he was one of the great Canadians of the age.[41] Certainly he was one of the few who had fought in what became, after the peace, the new Iraq. In any event, he outlived all his fellows from the school who had been in the War and died age 100 in Vancouver in 1991.

Angus's military activities bore testimony to the distribution of Victoria High School boys along many sections of the far-flung battle line. The school kept in touch with him, sending chocolates and cigarettes in its Christmas package of December 1917. The gift and the sentiments were welcome. Back came a letter from Angus to Miss Henry, the teacher and matron heading up this project, confirming that it was pleasant to feel he was still remembered by his old school. He wrote delightfully of the colour of the Near East:

> I am writing this in the house of an Arab Sheikh, converted into Brigade Headquarters and billets. The shamal, or north wind, is

blowing steadily, keeping the temperature bearable. In a few minutes the brilliant Eastern moonlight will throw into relief the dark masses of the palm gardens and light up the pale surface of the Euphrates.

In a few days I expect to visit Hillah, which is within a few miles of the ruins of Babylon. This part of the country is now under intensive cultivation and has a reputation already for its vegetables, its melons and its mosquitoes.

It is a curious backwater of the war in which we are condemned to drift till the end is reached somewhere else.[42]

The year 1917 also took from the school one of its finest teachers and greatest rugby coaches, the amiable Arthur Yates. We have met him before in various capacities—as champion for the boy's debating society, as the literary advisor to *The Camosun*, and as the proponent of the Matriculation Number of that magazine. Born in Darlington, County Durham, he moved to Montreal with his businessman father and family. At McGill, Yates did well and was selected as Rhodes Scholar for British Columbia in 1909. At St. John's College, Oxford, he took a degree in jurisprudence, spent his spare time in the debating society, and, of particular interest, thrice captained Oxford's lacrosse team in its games against rival Cambridge. We see that he also played ice hockey for the Oxford Canadians. In 1912, he came to Victoria and to his appointment at the school, where he brought the rugby team to a high level of achievement, with commendable victories over Vancouver and Royal Navy teams, many of whose members were far heavier than the VHS and Victoria College boys but far less disciplined, tough, or agile. He got the visiting New Zealand All-Blacks to give his squad various tips. Somehow he is forgotten among the great teachers and rugby coaches of the school, but that is an undeniable oversight. The War interrupted his progress, and many of his charges enlisted and went to the Front.

Born in 1885, Arthur Yates was scarcely ten years older than most of his students who were now in uniform. With conscription looming, he enlisted on March 29, 1917, and went overseas with the University of British Columbia, 196th (Western Universities) Battalion (Reinforcements). By the end of the year, Gunner Yates was in France with the 5th Division Trench Mortar Battery, 14th Brigade, Canadian Field Artillery—the same element of arms in which so many of the school's former students were serving.

Yates kept in touch with his former pupils and the school, and in spare hours near or at the Front, he wrote letters and word portraits, some of which were printed in issues of the school magazine. "It is of absorbing interest to any reader, but more especially to so many of us because of the bond of sympathy which exists between us and our master in his life at the front," wrote an editor of *The Camosun*, in preface to the following undated letter from Yates, printed here in full:

Some fate must have determined that my first experience of the war area should have been gained in one of the most famous and historical sections of the war zone, that is, the Ypres sector. When the war is won (as it will be soon), I daresay the English will maintain that this portion of the Front was the most critical, the most momentous in determining the war's issues, and the most decisive in the eventual outcome; the French will perhaps claim the Marne or Verdun. But at any rate, for us Canadians this sector will be forever memorable to our history—and with good reason, too. [Undoubtedly he had Passchendaele on his mind.]

Don't imagine I am depressed when I say it but I can't for the life of me understand why a Belgian's heart should palpitate patriotically over this portion of his native land. I could understand why he should cling most tenaciously to the soil—so would anybody—once in, you can't get out. The soil clings most tenaciously to you. I have not been in the firing zone yet—I don't know whether I shall go into it or not—but even where we are, well back from the firing zone, to describe the mud and conditions of living would really require a man who could "swear like a trooper." If it rains, we go to our meals to the mess house in mud, slime and filth quite six inches deep, and, if the man in front of you flounders, you make the trip twice over in order that you may clean the dirt out of your mess tin—that is if you are particular. But men coming down from the Front report even worse conditions— horses sunk so deeply in the mud, when they have gone off the beaten track that it is impossible to extricate them and they must perforce be shot. You can easily imagine the conditions under which the men exist. But the misery we endure (I can hardly call it that, for there is such an atmosphere of cheerfulness in spite of everything) is as luxury compared with the conditions under which some of the Canadians and Imperials have labored.

I do not seem to be getting much further ahead with my trip to Ypres, but the point of what I have written is this: I don't think that you who are almost citizens of Canada can have too much impressed upon you the misery and agony men have suffered in this part of the globe to make the world, not only safe, but hopeful for democracy. One of these days some great Canadian who has known and felt what has been suffered and endured will visit this area and consecrate the ground as Lincoln did for those who fell at Gettysburg . . .

I was fortunate in having the company of a man who knows the country fairly well. I said a moment or two ago that all the country-side was scarred and pocked with shell holes. I cannot vouch for the accuracy of the following information, but one of the first interesting bits my friend pointed out were two places quite untouched—two chateaux which he said were country seats belonging to Von Blissing who immortalized Miss [Dame Edith] Cavell [the British nurse, tried and shot by the Germans], and [Grand-Admiral] Von Tirpitz, of submarine and naval notoriety. Whether this was true or not, it is a singular fact that these two places are about the only untouched and undamaged houses in the vicinity! All else is ruin and desolation. In peace times I used to count it a pleasure when travelling on the continent to visit ruins of great places. It wasn't an altogether Byronic pleasure which I derived. I don't think I meditated upon decay and all that sort of thing, but now that I have seen how ruins are made, I must confess I do feel somewhat Byronic. It may be that Canadians making pilgrimages here, years hence, will feel only the thrill and awe, suggested by the memory of the almost superhuman things endured and deeds accomplished, but under present conditions, with all the desolation and awfulness and misery about, I can't quite conceive any other feeling than one of melancholy. One is too close to immediate grief . . .

Passing through Vlamertinghe, the signs of war quickly multiply. Trees lining the road are more frequently shattered, away on one side a working party is repairing a railway track where "Fritz" had dropped a shell or two the evening before; another working party is hauling a couple of dead horses from the roadway's innumerable shell-holes, great and small, camps, bivouacs, horse lines and dugouts, and before you know it you are jumping off the motor-lorry and stand at the entrance of the city. Immediately a watchful military policeman tells you to don your steel helmet and adjust your gas mask in the proper position of readiness . . .

I shall briefly mention a few things I noted: An observation balloon being "sniped" at by the Germans; the whining rush of three shells as they passed overhead to destroy some construction that "Fritz" had spotted farther back; the figure of Christ upon a church with a gaping shell wound in the body, but the look of physical pain and sorrow, petrified, as it were, after all these years. But one of the most remarkable sights of all is that of a water-tower which must have stood high up over the city reservoir. It is very strongly built of masonry; you will easily understand its strength when I tell you what has happened. It must be, so far as I could estimate, some 80 or 100 feet in height and as much in diameter. Some giant shell had come along, torn it from its foundations, and deposited it, as neatly as one could wish, upside down upon its cone-shaped pinnacle! Just imagine a fat, cylindrical elephant multiplied by three standing on its head and you'll have some idea how quaint it looks . . .

Coming home we passed a Canadian military cemetery. There are a number of such places in the old world which will always be Canadian soil. From the distance we could hear the Last Post being sounded and the firing party giving its salute to someone who had "gone west." One frequently hears the Last Post here, but, as you will find out from history, that is sometimes the way the work of the world goes on. Progress is not always a beautiful, peaceful Renaissance, but sometimes the progress is made, and the foundations of a Renaissance laid, at the cost of blood and tears and tragedy. Away and to the west was a glorious sunset with many a dark valley of shadows between; but after all there was light on the far hills. It's just symbolical of the dawning light that's coming to Humanity, and by all the signs it is coming. And I'm more convinced than ever that the change will only come rightly through right education.[43]

Yates is our eyewitness to history, writing not of the sharp end of war but of the life and times not far behind the front lines. With a literary bent, he had the capacity to see the oddities of war and some of its humorous sides. He also had the imagination to see regenerative aspects deriving from war.

We note here that at war's end, Yates returned to the school and the city briefly, only to tidy up affairs, then went to California to join his family— he was married to Dorothy Hazeltine (daughter of a local Victoria architect, the American Louis Hazeltine), and they had a son, Allen H. Yates. For two years he taught at Palo Alto High School, then became a publisher's agent in Boston, and in his last years until his death in 1956, he was attached to Long Island University, New York, as a professor of English. His love for rugby knew no bounds. He helped make Victoria into the nursery of Canadian rugby. He championed successfully the introduction of that sport to the Ivy League institutions. He arranged international matches for visiting Cambridge and McGill sides. He refereed top international fixtures. He deplored the decline of Classics as a subject of study. More, he deplored the professionalization of sport, and in that regard was the fading vision of the old spirit of "Play up, play up, and play the game!"[44]

We leave him now with a sigh of regret, for he indeed had fought for a different age and for different principles. Yet he left a remarkably strong stamp on the school.

*The year 1917* closed with a flurry of excitement at the school, for the long-anticipated visit of His Excellency the Governor General of Canada, the Duke of Devonshire, occurred on Friday November 23. The Duke, reputedly the wealthiest man in Britain, took a warm-hearted interest in Canadian matters, not only encouraging the Canadian war effort but also giving support to those at home who helped meet the social needs of the public. The auditorium was decorated with ferns and flowers, the back wall draped with the flags of the Allies (these same flags can be seen in the Roll of Honour). The proceedings opened with the national hymn, "O Canada." Then followed a short address by the principal, Mr. Smith. George Jay, the preeminent school board trustee, explained the aims of the Victoria schools. In his reply, His Excellency described the advantages of a good education and its beneficial effects on the character of the nation. He also said that Canada was at war for the maintenance of high Canadian ideals—"and that we must see the war to a successful end." In conclusion, he urged the students to do their part in carrying on the great heritage of Canada. After three hearty cheers for His Majesty the King and three more for His Excellency, followed by the national anthem "God Save the King," the school dismissed. "The Duke's visit was a great honor to the school and we hope that when he comes to Victoria again, he will not forget the V.H.S."[45]

*On reflection,* *1917* was the year of greatest Canadian triumph and greatest Canadian agony. Long will it be remembered as a turning point in Canada's history and the history of the British Empire as well. Sacrifices and tragedies have a remarkable way of developing the national legend that all nations possess. Vimy was the formative event, Passchendaele the horrid reminder that many great battles lay ahead before Germany could be defeated and an armistice achieved. On the Front, soldiers looked earnestly forward to a time when "the guns would no longer be heard."

Larger and more portentous events were also at work: the convoy system had reduced shipping losses to U-boats, and the Treaty of Brest-Litovsk had finally taken Russia out of the war. In consequence, the number of German divisions in the west at the end of 1917 had crept up from 149 to 161. Russia's collapse had special significance. Haig, who had seen his own great offensive, Passchendaele, end with such little gain and at such cost, told his army commanders on December 3, "The general situation on the Russian and Italian fronts, combined with the paucity of reinforcements which we are likely to receive, will in all probability necessitate our adopting a defensive attitude for the next few months. We must be prepared to meet a strong and sustained hostile offensive."[46]

One positive note: the Americans had finally entered the War and were landing in France in large numbers. In 1914, the US president had taken a path of non-intervention, but Germany's return to unrestricted submarine warfare early in 1917, and its sinking of several US merchant ships, provoked American anger. British interception of the notorious Zimmerman Telegram—a message from the German foreign minister offering aid to Mexico if it attacked the United States—caused the US public to support President Woodrow Wilson's move to declare war on Germany and

Austria-Hungary on April 6. American troops arrived on the front lines in late November, though they had been working behind the lines for most of that month.

In spite of this welcome addition, 1917 ended in gloom and uncertainty: for the Allies, no glimpse of a final outcome was in sight; the Central Powers believed one final great push might win the day. Deep in the background were the economic and social facts of the matter, for daily the Allies got stronger, particularly the British war machine backed by the empire's financial and trading might, ensured by British naval power. Daily, too, the Central Powers, especially Germany, suffered the slow strangulation of the British blockade. In the circumstances, Germany knew it would have to strike soon if victory were to be achieved, or if peace with honour were to be won.

*chapter 5* **1918**

## ROAD TO VICTORY: AMIENS AND MONS

N ew Year's Day brought no hint of an end to the War. Peace was only a dream. Nothing practical could be formulated in international diplomacy. The United States president, Woodrow Wilson, pressed for a peace along lines he had developed, but as long as the German high command and the generals in the field were determined to achieve victory, and as long as the Allies were determined to resist this, the War proceeded as before. Europe was being destroyed in the process. It all seemed so distant from the perspective of Fernwood and Grant Streets.

As they had since 1914, students of Victoria High School continued to watch the War from afar but ever conscious of the ties that bound them to those fighting. The May 1918 issue of *The Camosun*, edited by Ernest John Knapton, later a Rhodes Scholar and famed historian,[1] contained in its initial pages the enlarged Service Roll. The same issue printed the customary student literary efforts under the guidance of teacher Ira Dilworth. Knapton's editorial turned to more serious stuff—matriculating students, or some of them, were going to farms, engaging in "their patriotic labors" or alternative service. Roy Daniells, later a noted poet and literary giant, the matriculating class president, was one of them. A prominent debater and an associate editor, he made his exit, taking with him great good wishes from his fellow students.

There was news to report from the Front: Second Lieutenant Harry Brown and Lieutenant Everard Lynne Laundy had been awarded the Military Cross. Cecil Milloy, though he had come home wounded and been discharged, had actually re-enlisted. Henry George Sivertz had gained the Military Medal. So far as was known to that date, this made a total of eleven Military Crosses and seven Military Medals "for our school." Meanwhile, sad news had been received: Campbell Sanson and Claude Armour had been wounded in the performance of their duties. Elsewhere, Dudley Johnstone, an ex-VHS boy, training with the Royal Flying Corps in Texas, had recently won the high jump and obstacle race in the field sports there. For some time he held the high-school high jump record. In France, nineteen-year-old Private Norman Spencer, serving in the 7th Battalion, Duke of Cornwall's Light Infantry, was wounded in action and died in one of the hospitals near Rouen. Like the others, he is on the school's Roll of Honour.

Meanwhile, the Victoria High School Patriotic Aid Organization continued its noble work under student leadership. Helen Colpitts and Douglas Wallis, the latter the famed chemistry teacher of the school ("Test-tube Wallis"), were advancing the cause. Colpitts was an active debater in the Portia Society. Wallis was a lieutenant in the Cadet Battalion. Money was raised for the fund through the "Self-Denial Campaign." Boxes were placed in the hallways for donations. The group made scrapbooks for the amusement of soldiers convalescing in hospitals in England. The art teacher, Earl Clarke, devised the design and arranged for the brown wrapping paper that became the covers. On blank paper sheets, individual students could paste in their stories and good wishes. Brass-headed pins held the whole together. The covers bore inscriptions to the effect that the books were made by Victoria High School students. Old magazines were collected and shipped overseas. A visitor to the school, a Miss Clarke, who had nursed in English hospitals, spoke to the Portia and Beta Delta Societies, stirring up added enthusiasm; when she left to resume her work, she took away with her the wishes of the school's pupils. Christmas cards were organized to be sent in good time for reception, and included with them were perfume-scented photographs of school friends, lonely and adoring females in particular.

*The War's last* year saw great action in the air, some of it involving notable Victoria High School boys. Paul King (no relation to Albert Nelson King or his sister Jessie Nelson King) was a favourite at the school. Of independent, even rebellious, nature, he had been sent to a California military academy with a view to calming his instincts. Returning to Victoria, he had entered the school in 1914, excelled in science and dramatics, and shown full devotion to VHS. He had organizational and business talents, went into every kind of sport, and worked hard for the cadets. In acting and in directing Shakespeare's *Julius Caesar* and *Henry IV,* he shone, carrying the production by his zeal and leadership. It was no accident that he was elected president of his matriculation class. *The Camosun*'s tribute, written by his guiding force, Arthur Yates, upon his joining the CEF, shows him as a school idol, one of the brightest, the best, and the most popular: "It had been known for a long time that he had a great desire to serve his King and country, and a few years after his eighteenth birthday he left us and enlisted as a Private in the C[anadian] A[rmy] M[edical] C[orps], from which he has lately been transferred to the 13th Overseas Field Ambulance." His mother, an American of Irish stock, did not want her son to go to war, for he would be fighting for the British. This perhaps explains why young Paul King entered the medical corps. (All that was soon to change.) King expected to leave for the Front in a few weeks. He went with the heartfelt wishes of the school: "Every student to whom he is known wishes him great success in his military life and hopes that he will return safely from the war to renew his friendships among us."[2]

In September 1918, having earned his "wings" in England, we find him in 204 Squadron RFC at the controls of a Sopwith Camel, a single-seater scout. This aircraft had twin Vickers machine guns and a rotary engine that made it tricky to handle. Right to the end, Lieutenant King was in the thick of the air war. He showed the greatest courage and devotion to duty and took part in twenty-two low-level bombing raids in Flanders, bombing and strafing at elevations from 500 feet to 50 feet. His commanding officer praised him highly for his exceptional daring in attacking anti-aircraft batteries from low heights, in several cases obtaining direct hits on gun emplacements and causing severe casualties among the crews by his marksmanship. He was also credited with destroying two enemy aircraft. Nowadays, he would be classified as an expert in tactical air fighting. He was awarded the Distinguished Flying Cross.[3] We return to his story at a later time. But from his postings overseas he often wrote home to his friends at the school. On one occasion he wrote: "Since leaving school and Canada subsequently, we have just had one round of experience—at times pleasant and at times the reverse—but I wouldn't have missed this show for anything, for I see now that I can help pals that are unable to help themselves."[4] This was the essence of this man's humanity.

*The story of* Cecil John Clayton forms another chapter in military aviation history and, particularly, gives us a chapter of the war at sea. Originally from Manitoba, Clayton arrived in Victoria with his parents in 1893 and was a graduate of the school, Class of 1907. A popular and gregarious fellow, he possessed a quiet but effective sense of humour. He was in the employ of the *Daily Colonist*, but in mid-1916 left Victoria for Port Credit, near Toronto, to take a course in aviation at the Curtiss School. "The weather down here is abominable," he wrote home to friends, commenting on the heavy rains. "The work is very interesting, and I like it immensely. The only trouble is that we don't get enough of it. On the first flight they give it to you a bit rough to see how your nerves are. The instructor takes the pupil up 2,000 or 3,000 feet, and does a few stunts there. Then, when it is time to come down, he gives you a spiral dive. You get the sensation of falling, and the earth seems to be coming up towards you at a tremendous rate." After finishing the course on the land machines, students were given thirty minutes extra on the Curtiss H.4 "Small America" flying boat. There was a big waiting list at the Curtiss School, and Clayton was one of thirty at the time, while there were another hundred anxiously awaiting instruction and training, so popular had the war in the air become. One of the tests, completed successfully, was to attain an altitude of 400 feet, shut off the motor, and make a landing. Clayton passed, and was made a flight sublieutenant. Archie Wills, formerly a reporter on the *Victoria Times* (and also a graduate of Victoria High School), saw Clayton "performing in the air" and thought he certainly was doing fine.

There was romance ahead, for he received some training in the officers' scheme at the legendary Crystal Palace, built for the Great Exposition of 1851. Then it was to unpleasant Redcar, near Hartlepool, where cold winds cut like a knife. On another occasion he was at Witley Camp, where he found a number of old Victoria boys. While there he got hold of some mangled and well-read issues of the *Daily Colonist*, the first he had seen for months. "I was certainly glad to get some home news and a chance to look at a decent paper," Clayton wrote in a letter. He mentioned he had received a letter from Jimmy Rowe, written in the trenches: "He isn't in love with the mud in Flanders." "Was sorry to hear that Ernie Elford had been killed and some of the other Colonist boys wounded. Everybody seems to get it sooner or later." He may have been thinking of Nelson King.

At Cranwell it was judged that Clayton was a very good pilot, a very good officer, and very keen. He was recommended for seaplanes. In March 1917 he took instruction at Calshot, Hampshire, for the seaplane service. He was sent to Felixstowe Air Station, the headquarters for seaplane operational development, for advanced training, probably in Squadron No. 230 or No. 7 wing flying F.2As. Of seaplanes, Clayton wrote with understatement that they were quite nice to fly, though not nearly as easy as the land machines. In time he came to pilot the "Large America" flying boat, a seaplane capable of delivering a heavier bomb load to its target.

Clayton entered the scene when the War was far from won, and his dogged experience gives us a window on its last years, right to the surrender of the U-boats. He is possibly uniquely important in that he had sharp-end action against German air power in the form of Zeppelins, bombers, and fighters, as well as against U-boats.

The U-boat operated by stealth, capable of disappearing in its own environment. Anti-submarine methods were rudimentary. In 1918, the aerial torpedo was in its infancy, and the depth charge was useless against U-boats unless they could be found, which meant catching them on the surface of the sea and bombing them. In inshore waters, air patrol was largely ineffective, but offshore, air power on reconnaissance patrol increased the chance of detecting U-boats. The Royal Navy established the Dover Patrol, with ships and aircraft, to halt any U-boat transits from German and occupied Belgian ports to the Atlantic via the English Channel. All other enemy shipping was also hunted. Farther north, at the Thames Estuary, air power was central, as any Zeppelins or other hostile aircraft were to be intercepted, shot down, or driven away. The British developed the ingenious "Spider's Web" patrol system, with eight radial arms defining sectors to be systematically patrolled, using North Hinder light vessel as the base point.

On February 1, 1917, the German high command instituted unrestricted submarine warfare, and by April the losses in merchant shipping sailing to and from the British Isles reached alarming proportions. The Admiralty instituted convoys, with warships and aircraft accompanying the merchant ships, and the losses began to drop, though they remained high. This measure also drove U-boats more into inland waters than ever before. The war had to be waged in the Narrow Seas—the waters of the English Channel and north along the coasts of England on one side and France, Belgium, Holland, and Germany on the other. There were rich pickings in these waters for the British air forces. Clayton and others had another task: to guard against German destroyers making "tip and run" raids into the English Channel.

On September 3, Clayton was flying as second pilot in "Large America" seaplane 8676 when he and another RNAS aircraft surprised an ocean-type U-boat, *U.66*, running on the surface at fourteen knots off North Hinder. Bombs were dropped and the U-boat heeled over, probably never making port. Clayton was among those mentioned in despatches for this action. On December 19, 1917, he was again mentioned in despatches for "Services in Action with Enemy Submarines" and was promoted to flight-lieutenant.

On December 19, 1917, writing of another episode, he noted that he had made a forced landing forty miles out to sea but managed to get off the water after a great deal of bouncing on the waves, "which put most of my instruments on the blink."

All through that last winter of the War, the RNAS continued to take the fight to enemy submarines and any enemy surface ships they could find. They were driving the Zeppelins from the sky and intercepting German seaplanes. Clayton wrote on February 5, 1918: "I had a scrap with 5 Hun seaplanes. It lasted for 25 minutes and was rather exciting, but good sport. My gunner shot one of them down, and it crashed into the water. My machine was only slightly damaged." In the event, his air mechanic-gunner shot down a single-seater, one of two enemy craft, that had picked them out for easy prey. On another occasion, "Had another fight with them yesterday [March 12], which lasted for little over 15 minutes. We could see our tracers going into their machines, but we didn't bring any of them down. They put a few bullets into the tail of my machine, but none came very close to us."[5]

Clayton's war was important and eventful. He was again mentioned in despatches on June 3, 1918, and he was awarded the DFC in the New Year's List 1919. "You will be pleased to hear I have been awarded the Distinguished Flying Cross for worrying the Boche," he wrote to a friend in Victoria. By this time the U-boats that Clayton and the War Flight had daily sought out in the North Sea had been handed over to the British under peace treaty conditions.

Clayton had the honour of being senior officer escorting 150 surrendered U-boats to Harwich, and there the peril of the seas was destroyed, made scrap. "We had the agreeable job of escorting the blighters into Harwich, and I can assure you it was a great sight when they were all moored together up the river."

Now a squadron commander in the newly constituted Royal Air Force, he was promoted to major's rank about the time the Armistice was declared. He closed his war as deputy-commander at Felixstowe and returned to Victoria in October 1919 to a hearty welcome of friends.

In subsequent summers, Clayton flew in the Ontario air service on forest fire protection, spotting any smoke rising, placing it on maps, then notifying the district forester, who took steps to get it under control. He was headquartered one winter at Sault Ste. Marie. He attended the University of Toronto, graduating in dentistry. He died in 1965, a resident of 2323 Oak Bay Avenue, Victoria.[6]

Clayton was one of 944 Canadian airmen who flew with the RNAS. Well might they regard themselves as the cream of the crop, for recruiters called for very high physical and educational standards—and only British subjects need apply. Clayton's war was one of romance and opportunity, and he was one of the few who were, at the end of the War, able to claim naval aviation as the new and powerful weapon that would determine the future of war.

*On the Western Front,* 1918 had opened with continued uncertainty. The opponents were making plans for breaking the deadlock. The French army, mutinous the year before, had been revived under Marshal Pétain, who knew how to bring order and strengthen morale and organization. The British Army deployed in the field as the British Expeditionary Force was plugging gaps and potential weak spots on the line. The Australian Imperial Force was reaching powerful strength of purpose. The United States Army, fresh in the field, could be counted on—especially by the French—as a revival of fortunes, a trump card. Against all these armies, and other allies, stood the German army under Erich Ludendorff. During the previous winter, Ludendorff had determined on a final effort to break the opposing forces, split the British from the French armies, and advance on Paris and ultimate victory.

Ludendorff began his ill-fated Spring Offensive on March 21 with the super-heavy guns and the field artillery aimed at Allied guns, command posts, camps, and telecommunications centres. Then came the gas shells, again aimed at enemy positions. And then the explosive shells, the shrapnel, aimed at forward enemy positions. For five hours the bombardment continued, the guns switching between gas and high explosive. The damage done to the British Armies was incalculable. "I awoke," recalled a British artillery officer, "with a tremendous start conscious of noise, incessant and almost musical, so intense that it seemed as if a hundred devils were dancing in my brain. Everything seemed to be vibrating—the ground, my dugout, my bed . . . It was still dark."[7] Fog lay thick on the ground, but by mid-morning the air cleared. German fire changed to a creeping barrage, and in its wake advanced the German infantry. The Germans came forward in small groups or platoons, and they took the devastated ground that the guns had opened for them. The British units were in disorder, losing a quarter or more of their battalions and a large proportion of their machine guns. That day the Germans broke into open country. Now the British Armies, including the Canadian Corps, which had lost so many of its best soldiers at Passchendaele, were placed in a position of plugging the great gap.

Ludendorff had his eye on Amiens as the road to Paris and to victory. Haig, by contrast, was facing a catastrophe. The Fifth Army, under General Sir Hubert Gough, was ceasing to exist along the breach of forty miles of Front. In the circumstances, Haig's goal was to make sure the British and French armies remained united in command and purpose. A breakup of the alliance would spell disaster. It was clear to Haig that unless the French gave assistance, the British Armies would be confronting the weight of the German Army alone. But Ludendorff did not press his advantage. Rather than splitting the opposition, he ordered some small-scale actions. The British and French reserves arrived. The Germans lost the initiative and recoiled in exhaustion—though they were not yet finished.

The Canadian Army was now in a critical position, for Gough's Fifth Army disaster had led to the loss of about four miles of front lines. Byng's Third Army, which included the Canadian Corps, was pushed back even further. Its position was on the left flank of the Fifth Army. It was a desperate moment, and Haig told his commanders that his object now was to gain time so as to enable the French to come in support. To that end, the British Armies were to hold their ground, especially on the right of the Third Army, near Bray, on the Somme, "where *we must not give up any ground*."[8] Three Canadian divisions concentrated behind the Third Army.

Ludendorff shifted his plans with the moment, and all along the Front (rather than in a concentrated point in the line) he ordered his armies to advance. It was a fatal blunder. The pulse of war soon changed. The paralysis that had been the Western Front lifted. Instead of fighting in the trenches and in no man's land, mobility returned to the battlefield and remained there until the end of the conflict.

The British high command, which worked in concert with the French supreme command,[9] was planning its own campaign, following much the same lines as previous years except gunnery was now reaching a new effectiveness, air power was asserting itself in reconnaissance and tactical actions that won it supremacy over the battlefield, the tank was a force in the field, and staff planning had become so effective that well-conceived and directed action against the still formidable enemy would have desired results. There were to be no further battles such as the Somme or Passchendaele.

Meanwhile, at Canadian Army field headquarters, the quiet Canadian who had risen to the top in the army's command structure—the Canadian Corps in the field—Lieutenant-General Sir Arthur Currie, now a Knight Commander of the Bath and Knight Commander of St. Michael and St. George, sat at his desk drafting the Special Order dated March 27. His motto was "Neglect Nothing," and he heeded those words. Since July 1917, he had seen the Canadian Corps in action. He had felt the agony of the losses at Passchendaele and was set on preserving the lives of the soldiers under him. Although not unique among generals in this respect, he had seen warfare up close, first in charge of a brigade of the First Canadian Division and then, with promotion after promotion, right up to the top as commander of the Canadian Corps, and it was he, we recall, who had written letters home to Victoria's grieving families who had lost a loved one in the line of duty. Still, he also knew that Canada would do its part.

As he sat at his desk drafting the Special Order, he was preparing what we can now say is the most famous speech in Canadian military annals. We can also, incidentally, term it the last clarion call of the British Empire—at least as far as Canada was concerned. It was an appeal to patriotism and to utmost duty, and it made clear that people at home in Canada had the highest expectation of what the soldiers could do. The Order of the Day on the eve of the final battle of the Somme 1918 was passed to all senior and junior officers of the Canadian Corps to be read to each and every soldier who formed the

Corps. The words of the king in Shakespeare's *Henry V* come to mind, with its reference to "we band of brothers." The honour of waging war, the essential responsibility of action, the appeal to a greater and higher requirement with an immortal calling under God, are all present as Currie rallies his men to the flag in that urgent and fatal hour.

A few sentences make clear the lines of reasoning that Currie was advancing in the face of Ludendorff's mighty effort:

> In an endeavour to reach an immediate decision the enemy has gathered all his forces and struck a mighty blow at the British Army. Overwhelmed by sheer weight of numbers, the British Divisions between the Scarfe and the Oise have fallen back fighting hard, steady and undismayed.
>
> Measures have been taken successfully to meet this German onslaught. The French have gathered a powerful Army commanded by a most able and trusted leader and this Army is now moving swiftly to our help. Fresh British Divisions are being thrown in. The Canadians are soon to be engaged. Our Motor Machine Gun Brigade has already played a most gallant part and once again covered itself with glory.

Currie now turned to the matter at hand, calling for the last great sacrifices to be made:

> Looking back with pride on the unbroken record of your glorious achievements, asking you to realize that today the fate of the British Empire hangs in the balance, I place my trust in the Canadian Corps, knowing that where Canadians are engaged there can be no giving way.
>
> Under the orders of your devoted officers in the coming battle you will advance or fall where you stand facing the enemy.
>
> To those who will fall I say, "You will not die but step into immortality. Your mothers will not lament your fate but will be proud to have borne such sons. Your names will be revered for ever and ever by your grateful country, and God will take you unto Himself."
>
> Canadians: in this fateful hour, I command you, and I trust you to fight as you have ever fought with all your strength, with all your determination, with all your tranquil courage. On many a hard

fought field of battle you have overcome this enemy. With God's help you shall achieve victory once more.[10]

Currie's urgent command actually preceded Haig's desperate and dramatic "back to the wall" statement of April 1, a message that sent ripples through all the British Empire forces on the Western Front. Two days previous, Winston Churchill, who was in Paris attending a conference of all the great commanders —Haig, Foch, Pétain, Weygand, Rawlinson, and others—wrote to his wife, Clementine, and quoted Shakespeare's *Henry VI, Part 3*: "This battle fares like to the morning's war, When dying clouds contend with growing light." He added this chilling note: "a most formidable prolonged tremendous struggle is before us—if we are to save our souls alive."[11] That was then the desperate state of affairs. Currie was among the first to recognize it.

Dying during the German Spring Offensive was Verner Lovelace Plant, formerly of Victoria High School in the early 1880s, a lieutenant in the 8th Battalion, Somerset Light Infantry. He was killed on April 5, 1918, at age thirty-seven, one of the oldest former students of the school who died in the War.[12] His name is remembered with honour on the Arras Memorial, which commemorates 35,000 British, New Zealand, and South African service personnel. Five days later, on April 10, Lieutenant Hugh Searle Coppock, 3rd Battalion, South Lancashires, died age twenty-one. He had been mentioned in despatches and was killed in action, with no known grave. He is remembered at Ploegsteert Memorial. He was the son of H. Carmock and Mrs I.V.O Coppock of Carmock Chase, Westholme, Vancouver Island.

On June 11, Lieutenant Evan David Spencer, serving in the 5th Battalion, Corps of Canadian Railway Troops, died of unspecified causes, age twenty-one. Born in Victoria to a well-known Methodist family, and grandson of the famed David Spencer, who founded Spencer's Department Store, he had been a student at Victoria High School. His father, the philanthropist Christopher Spencer, and his mother, Sara Spencer, lived in Kerrisdale, Vancouver. Lieutenant Sara Ellen Spencer was his aunt. Evan David Spencer had served in the ranks of the 72nd Seaforth Highlanders of Canada and went overseas with the 121st Battalion, Canadian Infantry. He was an accountant by profession, assigned to the Canadian Railway Troops. On any day at this stage of the conflict, 12,000 Canadians carried out the essential work of laying and maintaining railway tracks. By Canadian policy, every Canadian engaged at the Front on work of a technical nature first had to be trained as a fighting soldier. The work was hazardous and uncomfortably close to where the Germans were pouring in the heavy shells. Lieutenant Spencer was one of 1,977 casualties suffered by the Corps of Railway Troops from April 1, 1917, to war's end.[13]

In the middle months of the last year of the War, three Victoria High School men died, all of them older than the customary early twenties—Lieutenant John Spouse, 17th Battalion, Canadian Engineers, died July 21, age forty-seven (the oldest VHS boy to die in the War); Private Albert Waterhouse, Canadian Infantry, who had won the Military Medal for gallant conduct, died September 2, age thirty; and Driver Edwin Steele, Canadian Field Artillery, died September 3, 1918, age twenty-six. These hard-pressed days of heavy bombardments and much exposed movement in the field were claiming Canadians by the hundreds and thousands.

*As Ludendorff's Spring Offensive* ran out of steam, the German divisions faced battle exhaustion. The blitzkrieg tactics employed by the Germans and storm troopers could not be sustained, and all the while the enlarged salient extended the lines that needed to be defended. The soldiers moved largely on foot and had no tanks. Ludendorff now focused on the southern part of the Western Front, where the greatest success had been achieved. This took the pressure off the British communications and their ports on the French coast of the English Channel.

Late June saw a change come over the Front. Not only was the Royal Air Force (which superseded the Royal Flying Corps on April 1) the strongest air force, but the tank, which had shown its value at the Battle of Cambrai the previous fall, could now also be used as an instrument of war. Technology was ending the old siege warfare; everything was in motion. In July, the Australian Fourth Division, in cooperation with the Tank Brigade, showed what was possible in the occupation of the town of Le Hamel, one of those devastated villages on a tributary of the River Somme. Their actions suggested what could be done on a larger scale. Haig made the suggestion to French general Ferdinand Foch, and thus was born the concept of advancing the Allied front east of Amiens. General Sir Henry Rawlinson, in command of the Fourth Army, called together the three corps commanders, as well as commanders of the cavalry and representatives of the RAF and Tank Corps. The two significant figures here were Lieutenant-General Currie, Canadian Corps, and Lieutenant-General John Monash, Australian Corps. The Australians on the left and the Canadians to their right were to carry out the main attack, while a French corps and a British were to form defensive flanks on their right and left.

"We just sailed through that morning," recalled Gus Sivertz of the unfolding events at Amiens. "It was unlike anything we had known—no trenches, blazing sunlight and absolute gaiety among the troops."[14] August 8, 1918, seemed like a day of destiny and is now seen as the beginning of the end. At the time, however, nothing was quite so sure. Canadian, British, and Australian forces began an attack on strong German positions near Le Hamel. Canadians and others refer to this as the Battle of Amiens.

If anyone doubted it, the day of the tank had arrived. Instead of the great bombardment that had opened Ludendorff's Spring Offensive, 430 tanks smashed through the enemy's defences. The British commander was Rawlinson but the Australian, General Monash, guided the planning. The preparations were thorough, the planning likewise. Surprise and deception, signals and communications, the hiding of forces during the day, tank movements at night under cover of the noise of aircraft overhead, whirling over the intended battleground, and then an early bombardment and a forward dash of infantry—all these were used on the day.

A short, surprise action, it left the Germans reeling. "This is the way to do it!" said General Rawlinson triumphantly. He was right—and this became a model. One authority says that this was the first instance of blitzkrieg—the magic touch of movement and coordination—following up on earlier gains of April and early July.[15] This was the most remarkable and least appreciated victory of the British, Canadian, and Australian armies.

The road from Le Hamel and Amiens, through shell-pocked fields of the Somme valley, to Mons and Ypres, the war-scarred areas of Flanders so well known to British and Canadian armies, became the long axis along which the journey to victory was wearily travelled. They had fought over this ground in 1916, and earlier in 1918 the "Red Baron," Manfred von Richthofen, leader of the Flying Circus, had been shot down near here.[16] Canada's army, described elegiacally as the Shock Troops of the British Empire, rolled up no less than forty-seven German divisions between August 8 and November 11—the Hundred Days. Currie estimated that this was nearly a quarter of the total German forces on the Western Front.

The Hundred Days saw some of the hardest fighting and the heaviest Canadian casualties. It is true that the German army suffered mightily, but so did the Allied armies. In tallying up the numbers, we see that in terms of deaths to soldiers connected with Victoria High School, 1918 was the year of the greatest fatalities, more than any other year. So high were the Canadian losses that Canadian politicians began to point fingers at what they thought was an irresponsible Canadian Army high command. This is why General Currie began to come under the closest scrutiny. But once the army came out into the open, it was exposed to enemy fire. When the troops began to move, the Germans could deploy their excellent machine guns to great effect. The road to victory was fought in open ground and in the air.

During this time, Canada suffered 50 percent of its casualties for the War. The news filled Canadian papers, and Victoria High School casualties filled the local papers with greater frequency. Lieutenant Donald Bertram Hanna, 2nd Canadian Mounted Rifles (British Columbia Regiment), died age twenty on August 10 during the Amiens campaign. Private Alister McCallum, a Glasgow-born Victoria High School boy, employed as a clerk in Victoria, had gone to war in early 1917. In the Machine Gun Section of the 7th Battalion, he was wounded in almost his first tour in the front lines. A year later he was killed in action on September 27, 1918. After crossing the Canal du Nord during the Bolton Wood operation, he took an enemy machine-gun bullet in the stomach, a catastrophic wound. After receiving first aid he was taken to No. 30 Casualty Clearing Station, where he died the next day. He is buried in Bucquoy Road Cemetery, Ficheux, France. He had been eighteen months in the fighting line and was not yet twenty-one when he made the supreme sacrifice.[17]

Gunner Donald Morgan McCannel, 33rd Battery, 9th Brigade, Canadian Field Artillery, age twenty-two, died September 27, the same day as his fellow student McCallum. Born at Qu'Appelle, Saskatchewan, he had moved to Victoria with his brother, Neil Ross McCannel, who was two years his junior (and who, as we will see, was killed in action November 6, 1918). Donald Morgan McCannel, after matriculation, had gone to Queen's University (Science, 1917), where he was an excellent student and popular athlete. He joined one of the many military units of that university, and he died of gunshot wounds to the head. He and his brother were sons of Donald Sinclair and Margery McCannel of 650 Linden Avenue, Victoria. He is remembered in Queen's University's Memorial, where correspondence on him was kept, including a letter from his sister Margery McCannel, who wrote that in late 1929 she visited the graves of her brothers in France and found them beautifully kept.[18]

A third former VHS student to die on September 27, 1918, was Sergeant Adam Cuppage Knox, 1st Battalion, Canadian Machine Gun Corps. He was twenty-two, son of the late John Alexander and Fanny Emma Knox, 1517 Bank Street, Victoria. He had been born in Victoria and educated at local public schools. He won the Military Medal. His two brothers, both older than him, died in the War. Corporal Frederick Vivian Knox, who had been born in Ireland before the family came to Canada, died November 21, 1916, age thirty, while in the famed 2nd Canadian Mounted Regiment (British Columbia Regiment). A third brother, Private Uchtred Charles Guy Knox, served in the 7th Battalion until something went dreadfully wrong. The Canada War Graves Registers (Circumstances of Casualty) describe his final desperate hours, and I leave it to the reader to draw conclusions of this extraordinary ending: "He was found at about 4:30 p.m. on August 19, 1915, in a latrine at No. 3 General Base Depot, Rouelles, bleeding from self-inflicted wounds in the throat. He was at once bandaged but died before he could be removed to the Hospital. A Court of Enquiry after having inquired into the circumstances of his death was of the opinion, that at the time of his death he was of unsound mind."[19]

Private Harold Lane Campbell, Victoria High School Class of 1910, and the first of four generations of his family to attend the school, arrived in France in 1918. Already well established as a teacher in British Columbia schools, he was twenty-three when he joined up. Military affairs were not new to him; for three years prior to enlisting in the CEF he had been in the 6th Regiment, Duke of Connaught's Own Rifles, a militia unit headquartered at the new Beatty Street Armoury, Vancouver. In 1915, at the University of British Columbia, he enlisted in the 196th (Western Universities) Battalion. Of a strong, amiable, and imperturbable disposition, and leaving his sweetheart May Irene Noble behind in Vancouver, he went overseas in the late fall 1916. Each platoon had a rifleman trained in first aid. In competitions, Campbell proved to be very effective and was invited to apply for transfer to the Canadian Army Medical Corps, which was subsequently approved. Sent to England, he received advanced medical training at Cliveden, estate of the Astors in Buckinghamshire, where the Canadian Red Cross had a hospital.[20]

Life on the forty-acre estate, with rooms in the Italianate mansion on the banks of the Thames, contrasted greatly with what he soon faced as a surgeon's assistant, serving in casualty clearing stations close behind the lines in France. By war's end he was one of those sergeants essential to the smooth running of the units that dealt with the wounded and worked to save lives.

The horrors of war, and what it did to bodies and to minds, was traumatic to all who encountered them. Campbell, dealing with broken and shattered bodies daily, was perhaps closer than most to the aftermath of the conflict. He concluded that much of his religious upbringing was to blame for his assumption that God should have intervened in these circumstances. As he later told his son Peter, "If there is a God, He is not a kind, compassionate God who listens to and answers prayers." In earlier life he had been a Methodist. But like many another soldier of the Great War, he turned away from religion. He was in various casualty clearing stations from the time he arrived in France; these stations forwarded casualties to the Canadian Hospital in Mons. He served magnificently during the War, was at Mons when discharged in March 1919, and returned to Vancouver to marry his sweetheart. Back in Canada he continued his outstanding work as an educator—writing textbooks on English, instructing at the provincial Normal School in Victoria, and then rising to the highest post as deputy minister of education. In recognition of the fact that he was one of the architects of the modern system of education, the University of British Columbia bestowed on him an honorary Doctorate of Laws in 1955.

His brother Claude Lane Campbell, also a graduate of Victoria High School, was seven years younger than Harold and signed on for the Canadian expedition to Siberia but shortly after withdrew for family reasons before his planned departure for Russia. Claude joined the staff of Victoria High School straight from the University of British Columbia in 1927 and was appointed vice principal in 1934. During the Second World War he had three years commanding Royal Canadian Navy ships. At the peace he returned to the vice-principalship, though he found it confining. He was superintendent of schools for the North Island from 1946 until he retired in 1959.

In November 1918, Victoria received the sad news of the death of Henry George Sivertz, killed in action at age twenty-five. One of six distinguished brothers who matriculated from the school, he had enlisted together with two of his brothers, Christian and Gustav (or Gus). They joined the 103rd

Battalion (Vancouver Island Timber Wolves). They were truly brothers in arms until September 29, 1918, when Henry George Sivertz fell at Cambrai.[21] He had won the Military Medal and two bars, clear indications of courage under the most dangerous of circumstances. When at school, Henry George Sivertz had ranked as a campus idol. A light had now been snuffed out.

Henry George Sivertz's next-to-youngest brother, Bent Gestur Sivertz, later commissioner of the Northwest Territories, recounted how the news reached his devastated family at home:

My oldest brother . . . never returned . . . He was three times awarded the Military Medal, the common soldiers medal, though no one had heard of anybody winning it three times. Teachers, business men, and ordinary citizens alike remembered Henry with pleasure. Whenever someone learned my name I would be asked if I were a brother of Henry, and I seemed always to benefit from this. He wrote faithfully to the family when he was away at the war, and his letters are touching still for their sensitivity and intelligence. The day we learned of his death my younger brother Sam and I were walking home at lunchtime from George Jay School . . . We saw the small vehicle used by the military pull up to our house. A woman emerged . . . Sam and I watched the woman go to our door and my mother take a telegram from her hand. Our mother read the two lines at a glance and slumped against the door frame waving the woman away. She stayed there until Sam and I approached her and she handed us the telegram without saying a word. We all went into the kitchen and as she served us our lunch we sat in silent incompetence. Just then we saw my father coming down the side of the house and through the back door. He was never home at this hour. He reached out to take my mother in his arms.

She greeted him with a loud question, "You know?"

When he nodded my mother shouted, "How do you know?"

"Percy Marchant sent a message to the post office that I should come to his office before going home."

Percy was a lawyer and a warm friend of my parents. My mother and father dissolved in one another's arms.[22]

Henry's teacher, Miss Jeanette A. Cann, recalled that he was by nature a philosopher and an idealist. He had that particular refinement of mind that made it difficult for her to associate it with fighting and bloodshed on the field of battle. She counted him as among the school's early graduates, especially those of the old McGill days, who had stayed at the school until they had completed their second year in Arts. These were the fellows who stood out "with the greatest clearness in the long procession that memory passes in review." She continued:

> I never doubted he could play the soldier with the same conscientiousness that distinguished his work in schooldays, but I have to confess it was with a slight start of surprise that I heard of the honors he won. It is rather difficult to identify our sometimes dreamy philosopher with the man of daring action. *The war has shown us that we knew not one half of the capabilities nor a tenth part of the breadth of character of our best friends.*
>
> His last letter reached me a few hours after I had heard that he would not return to Victoria. It told me of a bar [actually his second] to his Military Medal—with strict instructions not to pass on the news. Though I grieved because I should not see my old friend again, should not enjoy again a friendly chat in which with some difficulty I might induce him to express his thoughts concerning this strange civilization of ours with its terrible social and economic problems—how vitally interested he was in those problems!—though all such possibilities had ceased to be, I could not find it in my heart to begrudge him his glorious end. He had conquered death long before he fell fighting and he could say with the Soldier Poet:

> *Safe shall be my going,*
> *Secretly armed against all death's endeavour;*
> *Safe though all safety's lost; safe where men fall;*
> *And if these poor limbs die, safest of all.*[23]
>
> [RUPERT BROOKE, "1914 II. SAFETY"]

On November 1, Sergeant Raymond Harlan Brewster, twenty-four, only son of the late premier Harlan Carey Brewster and the late Annie Brewster, was killed in action in France. Born at Winter Hill, Somerville, Massachusetts, on Christmas Day 1893, he had shown great promise as both a scholar and an athlete (he was a champion sprinter). After matriculation from Victoria High School, he had qualified as a dentist at Portland's North Pacific Dental College. The call to arms was strong. In May 1917 he went overseas with a detachment of a Canadian divisional ammunition column. He was in the 3rd Brigade, Canadian Field Artillery, at the time of his death. Sergeant Brewster is buried in Valenciennes (St. Roch) Communal Cemetery, Nord, France. In Ross Bay Cemetery is a marble standing stone to his memory. In April 1917 his father, then premier of British Columbia, participated in the ceremony planting the avenue of maple trees at the school in honour of the fallen Ypres heroes. (As an aside, his father had won a US medal for bravery after he saved the lives of American sailors cast ashore near Clayoquot. Brewster was owner-operator of a cannery near Tofino and had perfected a process of sealing salmon tins that prevented contamination. He had been swept to power as a Liberal in the September 1916 provincial election but died less than two years into his term, on March 1, 1918, in Calgary.) Raymond Brewster's death was widely mourned, particularly sad because it came so late in the War. As the *Daily Colonist* said three days after the Armistice, Sergeant Brewster had been "called upon in the very last hours of the great struggle to lay down his life with the last gallant men who fell fighting for justice and truth."[24]

The very day of Sergeant Brewster's death, November 1, 1918, Gunner James McNaughton Pottinger, who fought side by side with his brother Claude, was killed in action at La Sentinelle, near Valenciennes, France. Wounded with a nasty gash to the scalp, he was safely on his way to the dressing station (and carrying the corner of a stretcher for one of the men who had been hit) when another shell exploded behind him. "He would have made Blighty," Claude reported to their parents, but the piece that killed him was very small and hit him in the back of the head. "He was killed instantly and died with a smile on his face." Claude reassured his parents that James had a splendid record of service in the closing stages of the great conflict, and was much liked by all the men in the battery. "And oh, Mother and Dad, I know it's hard, but try and think it's for the best and be very proud of our Jim."[25]

News of Pottinger's death was published after the Armistice was proclaimed. His letters give an impression of an uncomplicated and lovely young lad who went away to war at age nineteen and became a man by the time of his death at age twenty-one. There were so many like him—boys when they went off to war. He came from an old Victoria family. His grandfather, from the Orkney Islands, arrived on Vancouver Island in 1864 to teach at Craigflower School. His father was foreman at the King's Printer, and his mother was from Nova Scotia. The large family lived at 634 Battery Street in James Bay. James McNaughton Pottinger, educated at South Park and Victoria High School, intended to be a teacher. He had a year at McGill and was taking teacher training at the Normal School when the irresistible call to arms came in December 1915. He enlisted in the 5th BC Regiment of Garrison Artillery, RCA, then joined the 15th Ammunition Column, which included so many of the young men from Victoria who gave up their studies to take up arms. In England, at Witley Camp, he trained further as an artilleryman. Then he was sent to France to join the battery commanded by Major T. Duncan Ringwood, half-brother to artillery lieutenant Raymond Castle, also of Victoria High School (Ringwood died in the battle of Amiens).[26] The *Victoria Times* reported of James McNaughton Pottinger: "He had shared in the big actions since he entered the war zone and had taken part in the final drives which have brought about the victory which he missed seeing by a few days."[27] Pottinger was buried in a British soldiers' cemetery, a quiet and pretty place. "It is a miserable wet muddy day," Claude wrote that evening to sister Alice in Victoria, "but every man who could get away came, and the Union Jack was covered with flowers. The boys must have scoured the country for them. Jim's body was carried shoulder-high down the pathway to the grave, by six of his best friends . . . I can't write any more now Al. dear, so I'll have to say 'au revoir' and oh Al. soften it for all the people if you can. I know, dearie, what it costs to carry on when you are heartbroken."[28]

The last Victoria High School lad to die in the War was likely Signaller Neil Ross McCannel, 9th Battery, 3rd Brigade, Canadian Field Artillery. He was gassed on August 19, released from convalescence in late October, and returned to his unit. Just turned twenty, he was killed November 6, five days before the ceasefire. His brother, Donald, had died of wounds six weeks earlier. His sister, Margery, was a Canadian nurse, and, as we have noted, she visited France in 1929 to pay grateful respects at the well-separated graves of her two brothers.

We know of others from the school who died late in the War. The day before Neil McCannel's death, nineteen-year-old Private Harold Marshall Pearce, 1st Brigade, Canadian Garrison Artillery, was killed. In the Royal Air Force, Lance Corporal Henry Arthur Bruce Jackson died October 28.

He had only just enlisted. The last officer connected to the school to die, Lieutenant Angus McCallum of the British Columbia Regiment, was killed in action on September 27. Victoria-born Surgeon Sub-lieutenant Alfred Edward Beckwith, lately of HMS *Oriole*, a destroyer, died in Royal Naval Hospital, Haslar, Portsmouth, of Spanish influenza August 1. A witty fellow, fond of his time at the school and his many friends, he had won acclaim as a debater. After Victoria High School he studied arts and medicine at McGill and enlisted in the McGill Siege Artillery, then transferred to the Royal Navy Volunteer Reserve. He is remembered in the McGill Roll of Honour 1914–1918.[29]

The costs in the air were heavy, for in 1918 the war above the ground reached levels previously unimagined. The previous November, Second Lieutenant William Reynolds Cutler, age twenty-one, had died—the first Victoria High School airman to be lost[30]—and in 1918 came a further long litany. Air Mechanic Frank Garland, age eighteen, died January 15. Second Lieutenant Albert Augustus Gerow, Royal Flying Corps, twenty-two, died February 28, and is buried in Penton Mewsey (Holy Trinity) Churchyard, Hampshire. His headstone reads affectionately TILL WE MEET AGAIN. Second Lieutenant Geoffry W.A. Green, age twenty-four, died February 28. He was in the Royal Field Artillery and attached to Squadron 59 as an observer. The plane he was in crashed in flames. He was the son of prominent naval architect Walter Ashdown Green and Mrs. Green of Rockland Avenue and is buried in Achiet-le-Grand Communal Cemetery, near Arras.

There were more: Cadet Richard William Reginald Litchfield died May 2 in an airplane accident. Second Lieutenant Arthur William Aird, 209 Squadron, died in France May 23, age twenty-three, and is remembered at the Arras Flying Services Memorial, Pas de Calais. Second Lieutenant Hugh Arthur Bruce Jackson, who had enlisted as a private and had risen quickly, serving in 104 Squadron in France, was killed, age nineteen, on June 25, 1918. He was the son of the prominent lawyer and King's Counsel Malcolm Jackson and Mrs. Lillian Jackson of Rockland Avenue.

Flight Cadet Arthur Edward Johnson, serving in the Royal Air Force, age twenty-three, died October 28 in an airplane accident near Bath. He was the son of Arthur and Ellen Johnson of 1521 Bank Street, Victoria. He had enlisted in the 13th Field Ambulance and went over with that unit in June 1916, serving in numerous dressing stations, including the vast underground one at Ypres. After witnessing that horrific aspect of war, he wanted to see it from the air; he applied to and was accepted into the Royal Air Force. He is remembered at Hollybrook Memorial, Southampton, Hampshire, buried with others who went down on transports or other vessels in home waters. The memorial reads TO THE GLORY OF GOD AND IN MEMORY OF OFFICERS AND MEN WHOSE NO OTHER GRAVE IS BUT THE SEA OR WHOM THE FORTUNE OF WAR DENIED THE KNOWN BURIAL GIVEN TO THEIR COMRADES IN DEATH.[31]

These are some of those who can be mentioned as deaths for the year 1918 before the Armistice. How many other casualties there were during these closing months cannot be calculated. But they are legion. The losses in pilots, observers, and all-important ground staff were vast, and they claimed many who had been connected to Victoria High School. The Canadians paid dearly for their success.

For many Victoria families the call to arms was answered by all the sons. Such was the case for the McCallums of Maple Bank, the family home at Foul Bay. The four sons, Arthur, Eric, Kenneth, and Richard, fought for King and Country for a total of about twenty-four years, for they were all of that generation (born 1891 to 1895) who saw the War from beginning to end. They were Anglicans, their father a farmer. All of the boys were born in Victoria, and all attended Victoria High School. All came home but one, and here we necessarily take them from war's end or near to it.

The youngest of the McCallum brothers, Arthur, returned home from the War on a summer's day in 1919. With him was his wife, Mary Frances Mackenzie McCallum. They had married in Victoria in 1915 before he went overseas. She went overseas, too, and was at an RAF hospital as a Voluntary Aid Detachment nurse or medical assistant, after which she was employed at the War Office, London. Arthur's life was all the more extraordinary because he, first, somehow survived all perils of aerial combat, including a crash on the same day as the opening attack at Vimy (April 9, 1917); second, lived through near starvation and enforced labour at an enemy prison camp on the Russian border for twenty months; and third, if that were not enough, endured all the vicissitudes of life, including the long voyage home.

What worlds he had seen since leaving Victoria! Following his three brothers, he had enlisted (in his case in the 103rd Battalion) and soon found himself in the trenches. The allure of the air led to his being commissioned, and later we find him as Major Arthur Howard Kirkham McCallum, RFC. Not long after he returned home, he divorced Mary—their marriage probably a casualty of the War—resided for a time in the Union Club, then married Sheena Armstrong in London and had a family. The call to war in 1939 brought him into uniform once again, and in 1945, Wing Commander McCallum was restraining RCAF personnel from participating in the drunken and high-spirited Victory in Europe Day riots in Halifax, a deed for which he was awarded the MBE (Military) by a grateful government. Some quietude now awaited him at last, and· he retired to the Okanagan among the apple trees and died at Coldstream in 1973.

Also to survive the war was his next-eldest brother, Eric, who was a noted rugby player when at school. A good student and competent debater, his greatest field for action was the rugby pitch, where he was an excellent punter and agile ball handler who could also give out a crushing tackle to an opponent. Matriculating mere months before the War began, he had plans to study for the law. The War changed all that (as it did so much else). He had been in the 5th BC Regiment of Garrison Artillery, RCA, and went overseas with the 48th Battalion. He was sent to join the famed Royal Canadian Regiment, where he won the DSO for conspicuous gallantry at Ypres in 1916. Here is the citation: "When on patrol with two scouts, one of the latter was killed and the other wounded. Although himself wounded three times in the back and once in the leg, he dressed the other man and carried him some 600 yards under shell fire to safety."[32] He was wounded and gassed at Passchendaele. On his return home, he began to invent and manufacture toys and games. In his time at the school he had been one of the specially anointed "tin gods"—an immensely powerful fellow, supremely athletic, with strong powers of concentration. He gave his best to the war effort. Major Eric McCallum, DSO, died in Victoria in 1957.

The next McCallum, likewise an officer (for they were all officers in the end), was Kenneth. For a time he was in the 2nd Battalion, Argyle and Sutherland Highlanders. We next find him as a naval pilot flying Sopwith Camels in the RNAS. In 1917, Flight Commander McCallum was in a flying formation covering a bombing mission when he was attacked by a more powerful Albatros D. III and shot down. On crashing, his left foot was shattered. The only course for the medical personnel was amputation, successfully completed. Although his war in the air had come to an end, he could still instruct those coming forward to take his place in those flying machines, and he completed his war as an aerial instructor. He was awarded the Military Cross.

The last, but not the least of the McCallums, Richard Arthur, had joined the 50th Regiment, Gordon Highlanders, gone overseas, and was flying in the RAF when, on September 6, 1918, during the Hundred Days, he was killed in an airplane accident, age twenty-five. He, too, was a foremost athlete in Victoria. He won no medals for his gallant conduct, and like many another in this war he gave up his life for his sovereign and his country.[33]

Here is the story of another family at war. All the Milligan boys, who saw hard service in France, were Presbyterians who left the family residence at 1738 Leighton Road to go to the War. In 1915, the most ardent patriots were drawn to enlist as soon as possible, and two of four Milligan brothers arrived at the Front that year, with the other two soon to follow. The Milligan boys, by rough calculation, spent at least a collective sixteen years trying to bring about the Kaiser's downfall. They were all Victoria-born and educated. We begin with the two principals, John "Jack" Mudie Milligan and George Berry Milligan, both of whom were British Columbia land surveyors. After their years at the school (where they had come under the influence of Arthur Currie), they took up a flourishing practice in engineering and surveying with J.H. Gray in Victoria.

John, who was mostly concerned with mining projects in the northwest corner of British Columbia, was the first to go to war. He enlisted in the 7th Battalion at the outbreak and arrived in time to become attached to the First Contingent under Currie. At the Second Battle of Ypres, he was taken prisoner and remained "a guest of the Kaiser" (at Lager No. 1, Munster, Westphalia) until the end of hostilities. On his return to British Columbia, he superintended the Dolly Varden Mine at Alice Arm, but serious illness (related to having been a prisoner of war) overtook him, and he died in Victoria in 1927.

His brother George Berry Milligan, a noted rugby player, popular in his hometown, who had played with the New Zealand All Blacks, was out on survey when war was declared. He had completed an examination of the unknown northeast corner of British Columbia, north of the Peace River Block, toward the sixtieth parallel. The wide Peace River valley was slated for agriculture, railway, and townsite development—a great Canadian northern frontier—but in higher latitudes lay lands needing examination. In eighteen months, including a winter in Edmonton, he travelled more than 7,200 kilometres, almost half on foot, another third by pack horse, and the rest by canoe, train, steamboat, wagon, and even dogsled. The intrepid land voyager, a lance corporal in the 5th BC Regiment of Garrison Artillery, RCA, was about to depart on another venture, into an entirely different topography, one of Armageddon.

Returning to Victoria to finish up reports for the provincial government, George Milligan enlisted in the Army Service Corps and found himself far from the Front, in Vernon, British Columbia. He apparently thought this a consignment to indolence, so leaving it behind, and at his own expense, he shipped for London, where he joined the Inns of Court Officers' Training Corps. He went to France as a newly commissioned lieutenant in the Royal Field Artillery in December 1915. For services in the field, he was twice mentioned in despatches and recommended for the DSO and the Military Cross. He lived through all the great battles, and at a time when there was one British gun for every seventeen feet of the German line. He was killed instantly on March 24, 1918, age twenty-nine, while engaged with his battery at Rouelles. He had been recommended for the Victoria Cross for heroic actions and now joined the hundreds of dead on the Roll of Honour of the Inns of Court.

Lieutenant George Berry Milligan, MC, was a Fellow of the Royal Geographical Society and a member of the Union Club of British Columbia. His business partner, J.H. Gray, gave this salute to his late friend: "The death of G.B. Milligan, BCLS, native son, explorer, athlete and all-round fine fellow marks not only an irreparable gap in his chosen profession, but a loss to the community, probably not manifested on account of his reticent nature, through the development of provincial resources, of which he possessed wide knowledge and in which he seemed destined to take a leading part."[34]

Of 250 British Columbia land surveyors, a remarkable 129 of them enlisted, "including, as far as is known, every able-bodied man of military age, and many, though over age, would not be deterred from answering the Call." In the latter category was Captain James Herrick McGregor, president of the Union Club at the time he enlisted and left with the 50th Regiment, Gordon Highlanders. He was killed before Ypres, on April 21, 1915. The McGregor Lounge in the club is named for him, while above the fireplace there is a plaque, on which his name (as well as that of George Milligan, Robert Branks Powell, and twenty-one others) is inscribed, that proclaims in hearty remembrance, TO THE MEMORY OF THE MEMBERS OF THIS CLUB WHO GAVE THEIR LIVES FOR THE EMPIRE, 1914–1918.

Their home province did not forget their sacrifice. George Berry Milligan is remembered by the Government of British Columbia in Milligan Creek, north of Fort St. John, while John Mudie Milligan is likewise commemorated in Mount Milligan.

Two other Milligan boys enlisted: Lieutenant Alexander Wilson Milligan, who was wounded in action March 25, 1915 (underwent three operations and then returned to the Front), mentioned in despatches, and died September 2, 1918; and Lieutenant Charles Napier Milligan, a soldier turned airman in the RAF, who survived the war unscathed, though he had been wounded in action while flying.

British Columbia, and Victoria in particular, made a remarkable contribution to the Great War in terms of human numbers: as of mid-1918, statistics compiled at the headquarters of Military District No. 11, comprising the province of British Columbia, showed that in the four years since Germany invaded Belgium "and let loose the war-dogs of the world," as the *Daily Colonist* reported on August 7, 1918, the number raised had been strong. From August 4, 1914, to July 15, 1918, 52,202 had been recruited. Of these, 43,300 officers and other ranks had left the district for overseas. Nearly 9,000 were still in the District in training or recruiting. The Military Service Act, which had become law a year earlier, in August 1917, seems to have had little to do with the response. Since the end of 1917, 4,183 officers and other ranks had been sent as reinforcements to France. Various units of the CEF remained stationed in the province and in the Yukon. Victoria seemed like an armed camp. There was a depot battalion (a general administrative unit) in Victoria; the Royal Canadian Garrison Artillery, Overseas Draft, at Esquimalt; the Army Medical Corps Depot, No. 11, at Willows Camp, Oak Bay; the 11th Detachment of the Canadian Army Dental Corps in Victoria; and the No. 11 Detachment of the Canadian Military Police Corps.

The provincial response was a source of satisfaction to the authorities and the public. The *Daily Colonist*, with patriotic zeal, put it this way:

Of the gallant army which has gone overseas from this Province many have given their lives, many more are still in the fighting-line and others are in the casualty clearing stations, hospitals, or convalescent institutions of England or France. The number which has come back to British Columbia wounded or disabled is approximately 10,000, of which

8,000 have been discharged as unfit for further service. The military convalescent hospitals of the Province or the special departments of the general hospitals contain the greater part of the 2,000 or more remaining men, although some of the returned soldiers who have sufficiently recovered to be of service have been transferred for duty to other units.

August 8, 1918, the first day of the Battle of Amiens, the day of destiny for the Allies, was also, according to Erich Ludendorff, "the black day of the German Army." Two months later he told Hindenburg that there was no alternative but to seek an armistice. The German position had been penetrated; the German army would not fight. The civilian population had lost heart. Peace was in the wind, and Ludendorff and Hindenburg might accept that their dearest hopes of victory had been buried. On October 26, Ludendorff's offer of resignation was accepted by Berlin. He told his wife, "In a fortnight we shall have no Empire and no Emperor left, you will see."[35]

On November 1, the British Armies made their last great assault on German forces. The road to victory was now assured but Mons, the final objective, was not yet taken by the Canadians. Ludendorff had been removed from his high command. The German army was in retreat and without hope. Semi-starvation faced the nation. The German navy was on the brink of mutiny and revolution inspired by Bolshevik doctrine and action. The collapse of the German Empire seemed at hand. The process was astonishingly sudden.

The German high command knew that an armistice must come at the earliest possible moment and that the Kaiser must go. Wilhelm II departed by train to Holland on November 10 and then abdicated. The terms of the armistice were established. The guns in Europe fell silent; the dreadful slaughter of the War came to an end.

On the following day, November 11, 1918, at 5:00 AM, the Germans accepted the terms of the Armistice. At 11:00 AM, the Armistice came into effect. So closed the long and catastrophic agony.

*For the British Empire,* including Canada, the war ended as it had begun, at Mons. The final days and hours had seen strong German resistance. There was much bitter fighting right up to the end. At 6:30 AM, Canadian Corps headquarters learned that hostilities would cease at eleven o'clock. About the same time, Canadian infantry units reached the centre of the city. At the silencing of the guns at 11:00 AM, the Canadians liberated Mons. They had come to accept the German surrender. The citizens were in a celebratory mood, liberated after fifty-seven months under German occupation. In the Victoria High School Archives is the statement of the citizens of Mons, grateful thanks for their liberation at Canadian hands (see below). A week later, General Currie led the mounted parade into the city's cobbled courtyard. "The killing had ended and we hoped for a rest period," wrote Archie Wills, former *Victoria Times* reporter, now in the Canadian Artillery. "Our thoughts raced over the miles to Victoria. When would we see it again? For three years it had been a treasured memory." It was, historian Ken Roeche says, "a treasured memory that some 700 young men from Victoria would never see again.[36]

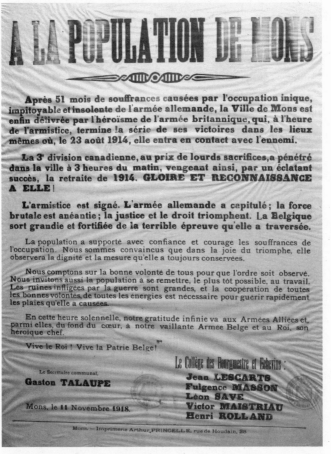

PHOTO COURTESY OF BARRY GOUGH

I was travelling northeast on the Soignies road northeast of Mons when my expert guide ordered our car to halt at the crossroads in the village of Casteau, Belgium. The place seemed entirely ordinary. I asked him why we had halted. Here, he said, the war had begun for the British Empire and here it had come to an end four years later.

At seven in the morning of August 22, 1914, he told me, the 4th Royal Irish Dragoon Guards, a mounted regiment, was patrolling the crossroads, the village, the woods adjacent, and the road to Soignies. German units were known to be approaching: the riders soon spotted four German lancers heading cautiously toward them.

Here, almost a hundred years after the event, I was on the exact spot where the action started. I could see the road disappear over the slight rise in the distance where the first Germans—a group of the Kurassier-Regiment 4 were seen. The second-in-command of the British unit, Captain Charles Hornby, drew his sword, spurred his horse, and led his troop in attack, cutting down a fleeing German. In this skirmish, too, the first shots of the First World War rang out. So that passersby may not forget the event, there is a memorial to mark the spot. (I also learned that Hornby's sword, German blood on the blade, has been preserved in the Regimental Museum, Royal Armoured Corps, Bovington, England.)

My guide now asked me to turn and look in the opposite direction, where an old inn stands. He asked me to stand just where the laneway from the inn meets the Soignies road. Here it was, he said, that my fellow countryman, Private George Price, against advice from his mates, put his head out round the corner. He was shot by a German sniper hidden from view in the bush beside the very same road on which the 4th Royal Irish Dragoons had made their charge four years previous. Price wanted to see what was happening. He knew that the bells of peace would soon ring out. Price, of the 28th North West Battalion, 6th Infantry Brigade, Second Canadian Division, took that bullet at 10:58 AM on November 11, 1918.

Nowadays, it all seems so futile, so useless. Price had proved nothing by his foolishness. But he had won a place in history: he was the last Canadian to die in this war. I found his headstone in nearby St. Symphorien Military Cemetery, possibly the most beautiful military cemetery. The headstone is not far from where you can find a companion stone for Private John Parr of the Middlesex Regiment, who died on August 21, 1914, the first British soldier to die in the war, right at the commencement of hostilities. He had been out on reconnaissance with his bicycle near the canal when he took a German bullet.[37]

A bombing raid on Etaples, France, May 1918. The photo shows the hospital dormitory where Clara Detweiler would have been had she not been on night duty. REID FAMILY

Canadian nurses mourn at a funeral following the bombing of Etaples, May 1918. REID FAMILY

A picnic of Canadian nurses and soldiers at Etaples. Private Clifford Reid is on the far left with his future wife, Clara Detweiler, beside him. SCOTT FAMILY

Aerial photo of the Western Front. SCOTT FAMILY

Lieut. William A. McKinnon,
Royal Naval Air Service,
later Royal Air Force.
VICTORIA HIGH SCHOOL ARCHIVES

Cadet Battalion Corporal John Gough
(the author's father), later a teacher at
the school, writer of textbooks, and, as
"Mr. Schools," District Superintendent of
Schools for Greater Victoria from 1951 to
1966. COURTESY OF SYLVIA PEARCE

Private Horace "Tod" Paul, died May 11, 1917, age 25. VICTORIA HIGH SCHOOL ARCHIVES

Private Harold Stanley Roe,
died April 10, 1917.
VICTORIA HIGH SCHOOL ARCHIVES

Lieut. Harold Eustace "Rollie" Whyte served
in the Army Service Corps. He survived to
fight again in the Second World War.
COURTESY OF ANNE MCKEACHIE

Two convalescents: Gunner Harry Cross *(left)* with an unknown companion.
VICTORIA HIGH SCHOOL ARCHIVES

Canadian soldiers march through the liberated streets of Mons, November 11, 1918.
SCOTT FAMILY

First World War medals: Military Medal with two bars, 1914–1915 Star, British War Medal 1914–1920, Victory Medal 1914–1919. TILSTON MEMORIAL COLLECTION, CANADIAN WAR MUSEUM CWM20040035-001

Canadian Expeditionary Forces (CEF) pin belonging to Harry Cross.
VICTORIA HIGH SCHOOL ARCHIVES

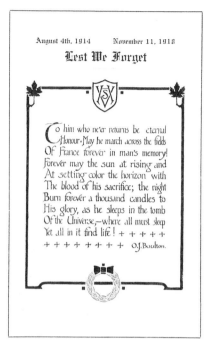

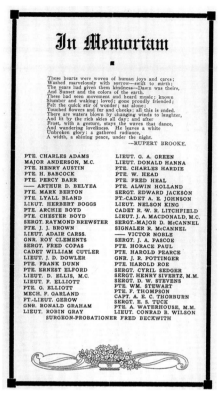

VHS Memorial Card sent to parents of boys who were killed or died while in service at the Front. VICTORIA HIGH SCHOOL ARCHIVES

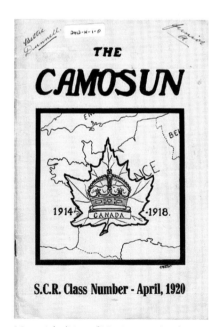

Memorial edition of *The Camosun*, April 1920.
VICTORIA HIGH SCHOOL ARCHIVES

*These hearts were woven of human joys and cares;*
*Washed marvelously with sorry—swift to mirth;*
*The years had given them kindness—Dawn was theirs,*
*And Sunset and the colors of the earth.*
*These had seen movement and heard music; known*
*Slumber and waking; loved; gone proudly friended;*
*Felt the quick stir of wonder; sat alone;*
*Touched flowers and fur and cheeks; all this is ended.*
*There are waters blown by changing winds to laughter,*
*And lit by the rich skies all day; and after*
*Frost, with a gesture, stays the waves that dance,*
*And wandering loveliness. He leaves a white*
*Unbroken glory: a gathered radiance,*
*A width, a shining peace, under the night.*

—RUPERT BROOKE

Memorial to the VHS Fallen in the December 1918 issue of *The Camosun*. The poet, Rupert Brooke, had visited Victoria in 1913.
VICTORIA HIGH SCHOOL ARCHIVES

The Roll of Honour bearing the names of 497 teachers and students who served in the War hangs today in the main foyer of the school. DESTRUBÉ PHOTOGRAPHY

A memorial service in 1920 featuring the nine-metre-high Banner of Honour and Sacrifice suspended from an upper window. VICTORIA HIGH SCHOOL ARCHIVES

The Banner is discovered in the school archives and displayed again for Remembrance Day 2011. Each hand-sewn maple leaf represents a Vic High teacher or student who served in the First World War. JOHN AZAR

The bronze Memorial Tablet listing the names of teachers and students who died in the War was cast during the 1920s by the school's art teacher, Earl W. Clarke. VICTORIA HIGH SCHOOL ARCHIVES

Signaller Harold Marshall Pearce
was the last of the VHS cohort to
die in the war, on November 5,
1918, age 19.
VICTORIA HIGH SCHOOL ARCHIVES

Gunner Ronald Graham *(left)* with brother
Stanley, also a gunner. Ronald died September 9,
1918, age 19. VICTORIA HIGH SCHOOL ARCHIVES

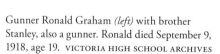

Sergeant Henry George Sivertz, died
September 29, 1918, age 25.
VICTORIA HIGH SCHOOL ARCHIVES

The Stained Glass
Wreaths of Victory and
Sacrifice. Ten of these
wreaths, designed by
Earl Clarke, were placed
in windows around the
school in the 1920s. They
provide a daily reminder
of the school's role in
the Great War.
ALAN MACLEOD

Plaque commemorating the Trees of Remembrance planted at the school in 1917.
ALAN MACLEOD

Rifle House Cemetery, Belgium. DAVID BOLER

Author Barry Gough at the grave of Lt. A. Nelson King, Rifle House Cemetery.
DAVID BOLER

Canadian National Vimy Memorial, France. WARREN SOMMER

Detail, Canadian Vimy Memorial. WARREN SOMMER

Private Price's headstone is one of many in this cemetery. But it is symbolic of the end of this war for Canada.

*Two days after* Private Price's death, somewhere in Belgium but near Mons, Matthew Scott, brother of Blayney and Gilling Scott, all of Victoria High School, wrote home:

My darling Mother,

The War is over at last. In the early morning of the Armistice our Division captured Mons—the place whose name is linked so affectionately in the hearts of the British nation, for it was here our "Contemptible" [the term was the Kaiser's in reference to the British Army] first came in contact with the Germans, and began their gallant retreat. It has fallen to the lot of the Canadians to retrieve the true foundation stone of the present mighty British Army, and we feel that it will be our great pride to always look back and remember the Canadians, and the Canadians alone, finished where the British Army first began.

Our reception by the Belgians in Mons was wonderful, and the Canadians will be remembered by the Belgians, as they are now by the French, with everlasting love and affection. As one old Belgian gentleman said, "You gallant Canadians, who never knew how to retreat, but always to advance."

Germany is beaten, and we are only beginning to realize now how really badly we have beaten her. One, however, cannot but respect her in many ways for the wonderful fight she put up before finally throwing up her hands for no matter what we say, she fought, until the very last, with a determination that was surprising and often made us wonder if we ever would be able to decisively beat her.

You must not expect me home soon, Mother. It will take months before we can ever hope to be demobilized and personally, I do not anticipate getting home for at least six months.

My fondest love to all,

Ever, Your affectionate Son,

"Matt"[38]

*Of all the* stories within the scope of this book, perhaps none exemplifies the trials, experiences, and sacrifice of the War more than the story of Blayney Scott. I relate it here because it seems to epitomize the whole long and gruelling episode of the War, at the same time showing the closeness of family, the brothers of that family at war, the ties binding the Front to that distant and far-away nest of civilization called Victoria, which had been irrevocably changed by the catastrophe that engulfed Europe in 1914 and spread to all quarters of the world.

Blayney Scott earned a rightful place in Canadian military annals because of his death-defying feat on the wing of an RAF airplane, high above the battlefield, bullets whistling round his head and body, and living to tell the tale. His military career was in every way outstanding, and the details reveal many harrowing escapes and several wounds suffered in combat—and decoration for gallantry in both the Canadian Army and the RAF.[39]

Blayney Edmund Scott was the son of Henry and Gertrude Scott, 1036 Craigdarroch Road, Victoria. The family was prominent in explosives manufacture, and during the War his father was active in what became Canadian Industries Ltd., with one of its plants on James Island, off Sidney.[40] Victoria-born Blayney, the eldest, had two brothers who also enlisted and served with bravery and distinction—Lieutenant Matthew Scott, who won the Military Cross in the time between Vimy Ridge and Passchendaele, and Sergeant Gilling Scott, in France with the 2nd Canadian Mounted Rifles. Here is another example of a family at war.

Blayney Scott had been an outstanding athlete: he was BC's middleweight boxing champion in 1913, was prominent in football and basketball, and was a noted sculler, the pride of the James Bay Athletic Association. A salesman, he enlisted as a trooper in the 2nd Canadian Mounted Rifles (along with his brother Gilling) and left Victoria with that regiment in 1915. He transferred to the Canadian Field Artillery. Trench mortars became his expertise—in essence, hurling shells at the enemy and then taking cover when the enemy returned fire. During the Battle of Hill 70, he volunteered to carry messages between the batteries and the rear when communication had been severed. To do this, he had to pass through three dense barrages. He won his commission for bravery in the field. Good fortune had attended him. He won the Military Cross at that time.

In 1917, now in his third year in combat, he decided to wage war in the air and was attached to the RFC as an observer and gunner, a trained expert in aerial artillery. He felt as easy up in the air as on land or on water. "This War is going to be won or lost in the Air," he wrote home.[41] "I was up at 4 a.m. this morning [May 9, 1918] doing a 3 hour reconnaissance over our front—everything was quiet and not a Hun in sight . . . Flying would be so the most wonderful sport in this world if it wasn't for the fact that you have to be forever screwing your neck off, looking for Huns and dodging 'Archies' [enemy gunfire from the ground] etc."[42] He was injured several times in crashes.

As if that was not enough, he got influenza the next month, but happily survived. At a Canadian Divisional sports meeting in late June he ran into Sir Arthur Currie, by now a famed general. The event reminded him of delightful fair days at the Exhibition in Oak Bay. Currie looked very well, Blayney related to his mother on June 26, 1918, and was seen patting everyone on the back. "He certainly knows what the troops like and how to give them a good time, such as they deserve when they come out of the line. We had a big feed of strawberries and cream (condensed) that night in the Battalion Mess and I must say I forgot completely all about ever having influenza."[43] Here we have another indication of Currie's respect for the soldiers, his concern for their well-being, and his appreciation of the importance of keeping up their spirits during the darkest of days.

Early in the morning of July 5, 1918, the plane in which Blayney Scott was flying (piloted by Lieutenant Duncan Campbell Dunlop) went through what their commanding officer, Lieutenant-Colonel A.S. Barrett, 2nd Wing, RAF, described admirably in fine English understatement as their "extraordinarily stout effort this morning." And what had transpired? The nature of the work was anti-battery attack—low-level flying so as to fire on the enemy's field batteries. At 1,500 feet, an aircraft would fly several miles behind enemy lines, do its lethal work, then return. During the hazardous mission in question, Blayney fired 200 rounds at horse-drawn transport with much effect. However, in the midst of this operation, the petrol tank on the wing was hit by a piece of shrapnel. Petrol streamed out, and Blayney, realizing the imminent danger, swung himself out of his seat, crawled along the wing, and stuffed a handkerchief into the hole. The petrol continued to stream out. He returned to the cockpit, stripped a piece of tin from the joystick, and with this and a piece of cloth torn from his cap, he blocked the leak.

Throughout all this time, he was under heavy attack from the ground, machine-gun bullets and anti-aircraft battery fire trying to bring down the plane. The pilot carried on with his mission. But the plane crashed behind British lines. For this act of gallantry, Blayney Scott, already winner of the Military Cross, was awarded the Distinguished Flying Cross—a rare double. But the episode had come at great cost to Blayney.

In returning to his seat, he was thrown into the cockpit and hit heavily against the joystick. He was invalided, recovered, and flew again, but on another occasion crashed and was severely wounded. The damage to his chest and heart from the first crash could not be mended.

Blayney Scott returned to Victoria wracked with injuries. He died November 9, 1919. "Throughout his illness," wrote the newspaper in San Jose, California (where he had family), "his infectious humour and happy buoyant spirit never left him. He was a model athlete, of splendid physique, in football, rowing, and boxing, he carried off many honours. In his death, Canada loses a gallant young officer and an athlete of unusual merit."

Then came the day of his funeral. The *Victoria Colonist* described the cortege. The gun carriage bearing his body to the last resting place in Ross Bay Cemetery was accompanied on its sad journey by a lone aircraft piloted by Lieutenant Harry Brown, MC, with Lieutenant Gordon Campbell as passenger. At a height of fifty feet above the gun carriage, Campbell released a wreath, which despite the wind blowing, fell within a few feet of its mark. It was placed on the gun carriage for the remainder of the journey. The funeral was attended by a large number of Scott's friends, including comrades from the 2nd Canadian Mounted Rifles, Canadian Field Artillery, and the Royal Air Force. The floral tributes were magnificent. The pallbearers were fellow Masons. Among the honorary pallbearers were many school chums. A memorial cot was dedicated at the Royal Jubilee Hospital, where Scott had died after being six weeks in bed, and on it was mounted a brass plate with the inscription IN MEMORY OF LT BLAYNEY SCOTT, MC, DSC, WHO SERVED WITH 2ND CMR, CFA AND RAF, NOV 9, 1919 "WELL DONE BLAYNEY."

Much has been written about Blayney, for he is an attractive figure on the stage of history. Equally significant in the outcome of the War, and equally part of the greatest generation, were his two brothers, Matthew Henry Scott, a captain in the infantry and later an officer in the Canadian Field Artillery in France. He was in all respects a lovely fellow, though much less charismatic than

Blayney. At one time or another he suffered minor injuries—a broken nose, loss of hearing for a time, a slight wound in October 1918—but escaped death. He was in on the preliminary bombardment at Vimy. In chemical engineering at University of California, Berkeley, when the call to the flag reached him, he returned to Victoria to join the 5th BC Regiment of Garrison Artillery, RCA.

The third son, William Gilling Scott, had joined the 2nd Canadian Mounted Rifles, which we note here was a mounted regiment raised mainly in Victoria, expecting that the cavalry would be the thing in the War. But once in England they found they were not needed, and accordingly Gilling volunteered to go into the infantry and the trenches. He was wounded twice, became a staff sergeant in the Canadian Pay Records Office in London for two years, then went back to the Front and was again wounded, taking a bullet in his left arm. He became a lieutenant after the War. In France he met Myfanwy Davies, an accomplished pianist, who after the War came to Canada as a nanny on Campbell Ranch, Alberta, and married Gilling. From this union came four children, Blayney, Megan, Ross, and Stephanie. While researching the papers of the Scott boys at war, I discovered what no one has ever seen or appreciated in our own time: the Victoria High School Entrance Certificate for William Gilling Scott, South Park School, dated July 20, 1910. At the risk of repetition, I note here that admission to Victoria High School was then by successful completion of an entrance examination, which Gilling had achieved.

We leave the story of Blayney, Matthew, and Gilling Scott with some regret, for there is much more to say—as there is of so many who fought for King and Country in this war. Their sacrifices and their martial toughness inspire us yet, even though a century has passed since they came forward without question to answer the call to duty and sacrifice. Theirs was a unique time in our history, and we look back on their experiences with some wonder, pondering whether such a thing could possibly be done again.

*chapter 6*

---

## ARMISTICE AND PEACE

*T*he doors of Victoria High School were bolted shut in the days running up to the signing of the Armistice. In fact, the very day the longed-for peace arrived, no observance of the Armistice could be held at the school: the dreaded appearance of Spanish influenza in October had obliged local health and civic officials to close public schools and other institutions. All sports were suspended. The flu had begun in the Near East, swept across Europe, killed 150,000 in Britain, and arrived in North America.

In Victoria and on Vancouver Island, medical officers took prompt action; they had had some considerable experience in dealing with diseases from faraway lands and were experts in the technique of quarantine. By their action, Vancouver Island was isolated. In addition, the civilian population proved cooperative. The mortality rates show the wisdom of strong and swift actions: in Victoria, 3.6 percent; in Vancouver, 10 percent. All the same, the flu struck irrespective of class. No known deaths were recorded of persons working at, or students attending, Victoria High School.[1] Near Victoria, in Sooke, an outbreak led to a call for nursing staff, which was answered, to deal with the medical crisis. As an early historian of this subject wrote, "The dual impact of war and epidemic rested heavily on a generation of child-bearing age. In Victoria, as elsewhere, families were broken or orphaned by the loss of parents.

In addressing these and other needs, women's organizations contributed unstintingly. They organized volunteer girls, nurses, clothing and food, soup kitchens and an endless host of supportive functions."[2]

On Armistice Day 1918, the *Daily Colonist* called on its readers to show "thankful appreciation of the noble work that has been done by Canada's sons, in keeping you in business, your country intact and undisturbed . . . Is it not your duty to think of the gallant lads, now resting in Flanders Fields, who will not return? . . . They have died to save you from the iron grip of the enemy. Peace brings rejoicing—but sorrow is brought in its wake—and more than ever the loss of a father, a son, or a brother encircles the happy, unbroken home of four years ago."

Meanwhile, *The Camosun* staff, forbidden to congregate by health regulations, continued their work. They joked that they were *en vacance*, but in spite of difficulties, they turned out an edition of the magazine.

The next month, the school principal, Herbert H. Smith, recalled, "During the period preceding the Armistice, the uppermost thought in our minds was an intense longing for peace, that the horrors of War, which so rudely and cruelly touched nearly every home throughout our own great empire, as well as those of our allies and enemies, might cease. With almost dramatic suddenness our wish was gratified."[3]

Principal Smith and many of the staff and students were aware that many great problems would occur after "so great a world convulsion." Few, he said, "had any conception of the tasks that were to be laid upon us in the succeeding period of re-adjustment." The necessity of several groups or nations getting together in the interests of peace was essential. A new prospect presented itself: a conference assembled in Washington, DC, made possible by the spirit of international cooperation. "As a school," Mr. Smith said, "we need to interject something of this same spirit into our life, for without it we shall fail to fulfill our highest resolves, and with a generous measure of it we shall overcome all difficulties, gain happiness, and mount to heights of which we had not even dreamed." Principal Smith had seen the human ravages that beset the school—student enlistments and deaths; unimaginable sorrows to family and friends; former students who returned maimed, blind, or gassed; the countless costs of war. His message was to the students of the post-war era:

> Those students, who in the Great War made the supreme sacrifice
> for their country, have pointed out the way to us. We, too, may serve

though in a different way, for it is within the reach of all to make a real contribution to the life of our school. Let each one of us, therefore, regardless of the group with which he is most intimately associated, search his own soul to discover the best means not of gratifying some purely selfish end, but of rendering to the whole student body a service that will abide forever."[4]

For years thereafter at Victoria High School, November 11 was commemorated as Armistice Day; it is now called Remembrance Day.[5]


*There was much* talk of "making the world safe for democracy" and bringing an end to war for all time. The diplomats gathered in Paris to discuss the terms of peace and the intended treaties. President Woodrow Wilson had proposed Fourteen Points. Upon these he hoped the Allies would build a peace once the War was won. Europe lay in chaos. The German Empire's collapse had brought down two other empires—the Ottoman and the Hapsburg Empire of Austria-Hungary. Russia had collapsed in revolution in 1917. A reordering of the Middle East occurred. German colonies in the western Pacific, Africa, and East Asia passed into other hands. The German fleet sailed into lonely and inactive internment at Scapa Flow, and some months later the German naval officers and men took matters into their own hands and scuttled most of the ships. The fleet that had caused so much trouble and anxiety was no more.

The terms of the Peace of Versailles were effective January 10, 1920. That treaty obliged Germany to accept the "war guilt clause." Germany would pay reparations. "Germany was not guiltless but it could hardly be said that Germany alone was guilty,"[6] wrote noted commentator Arnold Toynbee, shortly after the event, and German statesmen denied the responsibility assigned and called for a review. But Britain and France had borne the brunt of the fighting. David Lloyd George upheld the war guilt clause. So did Woodrow Wilson. Georges Clemenceau, who headed France's delegation, insisted that Germany must be punished.

Germany had been obliged to sign the terms of the Armistice and then to accept the war guilt clause. The horrors of what the German Army had committed in Belgium were not forgotten, nor was its trampling on the liberties of people of Belgium and Luxembourg. The victorious powers called for financial reimbursement for damages suffered. The world had been reordered. But could peace be kept up?

*chapter 7*

## THE RECKONING

*T*hree teachers and eighty-three students of Victoria High School died on the fields of France and Flanders in the Great War. Many others came home diseased, maimed, crippled, or victims of battle exhaustion, shell shock, and other psychological challenges. Female students served in nursing units. The school took pride in its eleven Military Crosses and seven Military Medals. Yet it mourned, from the very first casualty, the loss of the flower of this generation. The war memorials in the school entry hall, and the photographs of the Fallen in the School Archives, tell of heroic and unselfish sacrifice for the cause of Canada, the British Empire, and the Allies with whom they fought against Imperial Germany and the Central Powers.

The Roll of Honour of Victoria High School is the beginning point for anyone tracing the life of any one of the nearly five hundred names listed there. It is the only collective remembrance of all who served, a remarkable testament to dedication and sacrifice. It was the first of the school's memorials. Across the top are painted the flags of the Allied nations. In the middle is the famous etching by the famed English cartoonist Sir John Bernard Partridge, showing a soldier returning home from the perils of battle. Handwritten on the great field surrounding the etching are the names of those persons known to have been connected to Victoria High School who served in the War. The Roll, done in stages, was the work of the matriculation classes of 1917 and 1918, and was likely designed and inspired by Earl Clarke, the art teacher. First names are not given, only initials, and it seems likely that several inaccuracies have crept in. In checking the names of nurses, I have found there are many who, sadly, cannot be traced with thoroughness, while some known to have been connected with the school, including Jessie Nelson King, are not included.

*In all, about* 628,000 Canadians served in the armed forces. This was a very high proportion of Canada's small population. The total cost in human lives from all forces of the British Empire, including Canada and Newfoundland, Australia, New Zealand, India, and other states, was over one million dead, including those killed in action, died of wounds, or listed as missing. Of these, the Navy accounted for 33,361; the Royal Flying Corps and Royal Air Force 6,166. In all British forces, there was a total of 2,289,860 wounded (including 6,405 in the Navy and 10,457 in the RFC and RAF). The loss of life in merchant vessels and fishing fleets was more than 15,000. The number of civilians of the empire who lost their lives because of enemy bombardment or aerial strikes cannot be calculated. The French lost slightly more combatants. German figures on rolls of honour amount to two million but four million is likely more accurate. Australian casualties—killed, wounded, or made prisoner—reach over 60,000. The United States lost 250,000 killed or wounded.[1]

British Empire enlistment figures represented ethnic or racial realities. In the United Kingdom, the Scots joined up in the highest percentage, and the Irish the lowest, particularly after the troubles in 1916. The Australians never invoked conscription and, like the Scots, were eager in the line of duty. New Zealand, South Africa, and Newfoundland came forward strongly. But the Canadians sent the largest numbers of soldiers of all the dominions; though only 5 percent of these were French-speaking Canadians, despite the fact that they accounted for 40 percent of the population. In other words, French Canada, principally Quebec, accounted for 30,000 of the 641,000 from the dominion.[2]

How many Canadians died in military service in the First World War? The tally, based on Imperial War Museum statistics, is 64,665, of whom 19,507 are missing and have no known grave. Canada's Department of Veterans Affairs puts the figure at 66,000, though one would think they would have a more specific number.[3] What about the other dominions that now form the Commonwealth? Australia's dead number 61,860 (23,397 missing); undivided India 72,407 (64,518 missing); New Zealand 18,148 (6,299 missing), and South Africa 9,297 (2,815 missing).[4] Newfoundland's dead total is 1,570. And the bigger picture: casualties from the United Kingdom and British colonies totalled 888,367, including 412,991 missing. The grand total for all British and Commonwealth Great War dead is 1,114,744.

Figures for British, dominion, and colonial deaths are for those dying between August 4, 1914, and August 31, 1921, the date used by the Commonwealth War Graves Commission as a cut-off point for military personnel whose deaths from injuries are counted as First World War fatalities.[5] Sadly, many veterans of that war who were injured in action (including some from Victoria High School) and died shortly after the cut-off date are excluded from war memorials that give individual names. Such arbitrary exclusion has brought anguish to many a family contending that their deceased loved one deserved better.

Canadian historians and readers naturally look at the Canadian figures, which are alarming and profound. But they do not stand alone, for the First World War was fought by Canada as part of a grand imperial alliance. It was the British Army that took the lion's share of the casualties. All the same, the British imperial effort could not have ended in victory without the contributions of the dominions. The Canadian and Australian efforts during the Hundred Days are proof of that. Against considerable odds, unity of the British and imperial command was upheld but it would not last in the years after the Peace.

However, given that this book is about a Canadian high school, let us look again at the Canadian figures. No statistical report can do justice to the costs the peoples of Canada paid in blood and treasure. Many books have been written about the impact of the War on Canadians and their society. But few Canadians realize the exact scope or extent of the nation's military involvement. Gary Mitchell, archivist of the Province of British Columbia, and an expert on the history of the CEF, puts the remarkable story in these chilling words:

> With a population of over seven million and a peacetime military establishment of 74,213 personnel, the enrollment for military service

from 1914 to 1919 was 619,636 Canadians into the Canadian Expeditionary Force. Canadian Naval enlistments numbered about 10,000 but their service was in the Royal Navy and not as a separate naval force. The Royal Air Corps had a Canadian contingent of roughly 24,000. During the period of hostilities, 232,494 Canadians were listed as casualties, of whom over 60,000 died. Of the surviving veterans, 91,521 were classified as invalided and on military pensions at the end of 1919. Vocational school training programs had enrollments of over 20,000 veterans by end of 1919.[6]

He concludes, with undeniable clarity:

Overall, eight percent of all Canadian males enlisted, of whom one of every four was wounded and one of every ten died in military service. The sheer number of deaths and casualties had an influence on Canadian society without precedent in our history.[7]

*The War was* a great misfortune for Canada. The high immigration of the pre-war years was checked by the conflict. Canada could ill afford the men lost in battle or through other misfortune during the war. The national debt quadrupled in the four years. Income tax was introduced as a temporary measure. The conscription crisis of 1917–1918 strained the relations between the two European founding peoples. Against this stood the increase in national wealth and industrial development, and stimulus to the national spirit.

Many of the men who answered the call to arms (or were conscripted) were recent schoolboys. Back home in Victoria, or in many another Canadian town, stories of their prowess "came to our ears like some romance of other centuries." These were the words of an Australian, writing of similar experiences, who noted that, from a distance away from the fighting, the whole was hard to comprehend. News, reports from the Front, and photographs of "bayonets and bombs and shrapnel and trenches; barbed wire, night raids, shrieking shells; wild charges, sniping, dugouts, balloons, aeroplanes, tanks, spies" created a world of make-believe.[8]

How long would the memories last? Was this a fading vision of a world that we would prefer to forget? Or would Canadians realize that Vimy was perhaps Canada's greatest day?[9] The Australian asks, and the Canadian could do likewise: "Can they visualize what it all meant—the columns of marching men who, in the first flush of adventurous youth or from manly conviction, went out to that first baptism in a battle of giants—the remnants of war wreckage with us still, cripples in war hospitals and hostels . . . ?"[10]

The War gave to Victoria a host of grieving mothers, aunts, and sisters. It created an army of spinsters. In Victoria, hundreds of young women who had said goodbye to their sweethearts when they went overseas felt the heartbreak of loss, abandonment, and ruined hopes. These were the women who taught a couple of generations of British Columbia schoolchildren. They turned their attention to the classroom. Trained in the arts of teaching in the Normal School, they took their place as protectors of the memory of Canada's fallen ones. The Hazel Sargents and Jessica Roberts of this world, who had passed through Victoria's schools and then became highly educated and demanding teachers in Victoria High School, nurtured Canadian values of the new age, values based on British Empire traditions in the circumstances of the New World.

Many boys whose fathers suffered death or wounds or psychic damage paid the terrible costs of the War. Many grew up without a good role model at home. Male students at the school who did not go to war, primarily because they were too young to enlist, became ardent nationalists in these formative years of Canada's growing self-awareness. Some became diligent pacifists, others workers for Varsity Christian Fellowship. The students of the school who came under their tutelage not only had the powerful benefit of the old matriculation class development that Arthur Yates and others had nurtured: they also had a self-confident realization that this institution, which had been at the forefront of secondary level and even collegiate or junior college development, was very much a Canadian achievement forged by war.

Those of us who were of the next generation, the sons and daughters of this grey generation who believed in the Covenant of the League of Nations, grew up in an age of Canadian self-awareness. We took for granted that Canada had been central to the evolution of the Commonwealth of Nations. War, oddly, had given us the strength of nationhood. The costs had been enormous. They would never be forgotten as long as our teachers kept alive their own experiences of tragedy and loss. The First World War had been a tragic and unnecessary conflict. No teacher would proclaim it a heroic act without also counting its cost.

Over the years and months, the veterans returned from their various fields of engagement. They arrived, usually in clusters of six or seven, taking passage on the night or day steamer from Vancouver. A club room was set up for them in the 600-block of Fort Street, looked after by a veterans' association. Many men had become old before their time, world travellers to a nether world that few in the sanctuary of Victoria could understand. They returned home to a changed world. They were wheeled up the gangway and ramps at the CPR wharfs, or arrived on crutches, or limped along as best they could on two feet. Others walked without difficulty, some with eye patches, others skin grafts. Some were missing fingers, arms, or legs. Others were blinded or had lost their hearing. Some had glazed eyes or vacant faces. Some were "shell-shocks." Misfortune had come to ever so many. No cameraman recorded the scene. No reporter described it. You won't find photographs of them in the local papers. Even in group photographs of soldier patients at military hospitals, the best face is put on the rest and revival of those who at one time or another had been in the inferno or near to it.

Ypres, the Somme, Passchendaele, Amiens, and Mons were now far away, and so were the graves of many a dear comrade in arms. They had all been thrown together by the strange circumstances of this war. Did they count themselves lucky to be returning home? And how would they be received when so much had changed? How could their loved ones at home understand the horrors of the sounds and topography of the Armageddon they had somehow survived?

Harry Cross, whom we have already met, had been gassed by shell at Passchendaele while heroically warning a party of men who were in grave danger. This happened in the very last month of that dreadful campaign. Cross convalesced in an English military hospital until he could be shipped home. He had been remembered at the school as one of its most prominent debaters and an energetic supporter of *The Camosun*. For his part, in his travels the school was never far from his thoughts, and upon his return to Victoria he wrote for the magazine a powerful reflection that was published in its November 1918 issue:

> It is with gratification, tinged with the quieter feelings of reflection, that in these few words I renew my old acquaintance with the pages of The Camosun. The associations of the school, its life and activity, which

are brought to mind, are many and varied, but all very pleasurable. Where are all the participants in that old life now?

There are scores of those once the most prominent in school circles who are now playing the greater game of war with as fine a spirit as they ever contested the fortunes of the playing field in their student days. They are to be found in every branch of the service, and in every conceivable position, but it is for the same great cause they all fight. The Air Force has appealed to many of our adventurous spirits; the Navy has its adherents; but the Army seems to have had the greatest claim of all. A few of them had the pleasure of meeting while in England and France. Chance encounters they were, but very memorable ones for all that. Fit, healthy, keen, intelligent—there wasn't one who didn't measure up to the topmost mark of fighting efficiency.

Some, who unfortunately fell victims to bullet, shrapnel, or gas, already have returned from overseas after varying periods of life in hospital. The feeling that bulks most largely with these is the very keen appreciation of the beauty and sacredness of that word, "home."

Still others, sad to say, are sleeping their last in Flanders' fields. Such is the price we pay for victory. They have gone forth willingly to meet grim Death. "Greater love hath no man than this, that a man lay down his life for his friends."

When Cross wrote this, the War was not over, and he closed his letter with a powerful appeal to continue the struggle:

> Will you not prove worthy of their great sacrifice? Now that the great drama in France is drawing fast to its close—peace may even at this moment be an actuality—the world's whole system must be reconstructed. We shall face problems as difficult as any of those of war. Duty, in a different guise, calls again. Are you prepared?

We conclude Harry Cross's story by noting that back in Victoria, he was sent to the convalescent home Resthaven in Sidney, BC. Upon release, he entered the provincial Normal School and qualified as a teacher. He taught for a brief time at North Ward School in Victoria, but his brilliant career in that line of work came to an end. He never fully regained his health after the gassing. He died in hospital January 30, 1922. He had a full military funeral with cortege leading to Ross Bay Cemetery, where burial took place in the family plot. His headstone bears this fitting inscription from Thomas Campbell's "Hallowed Ground": TO LIVE IN HEARTS WE LEAVE BEHIND IS NOT TO DIE.[11]


*"Not all the* heroes of the Great War sleep across the seas," said the school's tribute, its *In Memoriam*, for Harry Cross and for St. Domenic "Dono" Macnaughton Heyland. Heyland had died in Victoria on January 18, 1922. Some had fallen in battle, others had come home maimed and wounded, and still others were wholly unscathed. Some returned broken in body or mind. They returned to the places of their happy youth, with all its memories. Cross and Heyland were two such. Cross was one of the most promising scholars, noted in debating and literary circles. Heyland, a talented student, had distinguished himself as an athlete and rugby player at the school and in the city. They had joined up as soon as they could, but they had paid the price for heroic deeds, for lingering illness had come upon them. Again from their *In Memoriam*: "With the strange waywardness of Fate, the two lads died within a few days of each other. But when a memorial comes to be erected to the honor of those of this school who poured out their blood as an offering, some fairer block of the marble, some more imperishable bit of the bronze, will alone be worthy to enshrine their names and memory. May the example of their devotion and exalted heroism never perish from the lives of all those who come after them."[12]

Now, in a unique way, the school played its part: from September 1919 to April 1920, it mounted a program of studies under the auspices of the Soldiers' Civil Re-establishment Department, a branch of the department of defence. The program was directed by the school principal, with seven staff members.[13] Among the teachers was C.M. Haverstock, a gunner who had gone overseas in 1917 and was now returning to his old post at the school after action in France. Another was Emsley Yeo, old boy of the school, basketball player, and *Camosun* staff member, another gunner, and now the newest addition to the teaching staff. Another new appointment to the school staff was T.S. Whittemore, former instructor in the Royal Navy, who on arrival at the school re-established the Victoria High School Orchestra: "Every school of any standing has its orchestra," said *The Camosun,* with undeniable truth.

The national government set up various schemes under the Soldiers' Civil Re-establishment (or the SCR, as it became known), which had as its focus academic preparation for more advanced education and professional development for the students. The VHS class included a number of former students who, after a long absence and thousands of miles of travel, now found themselves back in the hallowed halls at Fernwood and Grant Streets, taking part on the football field and in debates: class president Robert J. Renouf, who had gone overseas with the 2nd Canadian Mounted Rifles and was attached to the Signals Corps; class vice-president J.C. Foote, also a Victoria boy, who was in the 5th Division Signals; Cecil J. Clayton, the famed naval air service pilot described earlier; Albert R. Emsley, who had received his education in Victoria and had served with the 143rd Battalion; Clifford Duncan Reid, who had served in France with the Canadian Army Medical Corps; William Horace Ryan, who had been in France with the Canadian Field Artillery. Many of the others had connections with Vancouver Island, but there was a sprinkling of participants, English and Scots in origin, who had been assigned to the class, having been wounded in action and now happily under rehabilitation. Their photos, taken by famed local photographer Gibson, show each and every one of them to be well turned out and sharp-looking. There they are in their white shirts and dark ties, in suits, hair nicely cut, and altogether well groomed. The horrors of war in Belgium and France lay behind them now.

The scheme at the school was wound up in the spring of 1920. We know so little of what happened to them in later years, except for one or two. The SCR also set up a military hospital, housed at Craigdarroch Castle, for those who had been badly wounded. A number of hospitals were established in the Victoria area, which was regarded as an excellent place for rehabilitation. At the end of October 1918, Victoria had eight military hospitals, with bed capacity of 1,545, the second largest in Canada. Among the hospitals in Military District No. 11 (headquarters Victoria) were convalescent homes at Esquimalt, Resthaven, and Qualicum. These were in addition to the Military Station Hospital, Esquimalt, and Irving House Hospital, Victoria.[14]

*The battle-hardened soldier* might well return as a hero, then face the terrible tragedies of everyday life. Such was the case for Victoria-born Private Herbert William Lacoursiere. During his years at the school, his family had lived on Gladstone Street. His father was a contractor. Herbert had been a member of the school Cadet Battalion for three years. Then, as soon as he could, in his eighteenth year, he enlisted in the CEF on December 13, 1915. By occupation a stenographer, he may well have been employed by the gunsmiths Pichon & Lenfesty, to whom he sent a letter in 1917, reported in the *Daily Colonist*, about conditions in England. He became a runner—that is, a despatch rider—in the 29th Battalion.

He returned home on May 25, 1919, a hero, with three service medals. He had dodged every bullet, shell, and piece of shrapnel that had been fired his way. At a later date, he was doing carpentry work with two brothers at a house on Old West Saanich Road, near Mount Newton. It was here that tragedy struck at year's end in 1923. Herbert had been awakened by a fire in the house. Of a fearless disposition, and knowing that his older brother, Stephen, was still in the house, he went into the flaming building to haul him out. He did so successfully, though in this heroic effort suffered severe burns. First the brother died, then Herbert. They are buried in the graveyard of Our Lady of the Assumption Church, just north of Brentwood. A younger brother, also burned, survived. The service for Private Lacoursiere was well attended by a grieving community, and the customary military funeral was arranged. Representatives of various soldiers' associations were in attendance. Three rifle volleys were fired over the grave. A bugler sounded the Last Post.[15] Courageous in war, he had also been courageous in peacetime, risking his life for others.

Heroes' welcomes were hard to come by in Canada, for the nation had no traditions of heroes and shied away from hero-worship. General Sir Arthur Currie, the made-in-Victoria soldier who had risen to command the Canadian Corps, who had kept the four Canadian Divisions together, who had worked strenuously, against odds, to make sure Canadian soldiers were not unnecessarily sacrificed, and who had taken the German surrender at Mons, arrived back in Canada in August 1919. No welcoming parties, no flags, no bands greeted him. He returned to a sullen nation. But the ministers of government, the mayors and councils, the veterans' associations, and the old soldiers knew the importance of his return and what he had done as the personification of Canada's success in war. The politicians were wary of soldiers, slow to embrace the moment. They had no idea how to welcome home a real hero, a victor in a "foreign war." Already, an ill-founded campaign was underway impugning his integrity, a campaign viciously launched by the mentally unstable and scheming former minister of militia, Colonel Sam Hughes, who had been bounced from his job by the prime minister. The successful legal action Currie ultimately brought in his own defence necessarily placed him under a cloud for some considerable time.

But, as is often the case when Canadians of prominence are treated shabbily within the nation, he was highly decorated abroad. He was awarded the Knight Grand Cross of the Order of St. Michael and St. George, conferred by King George V in the old ruined town of Albert, France. The French awarded him the Croix de Guerre avec palmes. The Belgians conferred the Grand Officer de l'Ordre de la Couronne and Belgium's Croix de Guerre. A grateful United Kingdom government awarded him the Knight Commander of the Bath. He received the United States Distinguished Service Medal. The University of Cambridge awarded him the honorary degree of LLD. He was appointed McGill University's principal and vice-chancellor and remained in that position until his death in Montreal in 1933.[16] British prime minister David Lloyd George called Currie a "brilliant military commander," which indeed he was, having steered the Canadian Corps through its last sweeping Hundred Days. But, strange to say, empire had gone quickly out of fashion in Canada, and Mackenzie King and the Liberals who came on to dominate the age were not only opposed to imperial and foreign military and national decorations, but were also anxious to return Canada to a fireproof house, free from the searing flames of European nationalisms and ideologies. Somehow, out of the ashes of it all, a tribute had to be raised to the fallen and missing Canadian soldiers, and this brings us to the story of the Canadian National Vimy Memorial, an example of the alchemy of nation building, and a good one at that.

# chapter 8

# MONUMENTS OF VALOUR

A s early as 1917, the Victoria High School art teacher, Earl W. Clarke, a sculptor and an expert in design, began to conceive and execute memorials of sacrifice and endeavour. The school's motto was not his creation, though various VHS logos can be said to bear his imprint. Clarke had been born in Woodstock, Ontario. He came to Victoria in the 1890s and was a star student at the school—and its class valedictorian upon graduation. The talented Clarke, small in stature and reticent by nature, attended McMaster University, taking a degree in arts in 1908, and on his return to Victoria settled in at Victoria High School for a thirty-seven-year teaching stint that ended only with his retirement in 1945. "Bunny "Clarke, as he was affectionately known, seems to have joined the teaching staff in 1916. He and his wife, Ella, lived in an Arts and Crafts house he had designed at 1461 Pembroke Street, Fernwood district, now a heritage treasure. A student of Clarke's recalled that he put great emphasis on balance, colour, and proportion, and the relationships between and among them.

He became familiar with the classical motifs so popular in British and French sculpture of the age, a form of classical revival in an age otherwise dominated by Gothic architecture. The fourth building to house Victoria High School had been designed in Beaux Arts style, and the classical motifs

Clarke had in mind for his memorial projects were suitable to this style. His genius found full vent in the design and execution of the three great legacies, which we take chronologically by date of creation: the Great War Banner of Honour and Sacrifice, the Memorial Tablet, and the Stained Glass of Victory and Sacrifice. The Roll of Honour, which is the oldest of all these First World War memorials, probably bears his imprint as well. It was "Presented by the Matriculation Classes of 1916–17 and 1917–18."

The Great War Banner of Honour and Sacrifice, which dates from spring 1920, is made of linen flag cloth in red, white, and blue. This striking banner is purposely designed to hang from a window of the upper floor of the school on the east side, facing Fernwood Street, and above the field, sometimes called the grass hockey pitch, that served as the school's civic field and perhaps from time to time as a parade ground for the Victoria High School cadets.

The Great War Banner of Honour and Sacrifice measures 10 feet 6 inches wide by 30 feet tall. The main field is white, with a red border. Along the top side of the red border are ranged seven large white maple leaves, one each for the seven nursing sisters known to be connected with the school. Below these are the teachers or, as they were known at the time, the masters. They are represented in the uppermost portion of the field of white by nine large maple leaves, six in blue and three in red. Three blue leaves are in the top row, the three in red in the middle row, and the other three in blue on the bottom. The red ones memorialize the three teachers who were casualties of the War. We can see that those who survived the War still flank their fallen colleagues and, in effect, hold them in their embrace. The arrangement shows corporate unity.

Beneath the leaves commemorating the teachers are the maple leaves of the students, or, more correctly, members of the student body at one time connected to the school, some having been students before the War began. There are, by careful count, 53 red maple leaves and 397 white maple leaves. The 53 red maple leaves connote the casualties of War known to the date of the banner's hanging. The 397 white maple leaves are those who were not killed in the War.

A closer look reveals the 53 red maple leaves are arranged in the shape of an elongated shield. They are thus disposed in a similar fashion to the plaque of honour or shield on the Memorial Tablet, where their names are listed.

Thus we have the following totals of maple leaves: 7 for the nursing students, all female; 9 for the teachers, 3 of whom were casualties of the War; and 450 for the students, 53 of whom were casualties of the War and did not return. The grand total of maple leaves, each representing an individual connected to the school, is 466. It should be noted that these are the known and recorded ones. There are bound to be some unaccounted for, lost to history. For instance, it is impossible to know how many young male students entered the Royal Navy or the Royal Canadian Navy, or otherwise joined military units before the War and served for King and Country.

Clarke now turned his prodigious talents to another memorial, one in keeping with the general tendency of the age to provide something permanent in cast bronze. The names of the Fallen needed to be given. Then as now, a bronze memorial was an expensive proposition; such memorials depended on public subscription. (Even the cenotaph in Victoria, erected in 1924, was made possible only by public subscription.) In the circumstances, funds for the school Memorial Tablet had to be raised from the staff, students, alumni, and citizens. And what sort of design should be selected? The tendency of the age was to give an indication of sacrifice, quiet remembrance, and grief—all brought together in a Greek classical style.

Clarke's selection of a female figure to demonstrate motherhood and sisterhood, and the strong maternal characteristics of the age, was entirely in keeping with the times—and, more, the message. The woman symbolizes grief. She holds in her right hand a spray of flowers and supports with her left a shield. On the shield are embossed the names, over fourscore, of those who laid down their lives for their country, along with lines from Rupert Brooke's poem "The Dead."

*These laid the world away,*
*Poured out the red, sweet wine of Youth*
*That the world might be free.*

"The sacrifice of those students who perished during those four years of tragedy is commemorated in a significantly beautiful tablet," noted the April 1927 issue of *The Camosun*. And a sensitive and observant student, James A. Gibson, later a Rhodes Scholar, founding president of Brock University, and recipient of the Order of Canada, remarked that in its simplicity lay its beautiful significance. In an essay, "The Spirit Liveth," with the subtitle "To you from failing hands we throw the torch," from McCrae's "In Flanders Fields," Gibson recounted the unveiling ceremony, which occurred on Armistice Day 1925, giving us a unique student perspective and forging another link in the chain of traditions of the school.[1] He wrote, expressively:

> For the moment, [the Tablet] was enfolded, or draped, by a Union Jack. All the students had filed into the Auditorium. A large space had been reserved in the centre for the relatives and friends of the departed heroes. Expectation was in the air tempered by solemnity and sadness. The sound of bugles announced the arrival of the Lieutenant Governor, the Hon. Walter C. Nichol, who took up his place on the platform. With him were George Jay, chairman for the event, Principal H.H. Smith, the Bishop of Columbia, Schofield, Earl Clarke, and members of the faculty who had served overseas. Members of the School Board and officials of the Department of Education were there too. The program opened with the singing of the National anthem, followed by the hearty singing of "O God, Our Help in Ages Past." The Lord's Prayer was led by Reverend Bishop Schofield, after which two minutes of reverent silence was paid as a tribute to the fallen heroes. After the expiration of the time of silence, the Lieutenant Governor set forth, in a few words, how his task although a pleasure to perform, had also a measure of deep sadness. He expressed the wish that none of the young men present would be called upon to make so great a sacrifice. The Lieutenant Governor then passed out of the auditorium to unveil the memorial, and as the folds of the Union Jack were drawn aside, the notes of the "Last Post" resounded through the hall. Representatives of various organizations placed wreaths at the base of the memorial.[2]

The Memorial Tablet, a creation for the ages, remains for the school and all who pass by the centrepiece of sacrifice, grief, and memory of the Great War. We see in it, in miniature, many of the then-current expressions of art and beauty that are to be found on the Vimy Memorial in France, including the maple leaves, already adopted as a national symbol by that time. On the right toe of our lady of grief can be seen a gentle burnishing, the consequence of countless fingers that have touched it in passing remembrance. Those who look at the tablet today might not know that the right arm and hand of the lady of grief were modelled on those of the school's secretary, the long-serving Miss Margaret Hallam.

After the tablet was unveiled, the lieutenant-governor offered Earl Clarke a scholarship for a year's study in Europe. Clarke went to the British Academy in Rome, 1926–1927, then returned to the school. His enhanced knowledge of the art galleries and museums of Europe benefited his students. Much loved and fondly remembered, he died in 1958.

The last word here belongs to then-student James Gibson, whose words echo down through the decades: "May we, as students of a school which has a record to be proud of, cultivate the same spirit of courage and unselfishness in our associations of school activities, and afterward when we take up the responsibility of worthy Canadian Citizens."

*The Vimy Ridge* National Historic Site of Canada is on Canadian soil given to the people of Canada by the Republic of France. It stands above the wooded slopes of Hill 145, the highest point of the Ridge. Canadian sculptor and architect Walter Seymour Allward designed the monument. It is a gigantic edifice, observable from afar. Carved on the walls of the monument are names of 11,285 Canadian officers and men, "missing, presumed dead," who died in France and have no known graves. The wide stone terrace overlooks the broad fields and rolling hills of northern France, now lying so peacefully (though they again saw enemy occupying forces in the Second World War). Not far away are thirty CWGC cemeteries, the final resting place of thousands of Canadians and their allies.

On the Vimy Ridge monument may be read this inscription: "To the valour of their countrymen in the Great War and in memory of their sixty thousand dead this monument is raised to the people of Canada."

Twin white pylons or pillars, one bearing the maple leaves of Canada, the other the fleur–de-lys of France, symbolize the sacrifices of both countries in a common cause. At the top are figures representing Peace and Justice. Below them, on the back of the pylons, are figures representing Truth and Knowledge. Around these figures are exhibited the coats of arms or shields of Canada, Great Britain, and France. At the base of the pylons are a young dying soldier, the Spirit of Sacrifice, and the Torch Bearer. Each staircase has male and female Mourner figures. Elsewhere there are figures known as Breaking of the Sword and Sympathy for the Helpless. Above each grouping is a cannon, silent now and draped in laurel and olive branches. The dominant figure, standing above all, is a female—the sorrowing figure of a woman representing Canada, a young nation mourning her dead. There she stands, steadfast, shrouded head bowed forward, and weeps for her fallen countrymen. Below is a tomb, draped in laurel branches and bearing a helmet and sword.

The whole is a magnificent edifice to peace and sacrifice. The traveller examining it will surely comment on how unusual it is, both in its size and its modernity. It is different from the neoclassical, Norman, and sometimes Gothic edifices that other nations have put up to their dead. In many ways it is uniquely Canadian. Nowadays, the surrounding land is being reforested, but the grand view out toward Douai Plain is as clear as it is magnificent. And nearby, in fenced-off areas where sheep still graze, you can see the pockmarked ground with shell holes from artillery bombardment and mine craters from the fierce underground war. The trenches and tunnels have been selectively preserved. In all, it is a reminder of the magnitude of the task that faced the Canadian Corps on that distant dawn when history was made.

King Edward VIII unveiled the monument on July 26, 1936. It is estimated that more than 6,000 Canadians—the Vimy Pilgrims—sailed to Europe, while tens of thousands came from Britain and France to the site. This was the Vimy Pilgrimage. One historian, John Pierce, notes that the pilgrimage, like the Memorial, was full of ambiguities. "Was it a celebration of the achievement of the Canadian Corps or a ceremony mourning the dead? Was it an imperial event solidifying Canada's relationship with its new King or a statement about an independent Canadian nation? Was the monument to be seen as a remonstrance against war or a warning to the enemies of democracy that Canada would again play its part in defending Britain and France? It was all of these and more. It was, and is, quintessentially Canadian."[3] It is best a representation of what Allward wanted: Canada's mourning of her lost blood in battle and an eternal remembrance of the horrors of war. "It was 'over there' that Canadian armies fought and died. It is 'over there' that their final monument must stand," the King intoned.

*Epilogue*

## THE PITY OF WAR

I n August 1914, the bugles of England were calling from across the infinite seas. For the next four years they continued to sound. They were heard clearly in Victoria, as elsewhere. From far-off shores, the Empire answered the summons—from all parts of Canada, Newfoundland, South Africa, Australia, New Zealand, India, and other dominions and colonies. Germany had not counted on this imperial will to survive and not be vanquished. The Empire did not win this war (and if it did, it did not do so on its own) but it did not lose it. Its power in material and human strength, backed by ancient ties that bound (as they still bind some, though fleetingly), had made the difference in the survival of France and the rescue of Belgium. Victoria and its high school had done its noble part in the greater story. Even so, this terrible catastrophe had wasted Europe. That continent had but twenty years to rebuild before another storm came upon it, this one caused by Hitler's rise to power and his ambitions to dominate Europe and rid the world of the Jews. Once again the Empire answered the bugle's call, but this time more securely on its own terms.

No one who visits the graveyards of these wars can fail to be struck by the tragedy of it all. Wandering through the CWGC cemeteries of the 1914–1918 war, you see a headstone of a Canadian beside that of an Irishman, a

New Zealander beside a Scot, an Australian beside a Welshman, an Indian beside an Englishman. They had all come together under the same flag. You count the headstones not individually, because that would take too long, but by taking a sample row, determining the number in a row, then multiplying this by the number of rows to reach an approximate number. From Ypres and Passchendaele across to Amiens and beyond lies an archipelago of CWGC cemeteries. How many countless tragedies are told in these headstones, of lives cut short, of sad partings from loved ones, of minds and limbs disfigured and obliterated by the organized violence of war?

As early as 1916, Prime Minister Borden had written to the Canadian High Commissioner in London, stating that Canada deserved a place in the imperial councils. "It can hardly be expected that we shall put 400,000 or 500,000 men in the field and willingly accept the position of having no more voice and receiving no more consideration than if we were toy automata. Any person cherishing such an expectation harbours an unfortunate and even dangerous delusion. Is this war being waged by the United Kingdom alone, or is it a war waged by the whole Empire?"[1] Borden opposed committing a large number of Canadian troops to British military leadership. He resisted British plans to integrate the imperial forces, and he insisted on a role in the making of war policies. He sat on the Imperial War Cabinet and in 1917 introduced a resolution calling for a reappraisal of dominion status after the War. As he saw it, Canada and the other self-governing nations of the British Empire ought to have autonomy in domestic affairs and an equal voice in foreign policy.

By December 1918, Prime Minister Borden had made clear to the Imperial War Cabinet that Canada's future policy would be free of European entanglements. This view was the exact opposite of that of the British government: it wanted a stable Europe based on treaty arrangements and international obligations. Borden further made plain that Canada's interests were best met through friendly relations with the United States, and that the country would put its faith in the League of Nations. This last position also allowed the Canadian government to cut its military forces dramatically. A terrific turnaround had occurred: from unreservedly backing the Empire during the War, Canada would now act in its own interests. Isolationist thinking arrived for the first time. Borden resigned because of poor health. It could safely be said that he had given Canada a new status in the world. The British had accorded Canadians respect, he told his wife, and this was true. But that respect had been won at the sharp end, by Canadians fighting on and over the seas, mainly on the battlefields of Belgium and France.

All the battles fought by the Canadians in the First World War had resounding results. Although many a Canadian died in little-known episodes, the big events are of enduring importance. The first test of what became the Canadian Corps was the terrible gas attack at Second Ypres. Then came the hell of the Somme, then the splendid and symbolic victory at Vimy, followed by the agony of Passchendaele. At last came the Hundred Days—the road to victory. The cohesion of the Canadian Corps won the nation the admiration of its allies and the respect of its enemies. The Canadian Corps had been forged by Sir Arthur Currie and made possible by the determination of Sir Robert Borden. In all of Canadian history, no one had more difficult assignments or heavier responsibilities than Currie and Borden. The one fought on the battle-field, the other in the diplomatic halls of London, Paris, and Washington. Their legacy was Canadian nationhood.

*Within twenty years,* Canada, Britain, and other parts of the Commonwealth were facing the dictators—in particular, Hitler and his scheme of a Third Reich. But the causes of the Second World War are far more complex than merely the Allied demand for the "war guilt cause" or the economic consequences of the Peace, including the reparations imposed on the new Germany of 1919. These simple explanations deny this essential fact: Hitler's well-crafted rise to power had a hidden anti-Semitic policy (which was to become transparently clear when he became chancellor in 1933). The shame of losing the War and having the Allies dictate terms to a proud but defeated Germany was to Hitler something that needed overturning in the future.[2] When Nazi Germany began to rearm in earnest, the British government feared another war. This led to the policy of appeasement.

Appeasement had strong advocates in Canada and was the focus of national policy in external affairs. In 1935, Prime Minister Mackenzie King put it this way in the House of Commons in Ottawa: "The Government . . . regards the League [of Nations] as an indispensable instrument for orga-nizing and strengthening the forces of peace and goodwill in the world, and for effecting the adjustment of conflicting national aims, essential if the advance of science and the closer contact of peoples are to make for the advantage and not the destruction of mankind." But within a year the League had failed: it was unable to deal with Italy's ambitions in Abyssinia. Mackenzie King's views show a turnabout in Canadian foreign policy: "No happening of any magnitude abroad is without its repercussions on our fortunes or our futures." He went on in terms that would later be taken up by Lester Pearson: "We must continue to work earnestly toward the ideal of a world peace." Mackenzie King regarded the recent war as "the greatest international disaster of all time," a catastrophe that had dragged Canada into the European vortex.[3]

At Victoria High School, the head of the history department (who had himself been a VHS student during the War, graduating in 1919), the much-loved Henry "Harry" Drummond Dee, wrote an article for the 1936–1937 *Camosun*. Later a principal of the school, he was an imposing presence, with a solid and gracious manner. His opinions seem now, from our times, a cry in the wilderness, for the world was fast collapsing yet again. His words on the futility of war are worth quoting at some length:

> On the walls of the main corridor, beside our auditorium doors, there hang pictures of young men. Those photographs have been there for eighteen years. On a pillar across from them is fixed a bronze memorial inscribed with names. Today one wonders, and is afraid that the time will soon come for more pictures and another memorial. Yet those honored places are for those of our School who joined that great struggle "to end war" and to "make the world safe for democracy." It would be manifestly unjust to minimize the heroism and the self-sacrifice of those who fought for those ideals. Yet, how much of the lesson does the world remember today?
>
> After that war we hopefully placed our reliance upon the League of Nations and disarmament for world peace. They promised much and did much. Gradually, however, the old jealousies, the old rivalries came creeping back. Nations found excuses to avoid their obligations to the League and their duties to one another. Now those methods of obtaining world peace are discredited, and we go back to pre-war methods of alliances, secret treaties and armaments: those same things which your teachers claim were the fundamental causes of the World War.[4]

Harry Dee's appeal to the youth of the school and to its generation made clear that modern warfare was assuming staggering proportions, that the results would be stupendous—loss of life, increase of debt, reparations, and ruination of Europe. Armaments had steadily increased. He closed with this statement, which was as appropriate in our times now as it was in his: "Whether mankind will go forward to a new world order in which the strong cannot profit at the expense of the weak, or will relapse to the condition of international anarchy which produced the World War [of 1914–1918], is the supreme question of our generation. Upon the answer may well depend the fate of Western civilization. That answer is a challenge to the youth of today."

In 1939, the times grew dark again. In the school's main hallway is found the Memorial Plaque for the 1939–1945 war, which faces the Great War Memorial Tablet. It lists 115 Victoria High School students who DIED ON ACTIVE SERVICE. The epitaph reads THAT THE WORLD MIGHT BE FREE. Under the leadership of teacher L.J. "Lawrie" Wallace, students and staff raised the lion's share to build the VHS Memorial Stadium. A quarter-mile track was provided at the expense of the Victoria Gyro Club in 1951. The track encloses an infield for soccer, rugby, and field sports.

In the days of my youth, I would see the survivors of these wars parade bravely on Armistice Day, later Remembrance Day. They would come down the slight hill of Government Street past the Empress Hotel, then take up their position near the cenotaph, where, at the appropriate moment after the two-minute silence at eleven o'clock, they would lay their wreaths. The 5th BC Regiment of Garrison Artillery, RCA, the same that many had served in so long ago, would fire off the guns one at a time, the dull pounding of each echoing round the harbour, that same port from whence their steamer had first carried them away to war—first to England and then to Flanders Fields. Then the pipes and drums of the 16th Canadian Scottish Regiment (Princess Mary's) would break the greater silence and off they all would go again, forming up as they once used to do, wearing proudly caps and hats with regimental insignia on them, medals brightly on their blazers and rain-coats, following the flag to the applause of the grateful throng. No survivors of the Great War remain, and the numbers of those who survived the Second World War are dwindling. Now those who served in the Korean conflict or on UN duties or, more recently, in Afghanistan take up the old procession of yesteryear.

The days of empire passed away, too, and with it the poetry, the music, the art, and the photographs. Until about 1955, a large Union Jack provided the backdrop for the group photograph of the school graduating class, assembled on the auditorium stage. After that it disappeared from view. The graduates of 1955 sang "Jerusalem," with hopeful lyrics by William Blake, for the last time; they did similarly for the hymn "Old One Hundredth"—"All people that on earth do dwell . . ." The old values had been swept away by the modern, and a half century of war or recovering from war brought forth the period of disillusion. There were no more poems such as those written by Rupert Brooke, who at the eleventh hour before the Great War had spoken of an eternal England based on the old, secure understandings. A whole generation of poets had been swept aside by the War, and those who survived faced the uncertainties of the post-1918 world. The old note of Valiancy—"of the old Roman 'virtue' mated with cheerfulness"—had been forsaken.[5] A fashion of morose disparagement dominated poetry. Skepticism had replaced faith.

I have spoken of the poets and of the graduation exercises. I could also have written about the Victoria High School Band and Mr. Roland Grant, the band instructor. He used to tell us with glee about playing in a British regimental band during the First World War. On one occasion, as a member of the band, Dr. Maria Tippett, remembered, he told of how on the Western Front the line moved forward in the British Army's favour. "We all moved forward, including the band. The Germans had made such a quick retreat that their musicians left their music behind. We played it in the hope that they could hear it." Grant's story weakened, she noted, "when he told us that the opposite situation occurred—more than once!"[6] He brought discipline to the band room and outstanding musicianship that won for us, in 1955, the British Columbia Open Band championship against the formidable Kitsilano Boys Band, headed up by legendary Arthur Delamont—our finest musical hour. Our final rehearsal became the stuff of legend. En route to Vancouver, in the large aft drawing room, we entertained fellow passengers, while steadying shifting music stands, on the CPR day steamer that ferried us through heavy seas. High expectation was in the air, and for good luck we all threw pennies into the water as the steamer passed under Lions Gate Bridge. I can still recall Grant conducting band practice with one arm while gingerly playing his lovely silver cornet with the other, in that true tone that is the hallmark of English brass players. And one last anecdote: he told me that when he enlisted he was a very slender fellow, well below the weight limit. In order to pass the weight test, he drank several gallons of water before going in for the medical examination.

On cold blustery Remembrance Days, you could see us assembled on the steps of the Legislature playing the old tunes of empire: "Land of Hope and Glory," "Soldiers of the Queen," and, yes, "The Maple Leaf Forever." Something of the glory had departed, and the hope left had a hollow ring. The Canadian maple leaf flag had not yet been designed or adopted. We came of age slowly, even reluctantly. Traditions and connections die gradually, and empire eventually breathed its last. We of the 1950s now inhabited the world of the United Nations and NATO—and of ideological struggle between the West and the Communist Bloc. On the walls of our classrooms in the school, some of the old images, remnants of the imperial age, could be seen as late as 1956—a line of British dreadnoughts steaming in steady formation was one I particularly remember, for it was in my homeroom, where Mr. Douglas Smith was in charge. Alfred Lord Tennyson's words on that lovely image spelled out the old imperial message of consolidation and responsibility: "One life, one flag, one fleet, one throne. Britons hold your own." I have often wondered if that view inspired me to study the history of warships.

In another classroom, Miss Hazel Sargent, "the radiator queen," who had been a student at the school during the Great War, proudly displayed prints of the Group of Seven above her blackboards. They spoke of a Canada so far away from us who lived in the Pacific Province, one whose lands and trees we did not yet know; they looked noble and stark enough, though not like our own. Students chatted about the great shooting gallery that lay beneath the school's roof, and some of them, perhaps a little magically, could recall the whizzing of bullets there, and inscriptions written by cadets and others. And then, in 1949, the school opened its Memorial Stadium and Track as a tribute to those who had served in the Second World War. The cycle of the Great War went through another complete turn, and a new memorial list found itself in the great hallway. Yet still the old photos of the soldiers, sailors, and airmen of the Great War hung round the main hallway. When they were taken down is now lost to memory. They survive, no longer on public display but safely in the VHS Archives, that sanctuary of school history.

To conclude this history of Victoria High School and the First World War, I can think of no better words than those expressed in the hopeful editorial of the November 1918 issue of *The Camosun*. The author was probably Ursula

Edwards (Jupp), that year the school's top student. She wrote with a degree of wisdom far surpassing her youthful years, and her words echo down through the ages:

November 11th will be remembered while history endures as the day on which the nations of the world entered upon a new era—the day upon which a renaissance, so far-reaching in its influence as to eclipse all preceding ones, was ushered in. The breath of world-changing, epoch-making movements is in our nostrils. The dreams of visionaries, the seers of the past, which yesterday seemed but dreams, are today become the heritage of the man on the street. We stand linked in rejoicing, in aspiration, in hope, in the very problems which confront us with the whole world. International boundaries prove ineffective to check this new spirit. Henceforth man's conception of service is broadened to include the World and all Humanity. How many who have seen this day in youth will look back to it with thankfulness that they were then alive!

As we stand here with the light of Peace upon our foreheads, greeting the day which has just dawned for us, let no spirit of false exultation possess us, but one of humility and gratitude; let us not forget the sacrifice, the pouring forth of blood, the bitter tears and yet bitterer hours of tearless anguish which made this day possible; and let every nerve and muscle be tense with resolution as we descend from the mountain of visions into the valley of service and achievements.

## NAMES OF THOSE WHO MADE THE ULTIMATE SACRIFICE IN THE FIRST WORLD WAR, AS LISTED ON THE VICTORIA HIGH SCHOOL MEMORIAL TABLET

**MASTERS**

John A. MacDonald

Verner L. Plant

John Spouse

**STUDENTS**

Charles Adams

Arthur William Aird

John Gibson Anderson

J. Henry Austin

Arthur Babcock

Percy C. Barr

Alfred E. Beckwith

Arthur C. Belyea

Marc E. Berton

Lyall L. Bland

Herbert B. Boggs

Archie Boyd

Chester Boyd

Raymond H. Brewster

John James Brown

Adair Carss

Edgar W. Christie

Roy Clements

Frederick W. Copas

Hugh S. Coppock

William R. Cutler

Desmond S. Davis

John W. D. Dowler

Frank M. Dunn

Ernest R. Elford

Shirley D. Ellis

F. Fletcher Elliott

G.W. Elliott

Charles H. Fleming

Herbert French

Frank Garland

Albert A. Gerow

Ronald J. Graham

Robin Gray

G.W. Ashdown Green

Don. B. Hanna

Chas. M. Hardie

Walter G. Head

Fred G. Heal

Alwin Holland

A. Percy Huggett

Edward W. Jackson

H.A.B. Jackson

Percy James

Arthur E. Johnson

Charles Kennedy

Nelson King

Adam Knox

Charles Knox

Fred Knox

R.W. Reginald Litchfield
Ray B. McCallum
Allister McCallum
Donald M. McCannel
N. Ross McCannel
George B. Milligan
Victor Noble
J.A. Pascoe
Horace Paul
Harold M. Pearce
James M. Pottinger
Robert B. Powell
Jack Reid
Harold S. Roe
Cyril G. Sedger
Harry G. Sivertz

Alan Spencer
Evan D. Spencer
Norman Spencer
E.H.S. Steele
D. Vernon Stevens
William Stewart
Mortimer Tait
F. Thompson
A.E.C. Thurburn
Edwin S. Tuck
Albert Waterhouse
Douglas Whittier
Harry Wilby
Conrad B. Wilson
Frank Wood
Fred Wood

*Appendix 2*

---

## THE ROLL OF HONOUR OF VICTORIA HIGH SCHOOL, 1914-1918

\* Indicates those who died or were killed in the War (August 4, 1914–November 11, 1918)

NOTE: Names and ranks are as given on the original Roll of Honour. This list differs from original as follows: entries are arranged by surname; ranks have been abbreviated; ranks as given are not necessarily those eventually attained; medals won are not included. The list, which includes 497 names, may not be complete.

Gnr. Whitford Ackerman
Lt. L. Acton
Pte. Charles Adams*
2nd Lt. Arthur W. Aird*
Gnr. Creagh S. Allen
Pte. H.S. Allen
Nurse Anderson
Gnr. A.D. Anderson
Maj. John G. Anderson*
Pte. M. Anderson
Lt. Henry Angus
Cpl. W.C. Armour
Pte. Babcock*
Sgt. P.A. Babington
Pte. Hugh Baker
Q.M.S. William F. Baker
Sgt. William M. Baker
Gnr. Allan Ballantyne
Gnr. C.H. Bamford
Pte. Harvey S. Bamford
Cpt. R.C. Bamford
Gnr. E. Banner
Driver P. Bannerman*
Percy Bannerman
Pte. Percy G. Barr*
Cpt. Walter Barton
Lt. William Barton
Sgt. G. Beale
Fl. Lt. Percy E. Beasley

Surg. Alfred E. Beckwith*
Nurse Beeston
Pte. Arthur D. Belyea*
Cadet V. Bendrodt
Pte. George Bennet
Pte. Marc E. Berton*
Lt. G.W. Bissett
Pte. Lyall L. Bland*
Pte. J. Blandy
Lt. Arthur Boggs
Lt. Herbert Boggs*
Pte. Archie Boyd*
Cpl. C.F. Boyd*
Sgt. R.H. Brewster*
Lt. Charles Brown
Cpt. H.A. Brown
Pte. H.W. Brown
Pte. J.J. Brown*
Pte. J.P. Brown
Sub Lt. T. Brown
Lt. W.H. Brown
Spr. W.H. Brown
Pte. Malcolm Browne
Herbert Bunt
Cpl. Robert Burns
Fl. Lt. Somerlid Burns
Fl. Lt. Torquil Burns
Sgt. F.E. Burrell
Spr. S.E. Burrows

Pte. George Calder
Gnr. Gordon Cameron
Gnr. C.L. Campbell
Pte. Douglas Campbell
Maj. F. Campbell
Cadet Gordon Campbell
Sub Lt. G.M. Campbell
L. Cpl. H. Campbell
Pte. H.L. Campbell
Maj. J.T. Campbell
Pte. Walter Campbell
Lt. Morris Carmichael
Pte. Fred Carne
Pte. Harold Carne
Lt. Adair Carss*
Gnr. Elmer Carter
Driver Howard Carter
Pte. Robert Carter
Gnr. Vere Carter
Pte. C. Carver
Pte. Harry Carver
Lt. R.C. Castle
Stephen A. Chessman
Fl. Lt. Edgar W. Christie*
Pte. Cecil Clark
Sgt. Harold Clark
Gnr. Harry Clark
Pte. A. Clarke
Fl. Lt. A. Clay

Fl. Lt. C.J. Clayton
Lt. J.B. Clearihue
Gnr. Roy S. Clements*
Capt. D. Cleveland
Pte. Henry Clustin*
Nurse Elsie Collis
Pte. Clarence Colwell
Pte. Fred Colwell
Pte. Edwin Copas
Sgt. Fred Copas*
Pte. Roy Copas
Pte. Hugh S. Coppack*
Driver W.A. Craig
Gnr. Harry Cross*
Pte. Jas. Cummins
Gnr. William Cuthbert
2nd Lt. William R. Cutler*
Pte. Harold Davenport
L. Cpl. L. Davies
Sgt. Desmond Davis*
Sgt. H.E. Davis
Gnr. Lewis Davis
Gnr. C.W. Dawson
Driver Wilbur Dawson
Lt. William Day
Pte. A. Deacon
Gnr. Curtis Dean
L. Cpl. John Dee
Pte. Spencer Dee
Gnr. Jas. Denholme
Nurse Denovan
Pte. J.M. Denovan
Pte. M. Earle Dickinson
Allan Dorman
Wallace Dorman
Lt. Jack D. Dowler*
Sgt. Gordon Downes
Gnr. J. Duncan
Pte. Frank M. Dunn*
Lt. Harold Eberts
Sgt. H.A. Ede*

Driver Robert Edwards
Pte. Ernest R. Elford*
Lt. Fred F. Elliott*
Gnr. George W. Elliott*
2nd Lt. S. Duncan Ellis*
Sgt. T.B. Elworthy
Lt. R.F. Ely
Gnr. Claude F. Emery
Gnr. E.R. Etheridge
Gnr. R.S. Etheridge
Tpr. L. Fairburn
L. Cpl. S.E. Fairburn
Lt. L. Farguharson
Gnr. Fred Fatt
Capt. O.E. Finch
Cadet E. Finland
Pte. Charles H. Fleming*
Pte. Ellis Fletcher
Pte. F. Flinton
Pte. Claude Floyd
Pte. Thomas Floyd
Sgt. Thomas Forrester
Spr. D. Fort
G. Fort
Capt. R.H. Fort
Driver S. Foulkes
Pte. George Fox
Pte. Jas. Allan Fraser
Lt. Charles French*
Pte. Herbert French
Lt. Langford Fullerton
Lt. Lorne Fulton
Pte. S. Galbraith
Gnr. William Gale
Pte. L. Gannon
Mech. Frank Garland*
Pte. Arthur Gee
Lt. J. Ewart Gee
Pte. J.F. Geldard
2nd Lt. C.S. George
2nd Lt. Albert A. Gerow*

Cadet Walton Gilbert
Gnr. J. Gill
Spr. K.B. Gillie
Gnr. J. Goldie
Pte. Philip Goodwin
Gnr. Ronald Graham*
Gnr. Stanley Graham
Pte. W.H. Gravlin
Pte. H.S. Graves
Lt. A.J. Gray
Lt. G. Robin Gray*
Sgt. James Gray
Lt. G.W.A. Green*
Lt. Robert Green
Gnr. E. Greenwood
Pte. Ewart Gregson
Gnr. K.B. Greig
Pte. Charles
  Grenshaw-Gowen
Pte. Nelson Growen
Pte. R.N. Grubb
S. Fl. Lt. D.D. Hall
Fl. Lt. Ernest Hall
Gnr. Richard Hall
Gnr. J. Hamilton
Lt. Robert Hamilton
Pte. Evan Hanbury
Lt. F.C. Hanington
Lt. Donald B. Hanna*
Gnr. S.P. Hanna
Pte. Charles Hardie*
Sgt. Freeman Harding
Sgt. E.F. Hardwick
Maj. Barnett Harvey
Pte. C. Haverstock
Pte. Paul Hayward
Spr. Walter G. Head*
Pte. Fred Heal*
Pte. Lewis Heald
Pte. James Hector
Gnr. C.B. Henderson

Pte. Dono Heyland
Gnr. E.J. Hickey
Pte. Robert Hiscocks
Pte. Alwin Holland*
Lt. H. Cuthbert Holmes
Pte. H.J. Hopkins
Pte. T.E. Hopkins
Cpl. Stafford Horne
Lt. H.B. Hudson
Sgt. A.P. Huggett*
Pte. W.G. Hyatt
Pte. A. Jackson
Sgt. Edward W. Jackson*
L. Cpl. Hugh A.B.
  Jackson*
Gnr. William Jackson
Gnr. William James
Tpr. Kenneth Johns
Pte. A. Johnson
Pte. Alfred Johnson
L. Cpl. Arthur E .Johnson*
Pte. B. Johnson
Sgt. C.C. Johnson
Pte. Clarence Johnson
Pte. D. Johnson
Gnr. G. Johnson
Cpl. A.H. Jones
Pte. Aubrey Jones
Pte. Heber Jones
Pte. Percy Jones
Capt. G. Kenning
Gnr. Forrest Kerr
Pte. Edward Kershaw
Gnr. Edmund Key
Lt. Nelson King*
Pte. Paul King
Pte. J.W. Kinlock
Pte. H. Lacoursiere
Tpr. Stanley Langley
Lt. Thorlief Larsen
Pte. P.S. Langton

Lt. H.C. Laundy
Lt. E.L. Laundy
Gnr. Victor Lawson*
Gnr. Albert Leigh
Sgt. George Leighton
Pte. William Levirs
Gnr. Fred Lewis
Cadet Richard W.
  Litchfield*
Pte. Rt. Livingston
Pte. J. Longpre
Pte. Robert Lorimer
Pte. Sam Lorimer
Pte. Wtr. Lorimer
Tpr. Alva Lowery
Gnr. Alfred Luney
Pte. E. Lunsden
Gnr. Lussie
Pte. Norman Lynch
Lt. John A. MacDonald*
Gnr. G. MacEachern
Pte. E.A. MacLenran
Pte. A. Manson
Gnr. S.E. Marling
L. Cpl. G. Marwick
Gnr. Henry Matthews
Lt. J.H. Maxwell
Gnr. I.G. May
Gnr. Percy McAdam
Gnr. D.J. McBrady
Gnr. R.H. McBrady
Pte. Robert G. McBurnie
Lt. A.H.K. McCall
Lt. Angus McCallum*
Lt. E. McCallum
Lt. Ray B. McCallum*
Gnr. Neil R. McCannel*
Sgt. Maj. Donald M.
  McConnel*
Cadet Roy McConnel
Pte. H. McDiarmid

Sub Lt. N. McDiarmid
L. Cpl. A.S. McDonald
Cadet D. McDougal
Pte. Hedley McDougall
Pte. Athol McFarlane
Pte. John McGregor
Lt. M. McGregor
Pte. B. McIloride
Sgt. B. McIloride
Pte. Harold McIloride
Pte. H.G. McIloride
Pte. D.C. McIntyre
Pte. E.C. McIntyre
Capt. G.H. McIntyre
Pte. H.G. McIntyre
Lt. Vincent McKenna*
Gnr. Vincent McKinnon
R.A.F. William A.
  McKinnon
Pte. J. McLean
Gnr. Kenneth McLean
Spr. Evan McMillan
Lt. Leslie McNaughton
Pte. Rae McNeil
L. Cpl. H. McNeill
Pte. Proctor McPherson
Driver P.B. Mess
Pte. George H. Miles
Pte. Stanley Miles
Gnr. Gerald Miller
Lt. James Miller
Lt. George B. Milligan*
Pte. J.N. Milligan
Pte. Cecil Milloy
Pte. Gilbert Milloy
Driver F.C. Milne
Pte. A.A. Mitchell
Gnr. P.A. Moir
Lt. J.D. Moore
Lt. Arnold Morley
Gnr. A.E. Morrison

Lt. S. Morton

Nurse Moss

Gnr. A. Mulcahy*

Pte. Charles Munroe

Fl. Lt. D.F. Murray

Gnr. E. Myers

Pte. I.B. Nason

Pte. O.K. Nason

Pte. J.S. Ney

Pte. B. Nickells

Gnr. A.V. Noble*

Cpl. Stafford Norne

Gnr. George Norris

Lt. T.G. Norris

Lt. J.H. O'Keefe

Cpl. Stanley Okell

Pte. Robert O'Meara

Gnr. G. Parfitt*

Gnr. Ray Parfitt

Sgt. James A. Pascoe*

Pte. Thomas G. Pascoe

Pte. G. Patterson

Pte. Horace J.S. Paul*

Sgt. Sylvester Paul

Pte. Harold M. Pearce*

Pte. Phillips

Pte. Hiram Pickard

Gnr. J. Piercy

Sgt. Lew Pineo

Lt. Verner I. Plant*

Pte. Earl Pollock

Pte. Russell Pollock

Pte. Wilfred Pollock

Lt. Harold Pope

Pte. C.C. Pottinger

Pte. E.L. Pottinger

Pte. James M. Pottinger*

Pte. Charles Pratt

Sgt. Wilford C. Prevost

Nurse M. Redding

Pte. W. Redfern

Pte. Clifford Reid

Pte. Gordon Reid

Lt. Jack Reid*

L. Cpl. Jeffrey Reid

Pte. W. Revercomb

Sig. Arthur Riley

Lt. Harry Robinson

Lt. D. Rochford

Lt. W. Rochfort

Pte. Harold S. Roe*

Nurse Ross

Lt. Herbert Ross

Lt. William Ross

E.L. Rothinger

Gnr. W.H. Ryan

Pte. Campbell Sanson

Cpt. Albert Sargison

Pte. H.B. Sargison

Lt. Blayney Scott*

Cpl. Chester Scott

Gnr. Douglas Scott

Capt. Gilling Scott

Pte. Matthew Scott

Lt. William Scott

Pte. Clement Sears

Sgt. Cyril Sedger*

Pte. Reginald Sedger

Pte. Joseph W. Shakespeare

Pte. Alexander Shaw

Pte. Edward Shaw

Pte. H. Sherwood

Sig. E.P. Sidall

Sgt. Gus Sivertz

L. Cpl. C. Sivertz

Sgt. Henry G. Sivertz*

Lt. H. Skelton

Gnr. Ralph C. Smethurst

Pte. P.M. Smith

Pte. Thomas Smith

Pte. Southerland

Spr. Alan Spencer

Lt. Evan D. Spencer*

Pte. Norman Spencer*

Nurse Sara Spencer

Pte. Cecil Spring

Pte. Edward Sprinkling

Pte. C. Sprinkling

Cpl. G.R. Sprinkling

Cpl. P.D. Sprinkling

Lt. John Spouse*

Pte. Edwin H. Steele*

Lt. W. Steele

Sgt. David V. Stevens*

Gnr. Gerald Stevens

L. Cpl. Arthur Stewart

Pte. W. Stewart

Pte. William Stewart*

Gnr. Joe Stinson

Pte. Andrew Sykes

Capt. Edwin Tait

Cpl. Frank Tait

Pte. Harold Tait

Pte. Mortimer H. Tait*

Lt. D. Taylor

Lt. D.B. Taylor

Pte. T.T. Taylor

Sig. T.A. Temple

Sig. Kingsley Terry

Capt. M. Thomas

Pte. F. Thomson*

Pte. G. Thomson

Capt. Augustus Thurburn*

Gnr. Todd

Pte. Gerald Travis

Pte. Robert Travis

Lt. D.C. Tuck

Sgt. E.S. Tuck*

Pte. Frank A. Walker

Capt. Richard Wallis

Bomb. A.C. Walls

Pte. W. Walls

Capt. A.B. Walter

Sgt. Ernest Walter

Pte. W.C. Walton

Sgt. L. Warnicker

Pte. Albert V. Waterhouse*

Gnr. T. Watson

Capt. Virgil Wescott

Pte. Richard Wheeler

Lt. Harold E. Whyte

Pte. A. Wilby

Harry Wilby*

Capt. W.J. Wilby

Herbert William

Bomb. Archie Wills

Pte. Percy Wills

Lt. A.N. Wilmot

Lt. I.A. Wilmot

Lt. Conrad B. Wilson*

Gnr. R.S. Wilson

L. Cpl. Robin Wilson

Lt. W. Winsby

Capt. A. Wood

Driver Douglas Wood

F.A. Wood

Pte. Frank Wood

Pte. Fred Wood*

Lt. J.E. Wood

Pte. Leslie Wood

L. Cpl. Edward Wootton

Lt. Harry Wootton

Pte. F. Wright

Pte. A.W. Wylie

Pte. Arthur Yates

Pte. R.S. Yates

Pte. Emsley Yeo

Sgt. Sam Youlden

Pte. Stanley Young

Pte. Frank Youngs

Lt. Shirley Yuill

# *Appendix 3*

## VICTORIA REGIMENTS AND THE
## CANADIAN ARMY ORGANIZATION, 1914–1918

As of November 1918, the Canadian Corps, with a strength of 156,441, all ranks, consisted of the following:

CANADIAN CORPS HEADQUARTERS

CAVALRY—3 regiments, 1 squadron

ARTILLERY—4 field brigades, 1 anti-aircraft battery, 3 brigades garrison artillery

ENGINEERS—5 army troops companies, 1 searchlight company, 1 tunnelling company, 1 survey section, 2 tramways companies

MACHINE-GUN CORPS—2 motor machine-gun brigades

ARMY SERVICE CORPS—7 motor transport companies

MEDICAL CORPS—8 general hospitals, 6 stationary hospitals, 4 casualty clearing stations, 2 field ambulance units

RAILWAY TROOPS—13 battalions, 1 railway construction unit

LABOUR—4 infantry workshops companies, 5 area employment companies

Each of the 4 infantry divisions consisted of the following major units:

ARTILLERY—2 brigades field artillery, each of 3 field batteries and 1 howitzer battery

INFANTRY—3 brigades, each of 4 infantry battalions and a trench mortar battery

Each battalion had a strength of approximately 1,000 men, and a Canadian division had a total strength of approximately 21,000. In addition, each division had on its establishment one machine-gun battalion, one divisional train Canadian Army Service Corps, three field ambulances, and one employment company.

**REGIMENTS**—(First World War details only)

5th BC Regiment of Garrison Artillery, Royal Canadian Artillery, with head-quarters at Victoria, has the honour of being the oldest militia unit now existing in Western Canada. Artillery units served in many campaigns: Fenian Raids; North West Canada, 1885; Yukon Field Force, 1898; and South African War, 1899–1902. Organized October 12, 1883, it was an amalgamation of several other batteries and companies. The regiment was mobilized prior to August 4, 1914. In addition to manning coastal defences in Canada and St. Lucia in the British West Indies, the Canadian Artillery provided various divisional batteries, an army field brigade, an anti-aircraft battery, and three brigades of garrison artillery for the Canadian Corps in France. In addition, a brigade of horse artillery, the RCHA, served with the Canadian Cavalry Brigade. Two Canadian field batteries served in northern Russia and one in Siberia.

The Canadian Scottish Regiment (Princess Mary's), headquartered in Victoria, received that name in 1920. It derives from the 88th Regiment, Victoria Fusiliers, authorized September 3, 1912, which was amalgamated with the 50th Regiment, Gordon Highlanders, authorized August 15, 1913. The Victoria Fusiliers and the Gordon Highlanders were placed on active ser-vice on August 10, 1914, for local protective duty. They contributed to the 7th and 16th Battalions, CEF, respectively, on their formation in September 1914, and later were recruited for the 48th, 67th, 88th, 103rd, and 143rd Battalions. The 16th Battalion served in France and Flanders with the 3rd Infantry Brigade, First Canadian Division, from February 15, 1915, until the Armistice. Four members of the 16th Battalion won the Victoria Cross: Pte. (Piper) J. Richardson, Pte. W.J. Milne, Lt. Col. C.W. Peck, DSO, and L/Cpl. W.H. Metcalf, MM.

Sources: Army Historical Section, Minister of National Defence, *Regiments and Corps of the Canadian Army* (Ottawa: Queen's Printer, 1964); Donald J. Goodspeed, *The Road Past Vimy: The Canadian Corps 1914–1918* (Toronto: Macmillan of Canada, 1969).

# NOTES

## INTRODUCTION

1. Quoted by Max Hastings, *Finest Years: Churchill as Warlord, 1940–45* (London: Harper Press, 2009), xiii.

2. In 1921, Canadian legislation established Canadian citizenship, though Canadians were still British subjects. In 1947, Canadian nationality was established by statute.

As for the population of the city, the national census of 1911 tells us that the population of Victoria, Canada's twelfth-largest city, was 31,600. (The population of British Columbia was 392,480; that of Canada, 7,204,000.) Victoria's citizenry was predominantly Canadian-born (12,000, with 3,000 from Ontario). Of the Canadian-born, 8,000 were "born in British Columbia." Of those born in Great Britain, a total of 11,000, the English highly predominated at 9,000, with the Scots far behind at 1,400 and the Irish with only 700. (The Welsh numbers are included with the English figures.) A boosterish figure provided for the eve of the First World War suggested the city population was 50,000, with Vancouver at that time upwards of 125,000. Figures from Dominion of Canada Census 1911; also, R.E. Gosnell, *The Year Book of British Columbia and Manual of Provincial Information (Coronation Edition)* (Victoria: Government of British Columbia, 1911), 222.

3. John Canning, ed., *Living History: 1914* (London: Odhams, 1967), 13.

4. His Nova Scotia-born father, William Bissett, had been master of James Dunsmuir's yacht. Lieutenant-Colonel Bissett (1894–1958) served overseas in No. 16 Canadian General Hospital in the Second World War, and on the peace became president of the BC Medical Association, superintendent of Veterans' Hospital, Victoria, and commodore of Royal Victoria Yacht Club. Information from Leona Taylor.

## PROLOGUE—THE LONG AND SPLENDID AFTERNOON

1. John Ellis with Charles Lillard, *The Fernwood Files* (Victoria: Orca, 1989), 16.

2. This section is drawn from Gosnell, *Year Book of British Columbia*, 144–57.

3. Henry Boam, *British Columbia: Its History, People, Commerce, Industries and Resources* (London: Sells, 1912), 126.

4. Albert J. Pineo's testimony on Dr. Paul in *Camosun*, June 1908, 3–5.

5. Bruce Hutchison, *The Far Side of the Street* (Toronto: Macmillan of Canada, 1976), 41–42. He entered Victoria High School at age thirteen.

6. According to the regiment's page on the Department of National Defence website, "The 5th (British Columbia) Field Artillery Regiment, RCA originated in Victoria, British Columbia, on 12 October 1883." It underwent various name changes and reorganizations, outlined on the website, over the next 130 years. In this book it is referred to as 5th British Columbia Regiment of Garrison Artillery, Royal Canadian Artillery or 5th (BC Regiment) RCA. See www.cmp-cpm.forces.gc.ca/dhh-dhp/his/ol-lo/vol-tom-3/par1/art/5far-5rdc-eng.asp

7. The 88th Regiment, Victoria Fusiliers, and the 50th Regiment, Gordon Highlanders, were later amalgamated in the 16th Battalion (Canadian Scottish), which eventually became the Canadian Scottish Regiment (Princess Mary's). See the DND website, www.cmp-cpm.forces.gc.ca/dhh-dhp/his/ol-lo/vol-tom-3/par2/csr-eng.asp

8. Boam, *British Columbia*, 156.

9. "Cadet News: Sham Battle," *Camosun*, January 1913, 21 (details on Dowler, 19). Additional details: *Camosun*, November 1913, 20–21.

10. As late as the early 1950s, all except the original two-room high school remained on the site. The author can still remember the nooks and crannies and the various stairs and passages of the buildings on this site.

11. Ellis, *Fernwood Files*, 54–56.

12. Watkins was a graduate of the school, and his grandson, David Watkins, served as VHS principal in the 1980s.

13. *Camosun*, November 1912, 16.

14. *Daily Colonist*, May 2, 1914.

15. Esson Young's wife, the bright and charming Rosalind Watson, occupied a distinguished place in literary and social circles. Educated at McGill, with an MA in natural sciences, she was an expert in geography and taught at the high school and Victoria College until her marriage, when, on account of matrimony, she was obliged to leave. The Youngs were a formidable combination.

16. *Daily Colonist*, May 2, 1914.

17. Sandra Martin and Roger Hall, *Rupert Brooke in Canada* (Toronto: Peter Martin, 1978).

18. Arthur J. Marder, *From the Dreadnought to Scapa Flow: The Royal Navy in the Fisher Era, 1904–1919*, 5 vols. (London: Oxford University Press, 1970), 5:334–35.

19. The standard work on the lead-up to war is Michael Howard, *The Continental Commitment: The Dilemma of British Defence Policy in the Era of the Two World Wars* (1972; London: Ashfield, 1989), 9–52.

20. "The Winning Speech in the Frederic Wood Gold Medal Contest: Should the United States Intervene in the War?" by Strother Foulkes, *Camosun*, May 1915, 36–44.

21. Ibid, 38.

## CHAPTER I—1914: VICTORIA GOES TO WAR

1. John Buchan, *The King's Grace 1910–1935* (London: Hodder and Stoughton, 1935), 115; also, George Dangerfield, *The Strange Death of Liberal England* (1935; New York: Capricorn, 1961), 424–25.

2. Quoted in Peter Ackroyd, *London: The Biography* (London: Vintage, 2001), 721–22.

3. Moltke's memoir, quoted in Correlli Barnett, *The Swordbearers: Studies in Supreme Command in the First World War* (London: Eyre & Spottiswoode, 1963), 91.

4. Entry for Colonel Arthur William Currie, in F.W. Howay and E.O.S. Scholefield, *British Columbia from the Earliest Times to the Present* (Vancouver: S.J. Clarke, 1914), 4:168–72.

5. This sketch is drawn from the Currie's self-authorized entry in *Who's Who in Canada* (Toronto, 1927 ed.), 1519–20. I have left the charges of inappropriate fiscal arrangements in regards to militia development to those having a more scurrilous interest. In any event, it does not fall within the scope of this story.

6. *Victoria Colonist*, February 2, 1918, 5.

7. *Camosun*, December 1914, 16–17.

8. *Camosun*, November 1912, 8.

9. *Camosun*, November 1914, 12.

10. Julian Corbett, *Naval Operations*, vol. 1 (London: Longmans, 1920), 207; Nigel Hawkins, *The Starvation Blockades* (Barnsley: Leo Cooper, 2002), 20; H.W. Wilson, *Battleships in Action*, 2 vols. (1926; Annapolis: Naval Institute Press, 1995), 2:36.

11. Account of J. Spiess, torpedo officer on *U-9*, in Lowell Thomas, *Raiders of the Deep* (1928; Annapolis: Naval Institute Press, 2004), 29–31.

12. James Edmonds, *A Short History of World War I* (London: Oxford University Press, 1951), 77.

13. Quoted, Max Hastings, *Catastrophe: Europe Goes to War 1914* (London: William Collins, 2013), 248, 257.

14. *Camosun*, December 1914, 16–17.

## CHAPTER 2—1915: WELCOME TO FLANDERS FIELDS: SECOND BATTLE OF YPRES

1. *Camosun*, May 1915, 34.

2. Nathan M. Greenfield, *Baptism of Fire: The Second Battle of Ypres and the Forging of Canada, April 1915* (Toronto: HarperCollins, 2007), 15–16.

3. Tim Travers, "Currie and 1st Canadian Division at Second Ypres, April 1915: Controversy, Criticism and Official History," *Canadian Military History* 5, 2 (Autumn 1996): 7–15.

4. John P. Sinnott, "It was Algerian and Canadian Soldiers at Ypres who Suffered History's First Major Poison Gas Attack," *Military History*, April 1994, 12–16 and 81.

5. G.W.L. Nicholson, *Canadian Expeditionary Force, 1914–1919* (Ottawa: Queen's Printer, 1964) is the standard account. See also, C.R.M.F. Cruttwell, *A History of the Great War, 1914–1918*, 2nd ed. (Chicago: Academy Chicago Publishers, 1991), 159–61.

6. Beaumont Boggs entry in Howay and Schofield, *British Columbia from the Earliest Times to the Present*, 4:400–402.

7. Peter Smith, *Come Give a Cheer! One Hundred Years of Victoria High School, 1876–1976* (Victoria: Victoria High School Centennial Celebrations Committee, 1976), 56.

8. In 1913, large-scale riots had broken out in Nanaimo, caused by the mine owners' use of Chinese and Japanese strikebreakers. Widespread looting, burning, and destroying of property had led to the militia being called out in aid of the civil power. Militia forces were there at the outbreak of war in August 1914. Margaret A. Ormsby, *British Columbia: A History* (Toronto: Macmillan of Canada, 1971), 365–67.

9. Here I rely on the *Daily Colonist*, May 7, 1915, p. 1; further details and photos from May 15, 1915, p. 7, and October 3, 1915, p. 5. Other particulars from Sherri Robinson; also attestation papers and records of service, courtesy Jack Bates.

10. *Daily Colonist*, October 6, 1915, 5.

11. Information from his nephew, Brian R.D. Smith.

12. James Pottinger to his parents, March 23, 1918, Pottinger letters, Victoria City Archives.

13. Here I have drawn from Darrell Knight, ed., *Horace C. Singer, History of the 31st Canadian Infantry Battalion (1914–1919) CEF* (1938; Calgary: Detselig, 2006), 78–79.

14. War Diary of 5th Battalion, October 8 and 9, 1915, Library and Archives Canada.

15. *Daily Colonist*, December 18, 1915, 1.

16. Lord Beaverbrook, *Politicians and the War, 1914–1916* (London: Thornton Butterworth, 1928), 204.

17. Robert Graves, *Goodbye to All That* (1929; Penguin, 1960), 112.

18. See Reginald Roy, ed., *Journal of Private Fraser* (CEF Books, 1998).

19. Information from Leona Taylor.

20. *Camosun*, May 1915, 34.

21. *Camosun*, May 1915, 31.

22. Evelyn Rodgers, "Nurses Under Fire," *Victoria Times Colonist*, no date; information from Leona Taylor.

23. Sir Andrew Macphail, *Official History of the Canadian Forces in the Great War, 1914–19: The Medical Services* (Ottawa: King's Printer, 1925), 224.

24. Yvonne Van Ruskenveld, "Great War Nursing Sisters on VHS Roll of Honour," copy, VHS Archives.

25. Collis diary, October 8, 1915; Duffus, *Battlefront Nurses*, 36. Maureen Duffus, *Battlefront Nurses in WWI: The Canadian Army Medical Corps in England, France and Salonika, 1914–1919* (Victoria: Town and Gown, 2009), 8.

26. Milne's despatch, published in *London Gazette Supplement*, No. 2985, December 6, 1916; printed in Duffus, *Battlefront Nurses*, 97.

27. Duffus, *Battlefront Nurses*, 132.

28. Ibid., 8.

29. Twice the winner of the Military Cross, he later sat on the Supreme Court of British Columbia.

## CHAPTER 3—1916: THE SOMME: FIELDS OF FIRE

1. *Camosun*, June 1916; author unidentified.

2. This is drawn from Hutchison, *The Far Side of the Street*, 46–47. Benny Nicholas became coach of the boys' debating team at the school in spring 1917, taking up where Arthur Yates (who was away to the War) left off. Here I have also drawn on various issues of *The Camosun*.

3. Winston S. Churchill, *The World Crisis*, abridged ed. (New York: Scribner's 1931), 557.

4. Douglas E. Delaney, "Mentoring the Canadian Corps: Imperial Officers and the Canadian Expeditionary Force, 1914–1918," *The Journal of Military History* 77 #3 (July 2013): 931-53.

5. The 28th (County of London) Battalion of the London Regiment (Artists' Rifles), Territorial Army.

6. *Daily Colonist*, March 21, 1916, 5. WO 339/45154, the National Archives, Kew, UK, contains the essential details.

7. The Rhodes Scholarship was then in its infancy. Cecil Rhodes, the magnate of South Africa, who had made his money in gold, diamonds, and railway concessions, left a fortune to what became the Rhodes Trust. His scheme proposed that British, British Empire, German, and American graduates of exceptional promise should take up residence in an Oxford college. There they would earn an additional bachelor's degree and perhaps go on to more advanced study. Rhodes wanted future leaders, those with athletic or other prowess, the cream of the crop. To this day the Rhodes Trust continues this tradition, now offering scholarships to female recipients and non-whites, who at the inception of the scheme would not have qualified.

8. Duffus, *Battlefront Nurses*, 131–41.

9. Details on Jessie Nelson King from *Daily Colonist*, April 13, 1919; March 3 and 7, 1920; September 4 and 10, 1922; and October 14, 15, and 29, 1922.

10. MacPhail, *Official History of the Canadian Forces in the Great War*, 367.

11. *Military Operations: France and Belgium, 1916. History of the Great War based on official documents by direction of the Historical Section of the Committee of Imperial Defence* (London: Macmillan, 1932), 1:34.

12. Martin Gilbert, *Battle of the Somme: The Heroism and Horror of War* (Toronto: McClelland & Stewart, 2006), 179.

13. Particulars from McGill University Memorial Book, McGill University Archives. Photo available on Canadian Virtual War Memorial.

14. Ibid, 191.

15. Viscountess D'Abernon, *Red Cross and Berlin Embassy* (London: John Murray, 1946), quoted in Gilbert, *Battle of the Somme*, 212–13.

16. John F. Bosher, *Imperial Vancouver Island: Who Was Who 1850–1950*, 2nd ed. (Woodstock: Writersworld, 2012), 290–91.

17. Military record, Library and Archives Canada; other items, copies in Elford files, VHS Archives.

18. *Daily Colonist*, November 24, 1916, p. 5 (death reported), also, December 3, 1916, p. 10. Queen's University Archives files. 47th Battalion diary, from Jack Bates. Attestation paper, CEF. *Camosun*, December 1916, pp. 16–17. His parents were Roderick and Annie MacDonald of South Indian (now Limoges), Ontario. In Victoria, he lived with Mr. and Mrs. G.H. Christie ("Bon Accord," Princess Avenue).

19. *Daily Colonist*, January 14, 1917; May 21, 1918 (which also mentions Willis F. Barr).

20. His son fought and died in the Second World War.

21. Figures from Gilbert, *Battle of the Somme*.

## CHAPTER 4—1917: VIMY RIDGE AND PASSCHENDAELE

1. *Camosun*, May 1916.

2. Harry Cross files, VHS Archives.

3. *Glasgow Herald*, February 22, 1917; *Daily Colonist*, March 24, 1915, 5; June 11, 1916, 5; and February 18, 1917, 5. The 9th Battalion, Highland Light Infantry, war diary is available online at the Royal Highland Fusiliers website (rhf.org.uk). See also Alec Weir, *Come on Highlanders! Glasgow Territorials in the Great War* (Stroud: The History Press, 2013), unpaginated ebook.

4. Michael Boire, "Underground War: Military Mining Operations in Support of the Attack on Vimy Ridge, 9 April 1917," *Canadian Military History* 1, 1 & 2 (August 1992): 15–24.

5. CBC interview with G. Sivertz, Library and Archives Canada. The interview is also reproduced frequently on the Internet. See also Pierre Berton, *Vimy* (Toronto: McClelland & Stewart, 1986), 246–49. A sketch of Gus Sivertz appears in the rear endpapers of that book.

6. Little is known about his later years, and he died in Berkeley, California, of indeterminate causes in 1934, age forty.

7. Among other sources, mainly on the Web, *Daily Colonist*, May 4, 1917. Also Bosher, *Imperial Vancouver Island*, 598–99.

8. Figures from *The Canadian Encyclopedia*.

9. Graves, *Goodbye to All That*, 211.

10. Cruttwell, *History of the Great War*, 404–8.

11. Donald J. Goodspeed, *The Road Past Vimy: the Canadian Corps, 1914–1918* (Toronto: Macmillan of Canada, 1969), 93.

12. *Camosun*, May 1917.

13. Died January 24, 1915, age twenty-seven; serving in 10th Battalion, Canadian Infantry (Manitoba Regiment); buried in CWGC's Bulford Church Cemetery, Wiltshire, not far from the Bulford Camp training ground, near Salisbury Plain. Headstone inscription: GOD IS LOVE, DEARLY LOVED ELDEST SON OF FREDERICK & ANNIE HEAL. Parents were residents of Telkwa, B.C.

14. Died of typhoid at Work Point.

15. Drawn closely from "Our Fallen Heroes," *Camosun*, May 1917, 11.

16. Ibid. He was a law student in Regina when he enlisted.

17. *Victoria Times*, April 16, 1916, 11. The 11th CMR transferred to the 47th Battalion when overseas.

18. Information from Leona Taylor.

19. *Daily Colonist*, May 7, 1915, 1, 2; and June 3, 1917.

20. He was the third son of James Stuart and Annie Austin Yates according to the 1901 Victoria Census. Information from Leona Taylor. He died age fifty-two.

21. Information from Jack Bates.

22. In Google Earth, 2010, the Vining Street Memorial Trees can be seen from above and in leaf.

23. This comes from Paul Gross's *Passchendaele* movie, Norman Leach, historical advisor.

24. Information from Dr. Linda Reid; also various issues of *Daily Colonist*, notably June 3, 1917, and "Boys of the Old Brigade: Mr. Cliff Reid," *Veterans' Voice Memorial Pavilion*, February 1980, 1–2.

25. *Daily Colonist*, October 7, 1917, where his photo may be found.

26. J.C. Waters, *Crosses of Sacrifice: The Story of the Empire's Million War Dead and Australia's 60,000* (Sydney: Angus and Robertson, 1932), 74

27. The soldier was Private Pat Burns, 49th Battalion, CEF.

28. Haig's despatch on the Third Battle of Ypres, in John Buchan, *Nelson's History of the War* (London: Thomas Nelson, 1917), 20:225.

29. *Daily Colonist*, August 5, 1917, 5.

30. *Daily Colonist*, March 3, 1918, 5.

31. Ibid.

32. J. Allan Snowie, *Collishaw and Company: Canadians in the Royal Naval Air Service, 1914–1918* (Bellingham, WA: Nieuport Press, 2010), 37, 248–49.

33. Andrew Gray came to British Columbia, age eighteen, from Scotland in charge of steam tractors intended to be used by Barnard's Express on the Cariboo Road. Later he surveyed for CPR and then became manager of Albion Iron Works and part-owner of Victoria Machinery Depot. On selling out, he established Marine Iron Works, later managed by his son James. He was a keen angler and golfer and died in 1923.

34. *Camosun*, February 1918, 14 (which prints his *In Memoriam*). Also correspondence with, variously, Rear Admiral William Hughes, 2003, including commemorative information; Commonwealth War Graves Commission; Veterans Affairs Canada Remembers Project, (Virtual War Memorial); letter of James Gray to W. Hughes, n.d., and Ministry of Defence (RAF Records) to W. Hughes, November 15, 1978; copy, tracing records of Lieutenant George Robert Gray and Captain James Gray, all in Gray file, VHS Archives.

35. J. Gray to W. Hughes, n.d., and W. Hughes to Colonel [?], June 30, 2003, Gray file, VHS Archives.

36. Her attestation paper and her discharge certificate list her as Hon. Lieutenant, though I have referred to her here as Lieutenant Spencer. It was then not possible to commission women into the Canadian Expeditionary Force. See note 39.

37. Sara Spencer to Ira Dilworth, August 22, 1918, printed in *Camosun*, November 1918, 16.

38. Sara Ellen Spencer files, including her attestation paper, courtesy of Leona Taylor.

39. Howard, *Continental Commitment*, 64–70.

40. Ibid., 65.

41. H.F. Angus, memoir, copy, Archives of British Columbia; also, Bosher, *Imperial Vancouver Island*, 29–31; *Who's Who in British Columbia, 1953* (Victoria: Admark, 1953), 2–3.

42. H.F. Angus letter, undated, printed in *Camosun*, November 1918, 17.

43. *Camosun*, January 1918, 9–11.

44. *New York Times*, December 10, 1931, January 2, 1936, May 13 and December 28, 1940, December 16, 1942, and others.

45. *Camosun*, December 1917, 14–15

46. Barnett, *Swordbearers*, 264–66; also Haig, quoted in Edmonds, *Short History*, 276–77.

## CHAPTER 5—1918: ROAD TO VICTORY: AMIENS AND MONS

1. Knapton, a graduate of the University of British Columbia, went to Oxford as a Rhodes Scholar and took a doctorate at Harvard. An expert on Empress Josephine, he was a professor at Wheaton College, Illinois.

2. *Camosun*, 40 (from Krysteena White's files).

3. *London Gazette,* June 3, 1919.

4. *Camosun*, 20 (from Krysteena White's files).

5. *Daily Colonist*, April 13, 1918, 5.

6. *Daily Colonist*, February 5, 1918, 5. Adm. 171/85, TNA, gives details of the event of December 19, 1917 (also see *Supplement to London Gazette*, December 19, 1917). And see Snowie, *Collishaw and Company*; Gordon Kinsey, *Seaplanes–Felixstowe* (Lavenham: Terence Dalton, 1978), 50; Admiral Sir R.H. Bacon, *Concise Story of the Dover Patrol* (London: Hutchinson, 1923), ch. 16; S.F. Wise, *Canadian Airmen and the First World War* (Ottawa: Ministry of Supply, 1980), esp. ch. 8.

7. The quote and description are drawn from Barnett, *Swordbearers*, 306.

8. Ibid., 324.

9. In fact, in this unified command the French had the supreme authority, much to the distaste and opposition of Sir Douglas Haig, the commander in the field. Doubtless his subordinate commanders, including Currie, felt similarly.

10. Printed in John D. Robins, ed., *A Pocketful of Canada* (Toronto: Collins, 1946), 396–97.

11. Mary Soames, ed., *Speaking for Themselves: The Personal Letters of Winston and Clementine Churchill* (Toronto: Stoddart, 1998), 206.

12. At the time of his death, his parents, Henry Plant and Mary Cooper Plant, lived in Westmount, Quebec.

13. On railways, tramways, and Canadian contributions, see Nicholson, *Canadian Expeditionary Force*, 485–90.

14. Quoted, James L. McWilliams and R. James Steel, *Amiens: Dawn of Victory* (Toronto: Dundurn, 2001), 137

15. Col. John Hughes-Wilson, past president of the Guild of Battlefield Guides, personal communication with author.

16. Official records credit the Canadian Roy Brown with Richthofen's death on April 21, 1918, but Australians claim that their gunfire from the ground killed him. According to another account, two cooks in a nearby field feeding station, who got their rifles out for sport, may have killed the German flying ace, who had eighty victories in aerial combat, the highest number in any of the War's forces. The Australians gave Richthofen a military funeral, and rightly so, for he was a great warrior.

17. Alister was the son of Mr. and Mrs. John McCallum, 3245 Pine Street, Maywood P.O., Victoria. *Daily Colonist*, November 30, 1918; website Canada, War Graves Register (Circumstances of Casualty), 1914–1918.

18. Donald Morgan McCannel, photograph and correspondence, Queen's University Archives.

19. Entry for death of Uchtred Charles Guy Knox, no. 77047. He is buried in Ste. Marie Cemetery, Havre, France.

20. This was HRH Duchess of Connaught Hospital, essentially for the Canadian Army; it was re-established during the Second World War.

21. *Camosun*, April 1927 ("Old Students Number"): 14–15.

22. Tracy O'Hara and Bent Sivertz, *The Life of Bent Gestur Sivertz: A Seaman, a Teacher, and a Worker in the Canadian Arctic* (Victoria: Trafford, 2000), 9–10.

23. Jeanette A. Cann, "A Tribute to Sergeant Henry Sivertz," *Camosun*, December 1918, 14.

24. *Daily Colonist*, November 14, 1918, 10. Information from Leona Taylor.

25. Claude Pottinger to parents, November 2, 1918, Pottinger letters, Victoria City Archives (copy in VHS Archives).

26. Ringwood commanded the 60th Battery (Regina), 14th Brigade, Canadian Field Artillery. He was killed by shellfire when out with a reconnaissance party and died age thirty-one. Lieutenant Raymond Frank Castle, Victoria High School, later a noted stockbroker and entrepreneur (he built and managed the Oak Bay Theatre), joined the Royal Canadian Horse Artillery in 1915. In 1922, he married Katherine Fraser, born at Victoria, and died in 1949.

27. From Pottinger letters, Victoria City Archives; also *Victoria Times*, November 13 and 15, 1918.

28. Claude Pottinger to Alice Pottinger, November 2, 1918, Pottinger letters, Victoria City Archives.

29. Entry on Beckwith, *McGill Roll of Honour*, 1914–1918 (Montreal, 1926), 20.

30. He died November 18, 1917.

31. Information from Leona Taylor. Also *Daily Colonist*, November 5, 1918, 12.

32. *Supplement to London Gazette*, August 19, 1916.

33. *Daily Colonist*, February 22 and September 9, 1916; April 16 and 17, and May 1, 1917; January 25, September 6, and December 20, 1918. Victoria Census 1901. On Eric McCallum as "tin god": *Camosun*, March 1913, 22.

34. J.H. Gray, "Fellow Surveyor Pays a Tribute," *Daily Colonist*, April 2, 1918, 5; *Roll of Honour, British Columbia Land Surveyors: The Great War* (1919); *Daily Colonist*, various issues, including March 25, 1915, July 10, 1915, September 11, 1918; Obituaries, *Annual Reports of BC Land Surveyors*; Jay Sherwood, *In the Shadow of the Great War: The Milligan and Hart Explorations of Northeastern British Columbia, 1913–14* (Victoria: Royal BC Museum, 2013).

35. Quoted, John Keegan, *First World War* (London: Hutchinson, 1998), 444.

36. I am obliged to Ken Roeche for this research and for his text. Among Wills's various articles, the following are noteworthy: "The Last Hundred Days," *Daily Colonist*, September 1, 1968, and "The First Armistice Day, Nov. 11, 1918," *Daily Colonist*, November 10, 1968.

37. On the events of August 22, 1914, and November 11, 1918, I have relied on Rose E.B. Coombs, *Before Endeavours Fade: A Guide to the Battlefields of the First World War*, 13th edition (Harlow, UK: After the Battle Publications, 2010), 148–49; Don Farr, *Mons 1914–1918: The Beginning and the End* (Solihull, UK: Helion, 2008), 8, 157, 160; information from Colonel John Hughes-Wilson.

38. Matthew Scott to his mother, November 13, 1918, Megan Scott papers.

39. This account of Blayney Scott is taken from his attestation paper; *Victoria Colonist*, September 11, 1917, 5, and files at the time of his death and funeral; *San Jose Mercury*, November 22, 1918; also, Megan Scott papers.

40. Where my grandfather, Samuel Morton, a plumber, was employed.

41. B. Scott to his mother, October 7, 1917, Megan Scott papers.

42. B. Scott to his mother, May 9, 1918, Megan Scott papers.

43. B. Scott to his mother, June 26, 1918, Megan Scott papers.

## CHAPTER 6—ARMISTICE AND PEACE

1. Gary Sarian, "The 1918 Flu Epidemic in Victoria," *British Columbia Historical News*, 25, 4 (Fall 1992): 11–16. Available online at www.library.ubc.ca/archives/pdfs/bchf/bchn_1992_fall.pdf
2. Ibid., 15.
3. Herbert H. Smith, *Camosun*, December 1921, unpaginated foreword.
4. Ibid.
5. In the United States, November 11 is still called Armistice Day.
6. Arnold J. Toynbee, *Survey of International Affairs, 1920–1923* (London: British Institute of International Affairs, 1925), 85–100. This is a handy summary of the positions.

## CHAPTER 7—THE RECKONING

1. These figures are now regarded as low. See Edmonds, *Short History*, 426–27. James Edmonds was director of the Historical Section of the Committee of Imperial Defence and of the Cabinet Office, 1919–49.
2. Niall Ferguson, *The Pity of War: Explaining World War One* (New York: Basic Books, 1998), 199; also Elizabeth Armstrong, *The Crisis of Quebec* (New York: Columbia University Press, 1937), 250, and information from David Barnhill.
3. Department of Veterans Affairs, *Vimy Ridge National Historic Site of Canada* publication, [2013]. Also Coombs, *Before Endeavours Fade*, 89.
4. Coombs, *Before Endeavours Fade*, 227.
5. The CWGC cut-off date for the Second World War is August 31, 1947.
6. Gary A. Mitchell, "The Appraisal of Canadian Military Personnel Files of the First World War" (MA thesis: University of British Columbia, 1984), 68–69.
7. Ibid., 69
8. The quote comes from an Australian writer, J.C. Waters, in *Crosses of Sacrifice* (Sydney, NSW: Angus & Robertson, 1932), p. 9, but is nonetheless applicable to Canada.
9. As ANZAC Day, April 25, 1915, was for Australia and New Zealand at Gallipoli.
10. Waters, *Crosses of Sacrifice*, 10.
11. Letter from Mrs. Jocelyn Perry (née Rigby), September 20, 2003; copy VHS Archives.
12. Author unknown, but possibly editor-in-chief Ursula Edwards, *Camosun*, March 1922.
13. This section relies on various *Camosun* issues, notably, November 1919, 10, 13–17. C.M. Haverstock and E. Yeo are included on the school's Roll of Honour.
14. On military hospitals, see Macphail, *Official History of the Canadian Forces in the Great War: Medical Services*, 331.
15. His letter home was reported in the *Daily Colonist*, April 17, 1917; fire and burial, December 28, 29, and 30, 1923, also January 3, 1924. He first was assigned to the 103rd Battalion. Files are at Ref. RG 150 Accession 1992–93/166, Box 1 Box r 5290–68, Library and Archives Canada.
16. Entry on Currie, in *Who's Who in Canada*, 1520.

## CHAPTER 8—MONUMENTS OF VALOUR

1. Gibson's essay won a writing contest put on by the school, and he received gold cufflinks with the VHS emblem as his prize.
2. Reprinted in *Vic High 125* (souvenir program, 2001), 20. I have drawn liberally from Gibson's text.
3. John Pierce, "Constructing Memory: the Vimy Memorial," *Canadian Military History*, 1, 1 & 2 (Autumn 1992): 4–8.

## EPILOGUE—THE PITY OF WAR

1. Borden to High Commissioner, January 4, 1917, in Henry Borden, *Robert Laird Borden Memoirs* (London: Macmillan, 1938), 2:622.
2. Ian Kershaw, *Hitler* (London: Allen Lane, 2008), chs. 1–5.

3. Mackenzie King, speeches of October 29, 1935, and June 18, 1936, in Nicholas Mansergh, ed., *Documents and Speeches on British Commonwealth Affairs, 1931–1952*, vol. 1 (London: Oxford University Press, 1953), 142–43 and 144–50 respectively.

4. H. Drummond Dee, "The Futility of War," *Camosun*, 1937, 67–68.

5. Arthur Quiller-Couch, *Oxford Book of English Verse, 1250–1918*, rev. ed (New York: Oxford University Press, 1939), xii-xiii.

6. M. Tippett to B. Gough, May 19, 2014.

## SOURCES AND A GUIDE TO
## HISTORIES OF THE FIRST WORLD WAR

*T*he specific sources used in this book, especially for items quoted, will be found in the endnotes. Most of the documentation on individual soldiers, sailors, and airmen will be found in their individual files, kept by either the Government of Canada or the Government of the United Kingdom. Many Canadians, including Britons living in Canada, first joined the CEF, then transferred to the Royal Naval Air Service or the Royal Flying Corps (merged April 1, 1918, as the Royal Air Force); their files are to be found in Canadian and in UK repositories. Nowadays, diligent researchers, using various search engines, can locate on the Web the essential details on an individual in the services, though they might then have to do a follow-up application for documents.

On the Commonwealth War Graves Commission website (www.cwgc. org/find-war-dead.aspx), a deceased serviceman may be traced. Canadian databases also aid the reader, though the full military records of individual soldiers and airmen have not yet been digitalized. By way of Google, an investigator can readily find the various locations where such documentation is to be found, and there are many other ways of searching on the Web that bring remarkable results. This book has benefited mightily from Web searches, though there is no substitute for having the assistance of persons who know the records—and the methods of retrieving the important items.

Rather than give a long list of books in the customary order by surname, I am providing suggestions for reading by the categories indicated, which may help the reader explore in greater detail the phenomenally rich literature of the First World War, specifically those themes that relate to Canada's challenges, sufferings, and achievements.

### GENERAL WORKS ON THE FIRST WORLD WAR

On causes and circumstances, the reader should consult Margaret MacMillan, *The War That Ended Peace: The Road to 1914* (New York: Random House,

2013). Best introductions are John Keegan, *The First World War* (London: Hutchinson, 1998), and Max Hastings, *Catastrophe: Europe Goes to War 1914* (London: William Collins, 2013). Among the finest surveys are Hew Strachan, *The First World War*, Vol. 1. *To Arms* (Oxford: Oxford University Press, 2001), based on the most recent research; and C.R.M.F. Cruttwell, *A History of the Great War, 1914–1918,* 2nd ed. (1934; Chicago: Academic, 1991), which is still useful, especially for Salonika and Mesopotamia. For the reasons for the Allied victory, see Tim Travers, *How the War Was Won: Command and Technology in the British Army on the Western Front, 1917–1918* (London: Routledge, 1992).

### CANADA AT WAR, GENERAL

J.L. Granatstein, *Hell's Corner: An Illustrated History of Canada's Great War, 1914–1918* (Vancouver: Douglas & McIntyre, 2004) is the place to start. See also Tim Cook, *At the Sharp End: Canadians Fighting the Great War 1914–1916* (Toronto: Penguin Canada, 2007) and *Shock Troops: Canadians Fighting the Great War, 1917–1918* (Toronto: Penguin, 2008).

For the official account, see G.W.L. Nicholson, *Canadian Expeditionary Force, 1914–1919* (Ottawa: Queen's Printer, 1964). On aviation history, including naval air, see S.F. Wise, *Canadian Airmen and the First World War* (Ottawa: Supply and Services, 1980).

### ON INDIVIDUAL BATTLES AND CAMPAIGNS

Maureen Duffus, *Battlefront Nurses in WWI: The Canadian Army Medical Corps in England, France and Salonika, 1914–1919* (Victoria: Town and Gown, 2009). Martin Gilbert, *The Battle of the Somme: The Heroism and Horror of War* (Toronto: McClelland & Stewart, 2006), is a model, and for the war outside Europe, Tim Travers, *Gallipoli* (Stroud, UK: Tempus, 2002) is the most balanced of that campaign. For Second Ypres, these are recommended: Daniel Dancocks, *Welcome to Flanders Fields: The First Canadian Battle of the Great War: Ypres, 1915* (Toronto: McClelland & Stewart, 1988), and Nathan M. Greenfield, *Baptism of Fire: The Second Battle of Ypres and the Forging of Canada, April 1915* (Toronto: HarperCollins, 2007). An unequalled survey is Donald J. Goodspeed, *The Road Past Vimy: The Canadian Corps 1914–1918* (Toronto: Macmillan of Canada, 1969). To be treated with caution is Pierre Berton, *Vimy* (Toronto: McClelland & Stewart, 1986). Though handsomely built on soldiers' interviews for the CBC, the work is fatally partisan and veers toward exaggeration. Recommended is Ted Barris, *Victory at Vimy: Canada Comes of Age, April 9–12, 1917* (Toronto: Thomas Allen, 2007). This evaluates the views of a number of soldiers. In his article "'Junior but Sovereign Allies': The Transformation of the Canadian Expeditionary Force, 1914–1918," *Journal of Imperial and Commonwealth History*, 8, 1 (October 1979): 56–67 (reprinted in B.D. Hunt and R.G. Haycock, eds., *Canada's Defence: Perspectives on Policy in the Twentieth Century* (Toronto: Copp Clark Pitman 1993), 31–43), the learned Desmond Morton has explained, as subtext, that Canada "came of age" with the benefit of innovative political–military arrangements conducted in London and the ascendancy of the Canadian government's Overseas Ministry, created in November 1916. Once the appallingly bad leadership of Sir Sam Hughes was dispensed with and the interfering measures of Sir Max Aitken (Lord Beaverbrook) were brought to an end, Currie was in a better position (one he exploited and developed) to demand that the military interests of Canada be given full respect and attention.

### BIOGRAPHIES AND MEMOIRS

Two Victoria High School graduates have published their stories: Bruce Hutchison, *The Far Side of the Street* (Toronto: Macmillan of Canada, 1976), and Bent Sivertz, *The Life of Bent Gestur Sivertz* (Victoria: Trafford, 2000). Unpublished memoirs exist for Henry Forbes Angus and Joseph B. Clearihue (copies at BC Archives).

### VARIOUS

On matters relating to war and remembrance Canadian style, consult Jonathan Vance, *Death So Noble: Memory, Meaning, and the First World War* (Vancouver: UBC Press, 1997). For the history of Victoria High School, see Peter Smith, *Come Give a Cheer! One Hundred Years of Victoria High School, 1876–1976* (Victoria: VHS Centennial Celebrations Committee, 1976). For the relationship of Victoria High School, the cradle of Victoria College, to the University of Victoria, see, by the same, *Multitude of the Wise: UVic Remembered* (Victoria: Alumni Association of the University of Victoria, 1993).

Robert Ratcliffe Taylor, *The Ones Who Have to Pay: The Soldier-Poets of Victoria BC in the Great War 1914–1918* (Trafford, 2012), is worth reading though it has little school connection. The book has yet to be written about Victoria and the First World War. Ken Roeche, *A Fairfield History* (Victoria:

Trafford, 2005), and John Ellis with Charles Lillard, *Fernwood Files* (Victoria: Orca, 1989), provide essential information. Casey G. Williams et al., *100 Years of Valour: A Centennial Celebration of the Canadian Scottish Regiment (Princess Mary's)* (Victoria: Paradigm Publishing, 2012) relates the stories of piper James Richardson and others, and is handsomely illustrated. James A. Wood, guest editor, *BC Studies*, no. 182, Summer 2014 ("The Great War") deals in various ways with the province's involvement in the conflict.

## ACKNOWLEDGEMENTS

*My debt to* various institutions and individuals is considerable, and I am pleased to pay the following grateful tributes:

To Victoria High School Alumni Association for embracing the Great War Project, and to the team who aided the project in so many ways (Yvonne Van Ruskenveld, Leona Taylor, Keith McCallion, Gary Mitchell, Tim Travers, and especially Debbie Blackie for assistance in untold ways); to Victoria High School Archives for essential information; to Ms. Randi Falls, principal of Victoria High School; to Wendy Burleson, librarian of Victoria High School; to the City of Victoria Archives, the University of Victoria Archives, and the Archives of British Columbia. Special thanks to Deborah Morrison and Canada's History Society, and to the Canadian War Museum for the national launching of the Project. I benefited from the collections of the British Library, London Library, Athenaeum Library, Imperial War Museum, and the Army Museum. Many have helped with photos but more particularly Jim Buchan, Alan MacLeod, John Azar, Warren Sommer, Linda Reid, and Megan Scott.

I thank the following for special help: John Azar, CEF100 Commemoration Society, for information and also the opportunity to tell the story of the Victoria High School Memorial Trees to the Western Front Association, Pacific Coast Branch; Jack Bates, for information and inspiration; Jim Beatty and CHEK TV, for telling our story to the viewing publics; Captain Peter Campbell, for particulars on his father, Harold Lane Campbell, and his uncle Claude Campbell, all graduates of Victoria High School; Bruce Davies, for information on Craigdarroch Castle history; Jan Drent, for matters various; Paul Evans, Royal Artillery Library Woolwich, for particulars on A. Nelson King; Christina Nichol, for information on Conrad, Robin, and Jean Wilson; Barry Moen, for stories on the Victoria High School Alumni Association website; Barbara James, for bringing to life art teacher Earl W. Clarke; Susan Gibb, for permission to consult the letters of her great-uncles Claude Pottinger and James Pottinger; Rob Hanna, for assistance; Joan King, for details on her husband, Dr. Michael R. King, and his father, Dr. Paul King; Ross McKenzie, archivist, the Royal Military College of Canada, for details on Arthur Beaumont Boggs; Dr. Linda Reid, for particulars on the Reid brothers; John Orr, for information; Sherri Robinson, for help with Esquimalt particulars; Megan Scott, for details on the Scott brothers; Brian R.D. Smith, for particulars on the Parfitt family and Sir Robert Borden; J. Allan Snowie, for details on Canadians in the Royal Naval Air Service; Ray Travers, for professional knowledge of trees; Krysteena White and Andrea Cam Duhn, students at the school, for fresh insights; Joan M. Whiston (and Dr. Richard Mayne, the RCAF historian), for research on Cecil Clayton; John Whittaker, for details on surveyors; Glennis Zilm, for information on nursing sisters. I thank a number of historians for reading this book in earlier form, notably Lawrence Aronsen and Tim Travers.

David Boler and Colonel John Hughes-Wilson accompanied me to the battlefields of imperishable memory and helped find war graves of those connected to Victoria High School. I thank Audrey McClellan for editorial prowess. King Lee speeded the process in the last phase. Rodger Touchie, Lara Kordic, and Leslie Kenny saw this work through its various stages with professional zeal. I alone am responsible for any errors of omission or commission.

# INDEX

Manning, Frederic, 17
Metcalf, W.H., 202
*The Middle Parts of Fortune* (Manning), 17
Middleton, Joanna, 77
Milligan, Alexander Wilson, 157
Milligan, Charles Napier, 157
Milligan, George Berry, 155–56, 157
Milligan, John "Jack" Mudie, 78, 155, 157
Milloy, Cecil, 50, 78, 133
Milne, George, 75
Milne, W.J., 202
Mitchell, Gary, 171
Moltke, Hellmuth von, 45–46
Monash, John, 144
Mons (Belgium), 54, 55, 144, 147, 158–61, 178
Morris, John, 118
Moss, Alice Martha, 77
Mount Sorrel, 23, 65, 111
Mulcahy, Andrew, 35

Nicholas, Benjamin Charles "Benny," 81
Noble, Irene, 146
Norris, Thomas, 77

Odlum, Victor, 100
Okell, Stanley, 16
O'Meara, Robert, 78

Parfitt, Victor Raymond "Ray," 66–67
Parr, John, 160
Partridge, John Bernard, 169–70
Pascoe, J.A., 104
Passchendaele campaign, 62, 98, 111, 113–21, 126, 130, 139, 140, 174, 188
Paul, Ada, 107
Paul, Alexander S., 107
Paul, "Budge," 49
Paul, E.B., 32, 33, 107
Paul, Horace John, 104, 107
Peace of Versailles, 168
Pearce, Harold Marshall, 151
Peck, Cy, 100, 202
Pemberton, Philippa Despard, 92–93
Pierce, John, 185
Plant, Verner Lovelace, 142
Plummer, Mollie, 122
Pomeroy, S.J., 110
Pottinger, Alice, 151

Pottinger, Claude, 26, 150, 151
Pottinger, James McNaughton, 26, 67, 150–51
Powell, Israel Wood, 102
Powell, Jane Branks, 102
Powell, Robert Branks "Bobbie," 26, 102–3
Price, George, 160, 161
Pullen, Newton F., 95

Rattenbury, Francis, 32
Rawlinson, Henry, 143, 144
"Recessional" (Kipling), 15
Redding, M., 77
regiments and battalions, 48, 100, 201–202; 1st Newfoundland Regiment, 90; 5th Battalion, 48, 67, 68, 116; 5th BC Regiment of Garrison Artillery, RCA, 34, 39, 47, 48, 49, 58, 70, 108, 190; 16th Battalion (Canadian Scottish), 59, 100; 30th Battalion (Victoria), 59; 50th Regiment, Gordon Highlanders, 34, 47, 48, 59; 88th Regiment, Victoria Fusiliers, 34, 48, 49, 59; C Battery, 53rd (Howitzer) Brigade, 87, 88; Canadian Scottish Regiment (Princess Mary's), 190; Princess Patricia's Canadian Light Infantry (PPCLI), 91
Reid, Clifford Duncan, 111, 112, 113, 177
Reid, David Reginald "Reggie," 111
Reid, Janet, 113
Reid, John (grandson of Clifford), 113
Reid, John "Jack" Deighton (brother of Clifford), 111
Reid, John "Jack" (son of Clifford), 113
Reid, John, Sr., 111
Reid, Linda, 113
Reid, Reginald "Reg" Herbert, 112
Reid, S. Gordon, 111
Richardson, J., 202
Ringwood, T. Duncan, 151
Roberts, Jessica, 173
Robertson, William, 84
Robinson, G.W. (Ella), 64
Robinson, Henry L., 50
Roe, Harold S., 104, 105
Roeche, Kenneth, 16, 159
Rowe, Jimmy, 135
Roy, Alexander, 35
Royal Air Corps, 172

## ABOUT THE AUTHOR

Known for the vividness and authenticity of his histories, Barry Gough is heralded as one of Canada's foremost historians. Gough is the author of more than eighteen books on military and maritime history, including *Pax Britannica: Ruling the Waves and Keeping the Peace before Armageddon*, *Juan de Fuca's Strait: Voyages in the Waterway of Forgotten Dreams*, and *Historical Dreadnoughts*. He has won numerous literary awards, including the Lieutenant-Governor of British Columbia Medal, the Clio Award of the Canadian Historical Association, various BC Book Prizes, and awards from the North American Society for Oceanic History.

Gough is past president of the British Columbia Historical Federation; Professor Emeritus, Wilfrid Laurier University; and Archives Fellow, Churchill College, Cambridge. For civic contributions, he was awarded the Queen's Golden Jubilee Medal and the Queen's Diamond Jubilee Medal. Born and raised in Victoria, Gough graduated from Victoria High School (as did his parents) and was a teacher there. Today, he is chair of the Victoria High School Alumni Association. He lives in Victoria, BC.